CAREER OPPORTUNITIES FOR WRITERS

SECOND EDITION

Rosemary Ellen Guiley

Facts On File
New York • Oxford

Career Opportunities for Writers

Facts On File, Inc.
460 Park Avenue South
New York NY 10016
USA

Facts On File Limited
Collins Street
Oxford OX4 1XJ
United Kingdom

Library of Congress Cataloging-in-Publication Data

Career opportunities for writers
p. cm.
ISBN 0-8160- 2400-6.—ISBN 8160-2462-6 (pbk.)
1. Authorship—Vocational guidance.
PN151.G84 1991
808'.02'02373— dc20 90-49088

British CIP data available on request from Facts On File.

Facts On File books are available at special discounts when purchased in bulk quantities for businesses, associations, institutions or sales promotions. Please contact the Special Sales Department of our New York office at 212/683-2244 (dial 800/322-8755 except in NY, AK or HI).

Composition by Facts On File, Inc.
Manufactured by the Maple-Vail Book Manufacturing Group
Printed in the United States of America

10 9 8 7 6 5 4 3 2 1

This book is printed on acid-free paper.

CONTENTS

PREFACE
How to Use This Book

Purpose

Career Opportunities for Writers presents one of the most comprehensive catalogs of writing jobs available in a single volume. It does not focus on a single field of writing, but covers 91 jobs in eight major fields. Jobs are not merely summarized in a paragraph or two but described in detail, including duties, salaries, prerequisites, employment and advancement opportunities, organizations to join, and opportunities for women and minorities. It is intended to help both aspiring writers who are seeking entry-level jobs as well as experienced writers who are interested in making career changes.

Generally the jobs included in this book are open to persons with appropriate educational credentials (usually a bachelor's degree) and up to five or so years of experience. These are predominantly entry-and middle-level positions, those that are available to the largest number of candidates.

Sources of Information

Research for this book included the author's own experience, interviews with numerous professionals in various fields, and surveys, reports, facts, and other information obtained from professional associations, trade unions, the federal government and universities. The author has worked as a writer, journalist, or editor, either on staff or on a freelance basis, in newspaper and magazine journalism, advertising trade news and sales promotion, corporate communications, ghostwriting and collaboration, and scriptwriting.

The job descriptions are based on representative samples of actual job positions. In general writing jobs are broad in their responsibilities, and they can vary greatly from one employer to another. In many cases, a writing job is what the employee makes of it. Jobs at small firms tend to be broader in scope than those in large, structured companies and organizations. The descriptions in this book note some of the wide ranges of duties and responsibilities for various types of jobs.

Organization of Material

This book has nine parts: eight cover different fields and industries which employ many writers; the last section consists of appendices listing educational institutions and scholarships, associations and unions, periodicals, and a bibliography of additional sources, all pertinent to writing careers. While most of the 91 jobs listed are based solely on writing and editing skills, a few are writing-related; that is, in addition to substantial writing and editing skills, they require other skills or education. Some of the jobs that fall into this category are sales-oriented positions, research positions, and jobs requiring technical, legal, academic, or foreign language training. The Introduction gives an overview of job opportunities for writers, as well as explaining employment trends for the next decade or so.

Section 8, which covers freelance opportunities, has been significantly expanded in the second edition. There are two primary reasons for this. Economics will continue to force many employers to downsize, thus limiting staff opportunities but increasing freelance opportunities. And, advances in technology make it possible for freelancers to provide more sophisticated services.

Explanation of Job Descriptions

Each job description follows a basic format and is complete unto itself; the reader does not have to consult another section of the book to get a complete picture of a particular job. Therefore, readers may encounter some repetition from job to job within a given industry.

Jobs are listed by their predominant title, followed by a Career Profile, which summarizes main duties, alternate titles, salary ranges, employment prospects, advancement prospects, and prerequisites of education, experience, and special skills. A Career Ladder diagram shows a typical career path, including the positions above and below each job. If a job is entry level, school or other related positions are listed as preceding it.

The Position Description is a narrative that describes typical job duties and responsibilities, working hours and conditions, and optional duties which may or may not be part of an individual job. It includes peers and superiors, and it indicates the frequency of overtime or travel, wherever pertinent.

Salaries explains income ranges and factors, such as individual skills, size of employer, or geographic location, which affect how much a particular job may pay. Salary ranges are based on averages, and readers may find positions that pay less or more than the figures cited in this book.

Readers will find particularly helpful the sections on Employment Prospects and Advancement Prospects. Some jobs may sound terrific or be very glamorous, but they also may be extremely difficult to obtain. Others may prove to be dead ends, with advancement difficult or impossible. These are important factors to weigh in any job search.

Education describes academic requirements for various jobs. In most cases, writers who have earned undergraduate degrees in liberal arts or communications will qualify; some jobs require other educational backgrounds. Graduate degrees are not often required but are increasingly advantageous for many jobs. At the opposite end of the spectrum, some writing jobs require only high school diplomas.

In addition to education, many jobs require prior experience. The Experience/Skills section describes what background is essential or helpful in competing for a job. Previous experience may not be required for many entry-level positions, but candidates who have had some kind of related experience—even on collegiate, volunteer, or community levels—often have significant competitive advantages. In addition, this section spells out the skills and qualities employers look for, attributes which enhance prospects for success in particular fields.

Most communicators—a generic term that includes writers, editors and others in various communications jobs—do not belong to a union. Those who do, work for organized fields such as print and broadcast journalism, film and television entertainment, schools, and government. Even in those areas, unionization is not uniform throughout. Many do, however, belong to one or more professional associations, where they meet others who have similar jobs, exchange information and ideas, and make contacts. The Unions/Associations section, which ends each job description, lists the major associations of interest to professionals in a particular field, as well as the most likely unions, if any, that would represent them in wage negotiations.

Appendices

Appendix I, "Educational Institutions," lists colleges, universities, and educational institutions, in every state and the District of Columbia, which offer undergraduate degrees in major areas of communications—broadcasting, advertising, public relations, education, technical and specialized journalism, newspaper and magazine journalism, as well as courses in publishing. The list does not include every institution which offers courses or degrees in communications. The list also does not include two-year colleges, since most jobs require or give preference to degree-holders from four-year institutions.

The list gives each institution's address and telephone number, as well as the major programs, sequences, and courses of interest to writers.

Appendix II, "Professional, Industry, and Trade Associations and Unions," lists major organizations for writers, editors, and those in the writing-related fields included in this book.

Appendix III, "Major Trade Periodicals," groups such periodicals according to field or industry.

Finally, Appendix IV is a Bibliography of sources that give additional career and salary information.

ACKNOWLEDGMENTS

I would like to especially thank Dorothy Kroll for her assistance in researching material for the second edition. In so doing, Dorothy built on work done by Bruce S. Trachtenberg and Joanne P. Austin for the first edition.

Thanks also to The Newspaper Guild for providing information on salaries and minorities; Professor Lee B. Becker of the School of Journalism at Ohio State University, for providing a copy of his "Survey of Journalism and Mass Communications Graduates 1988: Summary Report July 1989," done in cooperation with Thomas E. Engleman, executive director of the Dow Jones Newspaper Fund; Linda deLaubensfels Russman, editor of *The Professional Communicator*, published by Women In Communications, Inc., for providing articles on salaries and trends; and Sharon Y. Richardson, publications director of the National Association of Black Journalists, for providing a survey of black media managers.

And finally, thanks to my editor, Neal Maillet, for his assistance and gracious support.

INTRODUCTION
The Job Outlook for Writers and Other Communicators

Communicators and writers are at the leading edge of society: they record its changes, document trends, help a wide variety of business enterprises meet its needs and help shape public opinion. With major societal changes already under way due to demographics, economics, health and environmental interests and global trade, the role of communicators promises to be exciting and challenging for years to come.

Since the first edition of this book was published in 1983, job opportunities have remained stable in some areas, decreased in others and expanded in still others. Throughout the 1990s and into the early 21st century, communications jobs in general will increase in the service sector due to rising needs and will decrease in the manufacturing sector due to continuing downsizing. Service sector jobs, however, tend to pay less. Specific areas expected to experience growth are health, environment, leisure, travel and international trade. The best jobs will go to candidates who not only excel in communications skills but also have knowledge of finance, economics and demographics. Many jobs will increasingly require a global perspective as the world marketplace continues to shrink.

Above all, job applicants must be computer literate. At the start of the 1980s, computers were just beginning to find their way onto desktops. A decade later, they had become commonplace, with increasingly sophisticated software and hardware options. Whether staff or freelance, the communicator who seeks to succeed must master the technology. More and more, information is created, stored and transmitted electronically. Desktop publishing software enables entire publications to be created and designed on-screen. Databases give communicators access to vast stores of information. Laptop computers enable people to take their office with them on the road, or boost productivity in library research.

Approximately 20,000 to 21,000 journalism and mass communications students graduate from colleges and universities each year, of whom 65 percent are women and about 10 percent are minorities. About two-thirds of all graduates find immediate employment in a job related to their major. Job applicants who had work experience as interns have an advantage in competing for openings. Experience at campus newspapers, publications and broadcast stations also is an advantage, yet fewer students are participating in such opportunities, according to a 1988 survey done by Professor Lee B. Becker of the School of Journalism at Ohio State University. Students who have yet to complete their degrees would be wise to investigate campus media experience. Undergraduate degrees are sufficient for most jobs, though candidates with master's degrees may be more competitive for certain select positions.

In the different fields of communications, the job outlook varies from field to field. Newspapers increased positions during the 1980s with expansion into suburban and special sections in an effort to capture more readers. This expansion is for the most part accomplished, and job openings are expected to have modest growth. Of the four major fields of mass communications—news media, broadcast, advertising and public relations—newspapers and wire services employ the most communications graduates, but only about two-thirds of those who seek newspaper and wire service jobs obtain them.

Magazines are a volatile field. There are approximately 11,000 periodicals, yet only about 400 of them are of significant size, accounting for 75 percent of all magazine circulation. The magazine field changed tremendously from the 1960s through the 1980s. Established general consumer magazines lost readers to new, narrow-focus magazines. Job opportunities increased rapidly during the 1970s and 1980s as numerous start-ups and spinoffs entered the marketplace. But by 1990, many of these specialized magazines were in financial trouble or had folded due to shrinking advertising. Mergers and acquisitions added to the uncertainty of jobs and job security. Retrenchment is likely to continue through the 1990s.

Openings in radio and television are expected to experience moderate growth. In the latter, more opportunities will be available in cable than at networks and independent stations. Slightly less than 9 percent of graduates take broadcasting jobs, more than half of them in television. Competition for television jobs is intense, for only about four out of every 100 jobs in the industry relate directly to producing news or entertainment programs.

In advertising, a merger mania during the 1970s and 1980s led to great consolidation among ad agencies. The result has been considerable staff trimming, with experienced personnel suffering the greatest number of cuts. Entry-level job openings are expected to remain good through the 1990s, but advancement will be more difficult. An increasing emphasis is being placed in global marketing skills as business enterprises seek to expand their markets around the world. Ad agencies and advertising departments of companies employ nearly 9 percent of communications graduates.

Public relations agencies and company departments hire a little more than 8 percent of graduates. The industry is still young, having barely established itself by the early 1950s, but has grown significantly in size and importance since the 1970s, as more businesses have recognized the importance of image and media and consumer relations. In an economic down cycle, however, public relations is often one of the first areas to experience budget cuts. Nonetheless, the increasing emphasis on communications and information in nearly all sectors will offer good job prospects in p.r. in the years ahead.

In the book publishing world, a decade or more of domestic and international mergers, acquisitions and bankruptcies have consolidated the number of major players in the field. Numerous jobs have been lost, and advancement prospects are more limited. Publishers continue to be notorious low payers. As the giants merge and downsize and smaller publishers are eaten up or go out of business, the small press field flourishes and grows, creating new job opportunities, though usually at low pay. Small presses exist all over the country, while most of the major houses are on the East Coast, and concentrated in the New York metropolitan region.

Glamour jobs such as author, playwright and screenwriter more or less follow the ups and downs in their respective fields. Book advances rose, and sometimes rose spectacularly, during the 1970s and 1980s, but financial troubles among many publishers by 1990 had depressed advances and the number of books purchased. At the same time, Hollywood had entered a big-spending period for screenplays. Competition is fierce, and to become a player in Hollywood screenwriting virtually requires residency in the Los Angeles area. Playwrights always face difficulties in getting established. While Broadway leans toward megahits and spectacles, the best opportunities, especially for drama, remain in regional and small theater.

Freelancers who offer multiple services—such as writing, editing, proofreading, indexing, scriptwriting, etc.—will find increasing work opportunities in the years ahead. Downsizing and mergers will keep the staffs at many businesses lean, yet workloads will increase. More and more, employers will look to freelancers to handle certain communications. In particular, communicators with technical skills will be in demand.

Freelance income is often irregular, and the uncertainties of work and pay require good sales skills, perseverance, self-discipline and organization and financial management. Freelancers also have to invest in office equipment and certain expenses of running a sole proprietorship. Most freelancers are versatile and don't bank on a single market or type of work, as market needs can shift and contacts can be lost. You're more likely to be successful as a full-time freelancer if you have at least several years' experience in staff positions.

With the exception of a small number of glamour jobs, communications jobs do not offer high salaries as may be found in other fields, but do offer better-than-average wages for all types of employment. The smaller the enterprise, the lower the pay scale, and many entry-level jobs across the board can offer as little as $10,000–$12,000. The Becker study found a median starting salary of $16,900 for the 1988 graduates, just slightly less than the wage earned by the average American. A communicator with several years of experience can expect to earn a salary in the mid-twenties to mid-thirties. Regional variations also apply, with highest-paying jobs located in the Pacific, Northeast and South-Central regions of the country, and the lowest-paying in the Plains and Midwest, with the Southeast in between.

Women will continue to dominate most of the communications field. A gap still exists between men and women in terms of salaries and percentages of managerial posts held: men hold more of the higher positions and earn more money than their female peers. In public relations, for example, men earn about 23 percent more than women in entry-level positions and about 27 percent more in executive posts. The gender gap has narrowed significantly in some areas, perhaps most notably in journalism, where women in entry-level positions earn about 95 percent of what their male counterparts earn. The gap widens at most higher levels, however.

No matter where you start your career in communications, you're bound to come in contact with creative people and have opportunities to stretch your creative wings yourself. You'll find enormous satisfaction in combining your imagination with your skill to produce a work that informs, sells or entertains. Communications professionals must constantly rise to meet the demands of an ever-changing world. A fresh challenge always lies ahead.

MEDIA

Newspapers and News Services

COPY AIDE

CAREER PROFILE

Duties: Assist reporters and editors in minor news-gathering and editing tasks

Alternate Title(s): Editorial Assistant; Newsroom Assistant; Copy Assistant; Intern

Salary Range: $8,000 to $11,000

Employment Prospects: Fair

Advancement Prospects: Good

Prerequisites:

Education—Undergraduate degree in journalism, communications, English, or liberal arts

Experience—None

Special Skills—Organization; writing; dealing with public

CAREER LADDER

Journalist; Copy Editor

Copy Aide

College

Position Description

Copy aides, the lowest rung on the newsroom ladder, are jacks-of-all-trades. Most of them are journalism or communications students who are working at newspapers while enrolled in college; a few are graduates who've been unable to find jobs as reporters.

At one time, it was customary for all reporters to start out as copy aides. The job consisted primarily of running copy from reporters to editors, doing errands, and disseminating materials throughout the newsroom.

Today, with most copy transmitted electronically, the job of the copy aide has changed. Copy aides monitor the wire machines of news services and see that the right editors get the appropriate stories (called "ripping the wire"), act as newsroom receptionists, and perform general news-related tasks. The job can provide excellent entry-level training. For example, a copy aide may help a reporter with research by going through clips in the news library, may make routine phone calls to police and weather sources, and may write up obituaries and other small news items. Copy aides may work under the supervision of journalists or editors.

Enterprising copy aides can turn their jobs into full-fledged internships, accompanying reporters on assignments and eventually writing their own stories. Copy aides can also learn the duties of the copy desk, doing minor editing and headline writing.

Salaries

Many copy aides are students who work part-time and are paid an hourly wage; some work full-time. Annual incomes can range from $8,000 to $11,000.

Employment Prospects

College programs and internships can lead to part- and full-time jobs as copy aides, though it is possible to get hired without help from a school. Many larger papers hire copy aides for evening and weekend work, which fits in with student schedules.

Advancement Prospects

Experience as a copy aide, particularly if the job involves research, writing, or editing tasks, can count heavily towards promotion to journalist or copy editor.

Education

Many copy aides are undergraduates in schools of journalism, communications, or liberal arts. Journalism study or background is desirable.

Experience/Skills

No experience is required to be a copy aide.

Unions/Associations

College students may join the Society for Collegiate Journalists; Quill and Scroll Society; and the collegiate chapters of the Society of Professional Journalists, and Women In Communications, Inc.

JOURNALIST

CAREER PROFILE

Duties: Gather and report information for news and feature stories for weekly or daily newspapers

Alternate Title(s): Reporter

Salary Range: $11,000 to $54,700+

Employment Prospects: Good

Advancement Prospects: Fair

Prerequisites:

Education—Undergraduate degree in journalism, communications, English, or liberal arts

Experience—Work on a college publication or internship for small daily or weekly newspapers; minimum one to two years' daily newspaper experience for large dailies

Special Skills—Aggressiveness; persistence; good interpersonal relations; good research habits; organizational ability; self-discipline

CAREER LADDER

Assistant Editor; Section Editor

Journalist

Copy Aide; College

Position Description

The journalist performs a vital service to his or her community—the gathering and dissemination of news and information about events on a local, national, or international level. The journalist must stay abreast of developments in his or her assigned area, called a "beat," to report the news accurately, to meet deadlines, and to generate story ideas.

Journalists work under the direction of an assistant editor or editor, who makes story assignments. Many journalists, particularly beginners, are general-assignment reporters,covering a broad range of stories at the discretion of the editor. These can range from a fire to a city-council meeting to a feature story about a celebrity.

Experienced journalists are usually assigned beats such as education, courts, labor, politics, or municipal government. The journalist must manage the beat—become acquainted with important news sources, monitor events, cover meetings, and look for stories of interest to the public. The journalist keeps the editor informed of news-gathering activities, as well as upcoming stories and their news significance. Beats are assigned customarily for a year or more, because it takes time for a journalist to build trust with news sources and become knowledgeable about issues. In addition to news stories, journalists are expected to generate features and occasional news analyses. Few journalists are "investigative" reporters, a pursuit glamorized by Watergate.

Journalists consistently work against deadlines, which vary according to particular newspapers' production requirements and publishing frequencies; a large metropolitan daily with several editions may have five or six deadlines around the clock, while a small daily may have one or two. Often news stories break close to deadline, and a journalist may have mere minutes to get the key facts and write a story. Long-range deadlines are set for in-depth articles that require more research and interviewing. Work schedules are subject to change according to the demands of the business, and night and weekend shifts are common. When out in the field, journalists may be required to file stories via modem or portable fax.

In addition, journalists may:

- take photographs;
- edit copy, and write headlines and cutlines.

Salaries

Most entry-level salaries are low, between about $11,000 and $17,000, depending on the size of the paper. Newspapers that pay union wages offer average starting minimum salaries of about $22,000 and average top minimum salaries (after about four to six years' experience) of $33,300. *The New York Times* pays higher wages, with a top minimum of nearly $55,000. Star reporters earn more.

Employment Prospects

Journalism jobs are expected to grow as fast as average for all occupations throughout the 1990s. The best employment opportunities are in small markets. Many large newspapers will not hire inexperienced journalists.

Advancement Prospects

Advancement prospects are fair; there are many more reporters than editors in a newsroom. Many journalists leave the field for public relations or corporate communications. The first promotion for a journalist is likely to be to section editor or assistant editor.

Education

Most newspapers require an undergraduate degree, preferably in journalism or communications. A liberal arts or any other degree is acceptable as long as writing and reporting ability is good. Specialized or advanced degrees in law or business can be advantageous.

Experience/Skills

Journalist is usually an entry-level job at a newspaper. Collegiate writing experience or internships are helpful.

Journalists should possess a keen curiosity and sharp observational skills. They should feel comfortable dealing with and interviewing persons in high positions of authority. They should know how to research and organize information, and be able to explain complex topics in a simple way. Speed and clarity in writing are essential skills. Journalists also must be self-disciplined and highly motivated. Computer literacy is a must.

Unions/Associations

The Newspaper Guild is the primary union for print journalists. Professional associations include the Society of Professional Journalists; American Society of Journalists and Authors, Inc.; Women In Communications, Inc.; National Association of Black Journalists; Investigative Reporters and Editors; National Sportscasters and Sportswriters Association; National Association of Media Women; and National Federation of Press Women, Inc.

COPY EDITOR

CAREER PROFILE

Duties: Edit reporters' copy for clarity, conciseness, organization, and grammar; write headlines and photo cutlines; lay out pages

Alternate Title(s): Copy Reader

Salary Range: $12,000 to $52,000

Employment Prospects: Good

Advancement Prospects: Poor

Prerequisites:

Education—Undergraduate degree in journalism, communications, liberal arts, or English

Experience—Often an entry-level position; experience desirable for large papers

Special Skills—Grammatical knowledge; speed; ability to spot weaknesses in articles; creativity

CAREER LADDER

Copy Chief; Editor

Copy Editor

Journalist; Copy Aide; College

Position Description

Copy editors are often the unsung heroes of the newspaper. The reporters may get the bylines, but the quality of their stories often depends on the copy editor.

The copy editor is often the last person to handle a reporter's story before it is typeset, after it has been read and edited by a news editor. For all but the smallest papers, there are usually several copy editors on duty who sit in a cluster or horseshoe near the news editor and copy chief.

Copy editors check the stories for spelling, punctuation, correct newspaper style, and other points of grammar. They may question reporters about vague sentences or inconsistencies. While substantial editing is the province of the news editors, copy editors can revise stories. Often the news editor is under too much pressure at deadline to spend a lot of time meticulously editing each story; consequently the task falls to the copy editor. Copy editors also write headlines and photo cutlines for the stories they handle, and they may do page layouts as well.

The work is fast-paced at deadline, and copy editors have to make quick and correct news judgment decisions. During slow times, enterprising copy editors research and write news or feature stories for the paper.

Copy editors report to the copy chief, who works in coordination with the news editor in charge. Sometimes the copy chief is also the wire editor or page-makeup editor.

In addition, copy editors may:

- monitor wire service terminals;
- write news and feature stories.

Salaries

Experienced copy editors earn about 10 percent more than journalists who have the same number of years on the job. Most beginners can expect annual salaries between $12,000 and $19,000. Copy editors with several years of experience command salaries up to $46,000 or more, depending on the size of publication. Most experienced copy editors earn from $30,000 to $40,000. Copy editors reach the top of their pay scales faster than journalists.

Employment Prospects

The overall journalism market is very competitive, but sometimes it's easier to get a job as a copy editor than as a journalist. In fact, many reporters take copy-editing jobs in order to get on a desired newspaper, then work their way into reporting by writing stories during slow periods or on their own time. Some papers require every journalist to spend a probationary period on the copy desk before he or she can join the reporting staff.

Advancement Prospects

Advancement for copy editors depends largely on individual career goals. Some copy editors enjoy working only with copy and have little interest in news reporting, while others aspire to move into reporter positions. Typical advanced copy editing positions are copy chief and wire editor. Copy editors with news reporting experience may be promoted to assistant news editor or assistant city editor, jobs which require supervising reporters and making decisions about news coverage. Most top level managerial jobs in the newsroom, such as executive editor or editor in chief, require news reporting experience.

Education

An undergraduate degree in journalism or mass communications is preferred. A degree in English may be especially valuable to a copy editor. Liberal-arts degrees also are acceptable.

Experience/Skills

Copy editing is often an entry-level job, although some large newspapers require experience. The copy editor must be skilled in grammar and be able to edit quickly and under pressure. Knowledge of type point sizes and column pica widths is needed for writing headlines and cutlines. The copy editor also should be creative in writing crisp headlines that influence people to read the stories. Most editing is done on a display terminal, requiring computer literacy.

Unions/Associations

The Newspaper Guild, affiliated with the AFL-CIO, represents copy editors on many newspapers. Related professional associations include Women In Communications, Inc.; Society of Professional Journalists; and National Association of Black Journalists.

ASSISTANT EDITOR

CAREER PROFILE

Duties: Assist news or department editor in news gathering and editing operations; assign stories to reporters

Alternate Title(s): Deputy Editor; Assistant City Editor; Assistant Metropolitan Editor

Salary Range: $15,000 to $55,000

Employment Prospects: Fair

Advancement Prospects: Fair

Prerequisites:

Education—Undergraduate degree in journalism, communications, English, or liberal arts

Experience—Background as a journalist essential

Special Skills—Editing; directing and motivating others; news judgment

CAREER LADDER

News Editor; City Editor; Section Editor

Assistant Editor

Journalist

Position Description

Most assistant editors serve on the general-news desk, while a smaller number serve section editors. Assistant editors are the front-line editors for nearly all copy, and they relieve editors of much work, giving the editors time for administrative and policy-making duties.

Assistant editors control the flow of copy through the editing process. They screen stories and do the preliminary editing. They have authority to ask reporters for changes and to decide on the importance of a story, determining its position in the newspaper. Decisions or editing that involves sensitive stories may be referred to the news editor or editor in charge.

Once assistant editors finish editing stories, they pass them along to the copy desk for additional editing and headline writing. They inform the makeup or layout editor of the positions the stories are to occupy on various pages and their approximate lengths.

Assistant editors help execute editorial decisions, field questions from reporters, and assign coverage of breaking stories. Some assistant news editors split their time between being journalists and working on the desk. The position is often a tryout to test a promising reporter's news judgment, editing, and management abilities.

Assistant editors may be assigned to work any shift, depending on the needs of the paper.

In addition, assistant editors may:

- write news stories;
- write headlines and cutlines.

Salaries

Along with copy editors, most assistant editors are paid slightly more than most journalists. Most experienced assistant editors earn between $30,000 and $40,000. Some earn more, depending on their years of experience and the size of the newspaper.

Employment Prospects

The assistant editor position is usually a training post, with candidates chosen from the reporting staff. Small papers offer the most and best opportunities for beginning assistant editors.

Advancement Prospects

The assistant editor's job is part of the track to middle and upper editorial management positions. Movement to another paper as assistant editor is unlikely; however, an assistant editor on a large paper may qualify for a news editor's post on a smaller paper.

Education

Most assistant editors have undergraduate degrees in journalism, communications, English, or liberal arts.

Experience/Skills

On small papers, a journalist with one or two years' experience may be promoted to assistant editor. On larger papers, four to six years' reporting experience is necessary.

Assistant editors should have good editing skills and news judgment. They should be able to meet deadlines and be well organized, in order to avoid copy bottlenecks at the last minute. They should be able to direct and motivate others.

Unions, Associations

Major professional associations include the Society of Professional Journalists; American Society of Newspaper Editors; Women In Communications, Inc.; National Association of Black Journalists; International Society of Weekly Newspaper Editors; Investigative Reporters and Editors; National Federation of Press Women; and National Association of Media Women.

NEWS EDITOR

CAREER PROFILE

Duties: Manage a news-gathering staff; determine the direction and content of the newspaper; make policy decisions

Alternate Title(s): City Editor; Metropolitan Editor; Executive Editor

Salary Range: $16,000 to $55,000+

Employment Prospects: Fair

Advancement Prospects: Fair

Prerequisites:

Education—Undergraduate degree in journalism, communications, or liberal arts

Experience—Background in reporting and copy editing essential

Special Skills—Ability to direct and motivate others; news judgment; editing

CAREER LADDER

Assistant Managing Editor; Managing Editor; Executive Editor

News Editor

Assistant Editor; Section Editor

Position Description

The quality of a newspaper often falls squarely on the shoulders of the news editor, who is in charge of the day-to-day operations of a newsroom. News editors must stay abreast of all major breaking and developing news stories, decide how the paper will cover them and play them on the page, and determine who will write the stories. They keep track of reporters' activities and make split-second decisions on how to handle breaking news.

News editors make story assignments and determine which reporters will handle what beats. In addition to editing copy, they monitor the progress of stories and the flow of copy through the editing process. They meet with high-level editors to determine the content and direction of the paper and discuss problems.

News editors are also administrators. They make up work schedules for reporters and assistants, arbitrate problems, write reports to upper management, and have a voice in the promotion, hiring, and firing of subordinates. They need to be informed on all labor laws pertaining to their employees. And, most important, they must be able to work within a budget.

Finally, news editors are community liaisons. Often they are called upon to speak for or represent the paper at civic functions and in the classroom.

On a small newspaper, the news editor may be in charge of the entire newsroom operation and have no assistant editors. On larger papers, news-editor positions are broken down into geographic areas, and each editor has one or more assistants.

The job is demanding, because a typical day can encompass a wide range of news and administrative tasks. News editors work regular business hours, but days run longer if a major story breaks. The counterpart of the news editor for the nighttime shift is the night editor, who oversees the operation of a daily paper after the news editor goes home.

Salaries

News editors earn approximately $16,000 to $55,000 or more. Most earn in the thirties and forties.

Employment Prospects

Skilled news editors are always in demand on papers of all sizes, though opportunities are best with small dailies and weeklies. The pool of competitors is much smaller than for journalists, but opportunities may be greatly restricted by the size of the publication and relocation requirements.

Advancement Prospects

News editors are in an excellent position for advancement into upper management.

Education

Most news editors have undergraduate degrees in journalism, communications, English, or liberal arts. Advanced degrees are not necessary but can be helpful. News editors should have additional training in management techniques.

Experience/Skills

On a very small paper, two or three years' experience as a journalist, section editor, or assistant editor can qualify someone for news editor. Five to ten years or more are required on larger papers. News editors should be adept at editing, rewriting, and making quick decisions, and they should be smooth in handling personnel matters. They must be detail-oriented and well organized, in order to handle administrative tasks. Experience and ease in public speaking helps if the job involves community liaison work.

Unions, Associations

Major professional associations include the Society of Professional Journalists, American Society of Newspaper Editors; Investigative Reporters and Editors; Women In Communications, Inc.; National Association of Black Journalists; International Society of Weekly Newspaper Editors; National Federation of Press Women; and National Association of Media Women.

SECTION EDITOR

CAREER PROFILE

Duties: Supervise content and layout of special-interest section or page

Alternate Title(s): Business Editor; Life-Style Editor; Sunday Magazine Editor; Sports Editor; etc.

Salary Range: $15,000 to $55,000+

Employment Prospects: Fair

Advancement Prospects: Poor

Prerequisites:

Education—Undergraduate degree in journalism, communications, English, or liberal arts; advanced degree desirable for specialized fields

Experience—Background as journalist, copy editor, or assistant editor

Special Skills—Staff supervision ability; news judgment; editing; graphics

CAREER LADDER

News Editor; Assistant Managing Editor

Section Editor

Journalist; Assistant Editor; Copy Editor

Position Description

Section editors are responsible for specialized sections or pages of a newspaper, such as business, lifestyle, arts and entertainment, real estate, suburban news, or Sunday magazine. They are responsible for determining content, assigning reporters and photographers to stories, monitoring deadlines, editing copy, and executing or overseeing page graphics. Most are expected to write for their pages as well.

Section editors may work under the direction of the news editor in charge, who may be called the city editor, metropolitan editor, or executive editor. Some section editors may be independent and work with other editors on a coordinating or advisory basis.

The job of section editor calls for a good sense of organization as well as the ability to manage others. The editor must monitor other sources of news, such as wire stories and magazines, for story ideas; must work on both short-term and long-term stories; and must coordinate the work of others.

On a typical day, a section editor may meet with other editors, review wire copy to determine which stories will be used in the section or page, assign stories, edit copy, and select photos and other artwork to illustrate the text. Many section editors do their own page layouts, while others work with the newspaper's art and photo departments. An editor of a daily page, such as business, must have good news judgment and be able to react to breaking news quickly.

The job can be especially rewarding, not only for the decision-making freedom that goes with it, but also for the leeway one has to put a personal "stamp" on part of a newspaper. Section editors tend to work regular business hours and usually are not subject to shift changes or weekend or night work.

Salaries

Section editors generally earn more than reporters. Their pay may be comparable to assistant editors, depending on a newspaper's hierarchy. Typical salaries are in the twenties and thirties.

Employment Prospects

Most section editors are promoted from within. Some newspapers, however, conduct national searches for talent. Journalists and editors with advanced degrees or specialized education in certain fields, such as law, business, or science, have a hiring advantage. Jobs are highly competitive.

Advancement Prospects

Section editors are in excellent positions to be promoted to higher level jobs, but competition is keen.

Education

Section editors should have undergraduate degrees in journalism, communications, English, or liberal arts.

Experience/Skills

Background experience required depends on the size of the newspaper. A journalist with only one or two years of experience may become a section editor on a small paper, while larger papers require four or more years of experience. Many section editors have served time as copy editors or assistant news editors.

Section editors should be thoroughly knowledgeable about their subject areas and the audience they serve. They should be good writers and editors, and be able to lay out pages.

Unions, Associations

Major professional associations include the Society of Professional Journalists; Women In Communications, Inc.; National Association of Black Journalists; International Society of Weekly Newspaper Editors; National Association of Media Women; and National Federation of Press Women.

EDITORIAL WRITER

CAREER PROFILE

Duties: Research and write editorials on issues; screen columns, letters to the editor, and other editorial articles; help decide newspaper's position

Alternate Title(s): Editorial Page Editor

Salary Range: $17,000 to $55,000+

Employment Prospects: Fair

Advancement Prospects: Fair

Prerequisites:

Education—Undergraduate degree in journalism, communications, or liberal arts; advanced degree helpful

Experience—Background as journalist and editor

Special Skills—Logic; persuasiveness; excellent, clear writing; thoroughness; objectivity

CAREER LADDER

Senior Editor; Managing Editor

Editorial Writer

News Editor; Section Editor; Journalist

Position Description

Editorial writers work away from the daily hubbub of the newsroom; they are concerned with the issues generated by events rather than the news of the events. They are responsible for the contents of the editorial page and the page opposite, called the "op ed" page. The editorial page is a sensitive area because it represents the quality and character of the newspaper.

Editorial writers comprise an editorial board, which also includes members of senior management and the publisher. A small newspaper may have only one or two editorial writers to share all the duties, while a larger paper may allow particular editorial writers to focus on special areas of expertise. On a large paper, junior editorial writers may do research for senior members of the board.

Editorial writers examine issues that arise, research them, and decide on a position. Some editorials must be timely, reacting to the latest news. Others, on topics of current interest but not related to breaking news, may be researched and written more slowly. Editorial writers do research the same way as journalists do, by calling sources and consulting library clips and other published sources. They may ask a journalist for additional information.

In examining an issue, editorial writers must be thorough, objective, and accurate. In order to be fully informed of local, national, and international news, most editorial writers do extensive reading of other news and commentary publications. All sides of an issue must be carefully weighed in order to arrive at a position.

In addition, editorial writers screen letters and columns for publication on the editorial pages. The "letters to the editor" column is an important public forum. Columns may be written by the newspaper's own news staff or by syndicated writers.

Salaries

The typical salary for experienced editorial writers is in the thirties. Only a small percentage, those at large newspapers, earn up to $55,000 or more.

Employment Prospects

Several years of seasoning are required to qualify for editorial writer. Candidates have to have demonstrated their reporting and analytical abilities as journalists first; editorial ability as newsroom editor is sometimes necessary as well.

Advancement Prospects

Fair opportunities exist to rise within the editorial board structure. Most senior managers, however, are selected from editors who run the daily operations of the newsroom. Many editorial writers, however, have no wish to leave the editorial department.

Education

Editorial writers should have at least undergraduate degrees in journalism, communications, English, or liberal arts. Degrees in business, economics, law, or other graduate degrees are likely to help career advancement because of the specialized nature of many editorial-writing positions.

Experience/Skills

Editorial writers have had at least several years' seasoning as journalists and, most likely, as newsroom editors as well. They have demonstrated their ability to write balanced, clear news analyses and accurate news stories. They have good news judgment, are objective, and are good editors. They do thorough research and stay abreast of public opinion through extensive reading.

Unions, Associations

Associations include the National Council of Editorial Writers; American Association of Newspaper Editors; Society of Professional Journalists; Women In Communications, Inc.; National Association of Black Journalists; International Society of Weekly Newspaper Editors; National Federation of Press Women; and National Association of Media Women.

BUREAU REPORTER

CAREER PROFILE

Duties: Manage or perform news-gathering activities away from newsroom, in a bureau located in a suburb or a different city; write and edit news, features, and analysis stories

Alternate Title(s): Correspondent; Bureau Chief

Salary Range: $11,000 to $55,000

Employment Prospects: Good

Advancement Prospects: Good

Prerequisites:

Education—Undergraduate degree in journalism, communications, or liberal arts

Experience—Background as a journalist helpful; sometimes an entry-level job

Special Skills—Self-motivation; good writing and editing ability; accuracy; organization; ability to direct others

CAREER LADDER

Bureau Chief; Assistant Editor; Section Editor; News Editor

Bureau Reporter

Journalist; Copy Editor; College

Position Description

Newspapers of all sizes maintain bureaus, which are news-gathering centers far enough away from the location of the newsroom to be independent operations. A bureau may be set up in a far-flung suburb of a large metropolitan area, a nearby city important to the paper's readers, the state capital, or the nation's capital. Newspaper groups and chains also operate bureaus; wire services, such as Associated Press and United Press International, have bureaus scattered throughout the world.

Some bureaus may be one- or two-person operations; others may have large staffs. In a small operation, the bureau reporter may be called bureau chief or correspondent; in a large operation, a bureau chief supervises a reporting staff.

The bureau reporter is responsible for monitoring news events within the bureau's jurisdiction and filing stories with the main newsroom. Copy may be transmitted electronically on computer terminals, sent over telephone lines on telecopiers or printers, dictated over the phone, or, if the bureau is close enough, delivered by messenger.

In a small operation, only the stories most important to the newspaper's circulation area can be handled. Wire-service bureaus, however, are also expected to file small and routine copy for their newspaper clients: minor accidents, arrests, weather reports, and commodity market prices, for example.

Bureaus keep the home-base news editor informed of events and stories as they develop. They also are assigned stories to cover. Bureau reporters often edit and rewrite copy written by other news sources for their own use. For example, a wire-service bureau will rewrite stories written by local papers and send the stories out over the wire. Newspaper bureaus, in turn, monitor wire copy.

Bureau reporting has many advantages for the correspondent. It allows him or her more freedom of movement and decision-making power, and it provides one with a chance to demonstrate journalistic and editorial ability. Many bureau staffers prefer the autonomy of their jobs to being a part of a newsroom.

Salaries

Pay for bureau staffers is roughly the same as that for journalists, ranging from about $11,000 to $55,000 or more. Some newspapers pay differentials that depend on the nature of the responsibilities. The chiefs of bureaus receive more.

Employment Prospects

All but the smallest newspapers have at least one bureau, in a suburban or capital area. In an effort to reach the spreading and diverse suburban readership, daily newspapers have established multiple bureaus in target areas. Associated Press and United Press International maintain more than one hundred bureaus each, many in small towns.

Advancement Prospects

The bureau, especially a capital one, is an excellent stepping-stone to an editorial position. Some reporters who are sent out to suburban bureaus, however, feel isolated from newsroom activities and politics; they often feel forgotten when it comes to promotion. It all depends on what the individual makes of the opportunity.

Education

An undergraduate degree in journalism, communications, English, or liberal arts is the minimum requirement.

Experience/Skills

Many beginning journalists are sent to small suburban bureaus before they join the general news staff; beginners also are hired for wire-service bureaus, small and large. Newspapers expect chiefs and reporters of major and capital bureaus to be experienced journalists.

Basic journalistic skills include quick and accurate reporting, good writing, astute news judgment, and aggressiveness. Bureau reporters also must be highly self-motivated, for many of them supervise their own activities. They must be well organized in order to monitor many events.

Unions/Associations

The Newspaper Guild wage bargains for more than 40,000 journalists. Major professional associations include the Society of Professional Journalists; Women In Communications, Inc.; National Association of Black Journalists; National Association of Media Women; and National Federation of Press Women.

COLUMNIST

CAREER PROFILE

Duties: Write daily or weekly columns

Alternate Title(s): None

Salary Range: $15,000 to $55,000+

Employment Prospects: Poor

Advancement Prospects: Poor

Prerequisites:

Education—Undergraduate degree in journalism, communications, English, or liberal arts; advanced degrees if specialized

Experience—Background as journalist

Special Skills—Good storytelling ability; creativity

CAREER LADDER

Assistant Editor; Section Editor

Columnist

Journalist; Copy Editor

Position Description

Columnists are regarded as having plum jobs on newspapers, but their job is harder than it appears. And, because they are showcased, they are also subject to more criticism.

Most columnists have human-interest, around-the-town or social-notes beats. Their columns may be collections of short, gossipy, or newsy items, or they may each consist of a single feature story built around an interesting person or someone's dilemma. Also common on most papers are political columnists who analyze or comment on the activities of politicians. A few columnists are nationally syndicated (see "Syndicated Columnist" in Section XIII).

Specialized columnists can write about any topic that catches the public's fancy—computers, pets, health, love and romance, plants, bridge, medicine—the list goes on and on.

Columns may be daily or weekly. Columnists are expected to generate their own material, which sometimes is not all that easy. The column goes to press regardless of material at hand.

Columnists usually operate autonomously and have a great deal of freedom. They become "personalities" and build up audiences, thus becoming promotional assets to their newspapers; consequently, some of them can negotiate higher pay than their fellow journalists. The position is usually an end goal rather than a steppingstone to something else. Few columnists want to give up their domain and their audience for something else.

Not all columnists work at their columns fulltime. Many report for the general-news pages as well.

Columnists who become syndicated can earn a good deal of money. Art Buchwald, humorist, and Jack Anderson, investigative reporter, reportedly earn well over $200,000 a year from their columns.

Salaries

Most columnists who work fulltime for a newspaper earn about $10,000 to $42,000 or more. Large newspapers may pay $80,000 or more for prestigious or popular columnists. Some journalists write columns in addition to their reporting duties, receiving no extra money for them. The visibility and experience, they hope, may catapult them into full-time columnist positions later.

Employment Prospects

Most newspapers do not hire journalists to be columnists unless they have established a track record and audience. The best bet is to use a journalist's position as the launching point to build a local readership for one's work.

Advancement Prospects

Few columnists aspire to managerial jobs; the column is the sought-after position. A popular column, however, can establish a writer as an authority in a certain area, and that can lead to syndication.

Education

Like their fellow journalists, most columnists have undergraduate degrees in journalism, communications, English, or liberal arts. A columnist writing about a specialized area, such as economics or medicine, should have the appropriate education and credentials.

Experience/Skills

Most columnists are experienced journalists; experience varies according to the market. Columnists must be creative. For human-interest subjects, they need to be good storytellers. Political columnists are expected to have good analytical skills. Since most columns are short, columnists must write concisely.

Unions/Associations

Many columnists are members of the Newspaper Guild union. Professional associations include the Society of Professional Journalists; Women In Communications, Inc.; National Association of Black Journalists; National Association of Media Women; National Federation of Press Women.

CRITIC

CAREER PROFILE

Duties: Review artistic performances, recordings, exhibits and books; write columns

Alternate Title(s): Reviewer

Salary Range: $15,000 to $55,000+

Employment Prospects: Poor

Advancement Prospects: Poor

Prerequisites:

Education—Undergraduate degree in journalism, communications, English, or liberal arts; specialization in a particular field

Experience—Background as a journalist and expertise in the area reviewed

Special Skills—Good writing ability; thorough knowledge of subject matter

CAREER LADDER

Section Editor

Critic

Journalist; Copy Editor

Position Description

Critics can wield a great deal of influence with the public and can affect the success of artists, films, plays, books, and musical and/or dance productions. Bad reviews can keep an audience away and close a play or kill a film. In 1981, for example, the $40-million film *Heaven's Gate*, starring Kris Kristofferson and Isabelle Huppert, closed within two days of its premiere due to scorching reviews.

Critics, many of whom work evenings and weekends, review plays, films, concerts, operas, exhibits, dance productions, books, records, nightclub acts—anything connected with the arts and entertainment field—and write their opinions in columns. They may be highly specialized; for example, a music critic may not handle films or plays. Some small to medium-sized papers, however, have one or two persons who handle all reviewing.

Critics are expected to be knowledgeable about their subjects and keep abreast of trends and news. They interview performers and celebrities, and they do extensive reading, even studying in their respective areas. They must be objective and have good judgment. Like columnists, they develop audiences who trust their judgment.

Besides review columns, critics often write celebrity interviews, feature stories, and in-depth articles on trends or other aspects of the arts.

Salaries

Critics earn roughly the same as, or sometimes more than, their fellow experienced journalists—approximately $15,000 to $55,000 or more. High salaries depend heavily on experience, credentials, and the size of the newspaper.

Employment Prospects

Many critics start out as journalists and work their way into full-time critic posts by doing occasional reviews. A position as a staff writer or assistant editor for the life-style or arts-and-entertainment sections is an excellent place to start. Once a critic is established, it is possible to change employers, though the job market is very small.

Advancement Prospects

Like columnists, many critics don't wish to do any other kind of news work. The most likely advancement is to become editor of the arts-and-entertainment section or book-review section.

Education

Critics are expected to have a background in their area of expertise; this may involve specialized or advanced degrees. Basic education is an undergraduate degree in journalism, communications, liberal arts, or other areas pertaining to the arts.

Experience/Skills

Critics should be thoroughly familiar with their specialization in order to give fair and objective reviews. This requires extensive reading and often periodic study. They should be good interviewers and be able to write quickly on deadline.

Unions, Associations

Professional associations include the American Theater Critics Association; Dance Critics Association; Music Critics Association; National Book Critics Circle; Television Critics Association; Society of Professional Journalists; Women In Communications, Inc.; National Association of Black Journalists; National Federation of Press Women; and National Association of Media Women. The Newspaper Guild negotiates wages for many journalists, including critics.

PUBLICITY/PROMOTION SPECIALIST

CAREER PROFILE

Duties: Write and disseminate news releases; write occasional speeches; create and manage contests; work with advertising staff; handle educational activities

Alternate Title(s): Assistant Publicity/Promotion Manager; Assistant Publicity/Promotion Director

Salary Range: Under $20,000 to $35,000+

Employment Prospects: Fair

Advancement Prospects: Fair

Prerequisites:

Education—Undergraduate degree in journalism, communications, advertising, or liberal arts

Experience—None necessary for entry level; background in advertising helpful

Special Skills—Flair for writing news releases and catchy promotional copy; speechwriting; outgoing personality

CAREER LADDER

Publicity/Promotion Manager

Publicity/Promotion Specialist

Copywriter; College

Position Description

Publicity/promotion specialists help shape the public image of a newspaper. On all but the largest papers, the functions of publicity and promotion are usually combined in one position. On small papers, one person may handle all duties and be called the director or manager of publicity and/or promotion. Sometimes publicity and promotion are part of the advertising department.

Duties include writing and disseminating press releases to the news and trade news media on upcoming major features or series in the newspaper, personnel changes (new hires, promotions, etc.), activities of major news executives (such as public appearances, speeches, and appointments to political and civic boards), and publicity stunts (such as sending a reporter around the state by bicycle to do "grass roots" interviews).

Publicity/promotion specialists handle questions and requests for information from other media. They may also write speeches for news executives, or write short radio spots promoting articles or publicity events sponsored by the newspaper. They frequently represent the paper at civic and public functions.

Promotion activities include creating ways to call attention to the newspaper, to attract more readers and subscribers. Such events could include subscription drives with premiums, contests, and drawings. Publicity/promotion writers may work with a newspaper's advertising agency in developing campaigns.

Many newspapers participate in an educational program called Newspapers in Education (NIE), which involves working with school districts to distribute newspapers in classrooms and encourage students to read them. Training workshops for teachers are conducted, and classroom appearances are sometimes required. The job is usually handled by an NIE coordinator, though publicity/production assistants may be called on for assistance.

Salaries

Publicity/promotion specialists can expect to start at under $20,000. Salaries tend to remain low, some paying in the thirties after 10 years' experience. Supervisory jobs pay more.

Employment Prospects

The job of publicity/promotion specialist is often entry level but, due to tight budgets at many newspapers, employment prospects are only fair. The best bet is to apply for such jobs at newspaper chains; these can lead to corporate opportunities.

Advancement Prospects

A beginning publicity/promotion specialist is in a good position to advance to manager or director. Further advancement, to vice president, often requires advertising sales experience. Newspaper groups and chains, such as Harte-Hanks, Gannett, and Knight-Ridder, offer opportunities for one to move into corporate public-relations management. A publicity/promotion specialist can also make a lateral move into corporate communications or to a public-relations agency. Jobs in public relations, publicity, and promotion seldom lead to top executive positions.

Education

An undergraduate degree in journalism, communications, advertising, or liberal arts is required.

Experience/Skills

No experience is necessary for some entry-level publicity/promotion writing jobs; others, with managerial responsibilities, require several years in this field or in advertising (either in account or creative services).

Publicity/promotion specialists develop different writing skills than journalists, therefore a background in advertising is helpful. Promotional copy is sales-oriented, while speeches are written for the ear. News releases, however, are written in news-story style.

Publicity/promotion specialists should be at ease in dealing with the public and with top executives. They not only must be creative but well organized, because publicity campaigns require thorough, detailed planning and coordination.

Unions, Associations

Major associations include the International Newspaper Advertising and Marketing Executives; International Newspaper Promotion Association; Public Relations Society of America, Inc.; International Association of Business Communicators; and Women In Communications, Inc. Some publicity/promotion specialists may belong to The Newspaper Guild.

Magazines

EDITORIAL ASSISTANT

CAREER PROFILE

Duties: Clerical and receptionist duties; errands; minor editorial and production tasks; research

Alternate Title(s): None

Salary Range: $13,000 to $15,000+

Employment Prospects: Fair

Advancement Prospects: Good

Prerequisites:

Education—undergraduate degree in communications, journalism, English or liberal arts; courses in publishing

Experience—None, for many positions

Special Skills—Editing; proofreading; secretarial skills; writing

CAREER LADDER

Associate Editor; Assistant Editor

Editorial Assistant

College; Secretary

Position Description

Editorial assistant is the entry-level position on a magazine's editorial staff. The job is more secretarial than editorial, but beginners are given a chance to learn on the job and work their way into more responsible editorial positions.

Editorial assistants report to higher-level editors, including assistant and associate editors, senior editors, and editors. They do library research for superiors who are writing articles, and they check the accuracy of facts in articles written by outside authors. They are responsible for reviewing other magazines and newspapers and clipping articles of interest for editors. Such articles may generate story ideas or provide helpful information on stories in progress.

They also proofread galleys and write headlines, photo cutlines, and "deck" copy, which consists of several lines of large type excerpted from the article to break up the gray type on a page. Secretarial functions include opening and routing the mail, answering the telephone, running errands, filing, and typing letters.

As experience is gained, editorial assistants are given more editorial responsibilities, such as editing manuscripts and suggesting article ideas. They may also be given a chance to write short bylined articles or columns for the magazine or be responsible for collecting short items for news-roundup columns.

In addition, editorial assistants may:

- handle production details, including trafficking copy, galleys, and artwork;
- give a first reading to unsolicited manuscripts;
- work with freelancers involved in writing and production;
- screen job applications.

Salaries

Most editorial assistants earn between $13,000 and $15,000. Some top magazines pay as much as $21,000. Trade publications sometimes pay more than average for those who have specialized education or experience, such as technical or computer-science backgrounds.

Employment Prospects

Competition for magazine editorial jobs is keen, even at the entry level. Beginners who have taken skill-oriented journalism or publishing classes in high school and college—writing and editing—and have had school newspaper or intern experience have an advantage.

Advancement Prospects

Editorial assistants have a good chance of working their way up the editorial ladder, though competition remains stiff at all levels.

Education

An undergraduate degree in communications, journalism, English, or liberal arts is necessary. In some cases, a master's degree in communications or publishing may be advantageous. Technical and trade journals may require specialized education in such fields as engineering, computer programming, science, law, or economics.

Experience/Skills

Although no experience is required for many editorial-assistant jobs, the candidates with the best chances of employment are those who've taken writing/editing journalism and publishing courses in school, been actively involved in school publications, and have had internships or summer jobs in the field.

Editorial assistants should demonstrate both editing and writing ability, though they may not immediately write articles. Production knowledge also is useful.

Unions/Associations

The American Society of Magazine Editors; American Society of Journalists and Authors, Inc.; and Women In Communications, Inc. are among the major professional associations open to magazine editors. Some editors also join specialized authors' groups or trade and industry associations. Those who work for major news and feature magazines may belong to The Newspaper Guild.

RESEARCHER

CAREER PROFILE

Duties: Read all stories and mark facts to be verified; check with author and sources; keep records of any changes and apprise editor of changes.

Alternate Title(s): Fact Checker; Research Editor; Editorial Assistant

Salary Range: $10,000 to $25,000+

Employment Prospects: Poor

Advancement Prospects: Poor

Prerequisites:

Education—Undergraduate degree in journalism, communications, English, or liberal arts; advanced degrees or course work for technical/scientific/business publications

Experience—Entry-level researcher does not necessarily require any previous experience; background as journalist, writer, or editor helpful

Special Skills—Meticulous attention to detail; organization; telephone skills; editing; writing

CAREER LADDER

Associate Editor; Assistant Editor

Researcher

Editorial Assistant; College

Position Description

Researcher is often an entry-level position with a magazine, but one that is usually understood to lead to more editorial responsibility. Researchers must verify each piece of information in a reporter's story and make sure that all corrections are made. Both the reporter and the assistant editor should be informed of any changes the researcher makes.

Smaller publications usually do not hire researchers but depend on their own reporters to verify facts and information. At larger magazines, the researcher not only checks data but shepherds stories under his or her responsibility through the entire production process, making sure that everything remains correct at each step.

To groom them for reporting and other editorial positions, editors may assign small, bylined stories or column features to researchers. Write-ups of personnel changes or new-business columns may be the regular responsibility of a researcher. Researchers may also be responsible for proofreading galleys and writing headlines and captions.

In addition, researchers may:

- handle other production details;
- attend seminars, workshops, and trade shows to keep up with industry trends.

Salaries

Pay depends upon the size of the publication and the applicant's skills and training. Beginners can earn as little as $10,000. Pay is substantially higher at large consumer magazines, where experienced researchers can earn in the twenties and thirties.

Employment Prospects

Since researcher is an entry-level job, there is more turnover at such positions than at higher ones. People who have patience and are capable of meticulous attention to detail are not always easy to come by, yet a magazine's credibility depends on the accuracy of its stories. Beginners with journalism skills and great organizational ability have less trouble breaking into the editorial staff by acquiring such researcher positions. Not all magazines employ researchers.

Advancement Prospects

Most researchers have fairly excellent advancement prospects. Often a researcher is hired with the understanding that, if everything works out all right, promotion to assistant or associate editor is quite likely in about two years. On smaller publications, a researcher may move up even sooner. As with all editorial jobs, however, competition is stiff.

Education

An undergraduate degree in journalism, English, communications, or liberal arts is essential. Any secretarial training that gives the researcher organizational skills is also a boon. Advanced course work, sometimes even an advanced degree, is necessary for researcher jobs on specialized publications, such as those for law, medicine, or high technology.

Experience/Skills

While no formal experience in journalism is necessary, aspiring researchers who have taken writing and editing courses, have been involved in school publications, and who have had summer jobs or internships have a leg up on other applicants. Many editors think a good researcher should have a background in liberal arts and have a strong interest in reading in general. Attendance at summer seminars or workshops is also advantageous.

Researchers should demonstrate good organizational skills, plus editing and writing ability. Knowledge of magazine production is very helpful.

Unions/Associations

Researchers are eligible to join the American Society of Magazine Editors; American Society of Journalists and Authors, Inc., and other writers' trade groups. All women journalists may join Women In Communications, Inc. The Newspaper Guild represents employees on some major news and feature magazines.

COPY EDITOR

CAREER PROFILE

Duties: Oversee all editorial copy for grammar and style; prepare copy for production; check facts

Alternate Title(s): Copy Chief; Assistant Managing Editor; Production Assistant; Proofreader

Salary Range: $12,000 to $40,000+

Employment Prospects: Fair

Advancement Prospects: Fair

Prerequisites:

Education—Undergraduate degree in English, communications, liberal arts, or journalism; advanced course work or knowledge of specialized fields necessary for certain technical publications

Experience—Not necessary for entry-level jobs; otherwise, work as editorial assistant or professor's assistant beneficial

Special Skills—Good command of English punctuation, grammar, and spelling; organizational skills; patience; attention to detail

CAREER LADDER

Associate Editor; Assistant Editor; Reporter; Researcher

Copy Editor

Editorial Assistant; College

Position Description

The copy editor takes each article through the successive steps of accuracy and fit, readying it for typesetting and, finally, print. He or she checks each story for grammar and magazine style, and may be responsible for fact-checking as well. On smaller publications without separate researchers, the copy editor handles fact research, working directly with the writers and editors.

Copy editors must have a good working knowledge of magazine production. If a story is too long or too short, the copy editor is usually the person responsible for cutting or lengthening it. If the piece is too short, the copy editor will prefer to go back to the original writer, but he or she may have to act alone if pressured by production deadlines. Copy editors often write headlines, captions, and "decks" (the large quotes which highlight a page of copy). They check relentlessly for typographical errors, misspelled words, and incorrect usage in the original manuscript, proofreading galleys and final page proofs for errors that may have slipped by earlier or have been incorrectly set by the typesetter. Other production duties may include working with the layout or managing editor to decide article placement, determining use of photos and other artwork, and giving final approval of page layouts.

Large publications usually employ several copy editors for individual sections, but one copy editor may serve for an entire small magazine. Copy editors are valued for their unruffled personalities and meticulous attention to the smallest details.

In addition, copy editors may:

- spend time with managing editors at typesetters' or printers' shops;
- substitute for the managing editors when necessary.

Salaries

Most small trade magazines start copy editors at about $12,000, while large consumer publications start copy editors at about $20,000. A good copy editor with experience can earn about $40,000, while those at large consumer magazines can earn up to $75,000.

Employment Prospects

Competition is stiff and is characterized by high turnover. Many copy editors work on a part-time basis for more than one publication, or work as freelancers (for freelance rates, see Section 8).

Advancement Prospects

Advancement potential for copy editors is fair. A beginning copy editor can move on to associate or assistant editor, perhaps eventually to senior editor. Knowledge of magazine production is always helpful at higher editorial positions, and the copy editor is in a perfect position to acquire such information.

Education

As with all magazine-writing jobs, an undergraduate degree in English, journalism, communications, or liberal arts is a must. After that, a copy editor would do well to brush up on grammar and writing skills through course work and/or seminars and internships. Advanced course work for specialized publications gives the copy editor familiarity with technical concepts and jargon connected to a particular field.

Experience/Skills

Although a background in writing or journalism is helpful, the copy editor's most important skill is a thorough command of English grammar, punctuation, and style. Copy-editing work for any general-interest publication stands as a good recommendation for any other general-interest magazine. Secretarial skills acquired along the way, for organizational purposes, are also helpful.

Finally, a copy editor would do well to learn how to communicate easily and courteously with people, since some writers are not predisposed to hear about their sloppy grammar, incorrect information, and terrible spelling.

Unions/Associations

There are no unions for magazine editorial personnel. Professional organizations available include the American Society of Magazine Editors, as well as writers' trade groups.

ASSOCIATE EDITOR

CAREER PROFILE

Duties: Assign, read, and edit articles; write articles, columns, and copy; handle production

Alternate Title(s): Assistant Editor

Salary Range: $12,000 to $45,000+

Employment Prospects: Fair

Advancement Prospects: Fair

Prerequisites:

Education—Undergraduate degree in journalism, communications, or liberal arts; advanced or specialized degrees for technical, scientific, or business publications

Experience—None for entry level; otherwise, background as journalist, editorial assistant, or as associate editor on a smaller publication is needed

Special Skills—Editing; organization; production skill; graphics sense

CAREER LADDER

Editor; Senior Editor

Associate Editor

Editorial Assistant; Journalist; Writer; College

Position Description

Associate editors have varying degrees of responsibility, depending on the size of the magazine. On a small trade magazine, for example, an associate editor can be second in command, reporting to an editor. On a larger publication, an associate editor may work under a senior editor and be assigned to a particular department.

Associate editors screen the unsolicited manuscripts that are initially screened and routed to them by editorial assistants; in some cases, they may do all the screening and routing themselves. They assign articles to freelance writers, edit manuscripts, plus write headlines, cutlines, and other copy as needed. They are responsible for assigning photographic coverage or art illustrations to accompany articles. They either direct editorial assistants in research and fact-checking or are responsible for those duties themselves.

Associate editors participate in regular editorial meetings at which ideas are suggested and content for future issues planned. They may be assigned responsibility to generate articles on certain topics, which they in turn assign to writers.

In addition, associate editors may:

- handle production tasks, such as proofreading galleys;
- represent the magazine at professional functions;
- attend workshops, seminars, and trade conventions to stay abreast of industry trends and techniques.

Salaries

Associate editors generally earn between $12,000 and $18,000. Trade publications that require associate editors with advanced or specialized degrees pay more. Large consumer magazines also pay more than $20,000, with some salaries as high as $45,000 or more. Top salaries at large consumer magazines are about $55,000.

Employment Prospects

The best job opportunities are on small and special-interest magazines, though job security is low. Many trade publications do not require experience or education in the industry they serve; background information is learned on the job.

Advancement Prospects

Work as an associate editor provides the necessary skill and background for higher editorial positions. There is a great deal of movement from one publication to another, especially in cities such as New York, which have a high concentration of publications. It is also possible to move into book-publishing editorial jobs.

Education

Associate editors are expected to have undergraduate degrees in communications, journalism, or liberal arts. Courses in publishing and advanced degrees in communications provide one with a competitive edge. Degrees in specialized fields are required by many technical, law, economics, scientific, and medical publications.

Experience/Skills

Prior experience as an editorial assistant, writer, or journalist is necessary for most associate-editor positions, though some jobs are at entry level. Also, work as an associate editor on a small magazine may be necessary to advance to associate editor on a large magazine.

Associate editors should be organized and deadline conscious. They should write and edit well, and understand the production process. They must be able to manage and direct others.

Unions/Associations

The Newspaper Guild represents employees of some major news and feature magazines, but by and large magazine editors are nonunion. The principal professional association is the American Society of Magazine Editors. Many editors join trade associations and are auxiliary members of writers' groups. Women In Communications, Inc. is open to women in all media.

SENIOR EDITOR

CAREER PROFILE

Duties: Supervise major editorial department; manage lower-level editors, freelancers, and/or photographers; write some articles and columns

Alternate Title(s): Executive Editor; Associate Editor

Salary Range: $22,000 to $50,000+

Employment Prospects: Fair

Advancement Prospects: Poor

Prerequisites:

Education—Undergraduate degree in journalism, English, communications, or liberal arts; advanced degree in journalism or specialized degrees for technical, scientific, or business publications

Experience—Background as journalist, writer, or editor essential; academic career sometimes beneficial

Special Skills—Editing; organization; managerial skills; knowledge of a particular field or specialty; production and graphics knowledge

CAREER LADDER

Editor; Executive Editor

Senior Editor

Associate Editor

Position Description

Senior editors may have almost as much responsibility for a magazine's content as the editor. On small trade magazines, senior editors usually write the longest, most comprehensive articles as well as news. They offer story ideas and may even pass these ideas on to other writers. On larger publications, especially consumer magazines, senior editors manage a single major editorial department. In fact, the senior editor's title may reflect his or her area of responsibility, such as sports editor or fashion editor.

Although associate editors under the senior editor's supervision may handle all of the day-to-day tasks—reading unsolicited manuscripts, working with freelancers—the senior editor has ultimate responsibility for this work. Senior editors may deal directly with freelancers and occasionally assign photographs and illustrations for particular stories. If there are any changes in an assigned article's composition, or if the writer is having problems, the senior editor should—and must—know about them.

Senior editors participate regularly in editorial meetings, keeping the editor informed of the department's progress and suggesting story ideas. On a large publication, the senior editor may have the freedom to assign stories or columns without first getting the editor's approval. Such assignments may be the senior editor's ideas, but it is usually the associate editor's responsibility to write the stories or else hire freelancers for the task.

Particularly on smaller magazines, the senior editor also writes. He or she may have a regular column or may produce articles or features as assigned. Senior editors for larger magazines rarely write; their supervisory and editorial duties take up a great deal of time.

In addition, senior editors may:

- handle production tasks, such as editing manuscripts and proofreading galleys;
- attend workshops, seminars, and trade shows to keep abreast of trends in the industry;
- represent the magazine at professional meetings and functions;

• handle day-to-day dealings with the printer.

Salaries

Many senior editors earn from $20,000 to $30,000. Trade publications that require advanced degrees or specialized experience often pay more, as do the larger consumer magazines. A good senior editor at a large consumer magazine may make as much as $75,000 a year.

Employment Prospects

The best job opportunities for senior editors are on small and special-interest publications, especially trade magazines. Such publications have smaller staffs and often need people who are experienced writers and editors. Background information may be learned on the job, but familiarity with a given industry is preferable.

Advancement Prospects

Opportunity to move up the ladder to executive editor and/or editor depends on the publication. Although senior editors at smaller magazines have more visibility and perhaps perform more duties—both writing and editing—advancement may be stymied if the longtime editor has no plans to step down. At a larger magazine, senior editors have more chance to change departments (often with more responsibility) or to be promoted to executive editor. This is because editors at large publications tend to move more frequently to other magazines or even decide to start their own publications.

Education

Senior editors should have degrees in journalism or English; communications or other liberal-arts fields are also acceptable. An advanced degree can give the senior editor an edge. For specialized fields, such as law, economics, medicine, science, or technology, course work or degrees in that specialty are essential.

Experience/Skills

Prior experience as a journalist or lower level editor is often required to become senior editor. Academic experience as a professor or researcher is often acceptable as one's only qualification for becoming a senior editor in a specialized field, such as medicine or science—particularly if he or she will be writing a regular column.

Since so much of the senior editor's duties are supervisory, he or she must be well organized and able to manage people well. Senior editors have to have excellent editing skills and should write well also.

Unions/Associations

The American Society of Magazine Editors is the principal professional organization for editors. Writers and editors also often join writers' groups, such as the American Society of Journalists and Authors, Inc. All women writers and editors are eligible to join Women In Communications, Inc. Editors of large news and feature magazines may belong to The Newspaper Guild.

EDITOR

CAREER PROFILE

Duties: Supervise magazine preparation; manage staff; rewrite and edit

Alternate Title(s): Editor-in-Chief; Editorial Director

Salary Range: $20,000 to $100,000+

Employment Prospects: Poor

Advancement Prospects: Poor

Prerequisites:

Education—Undergraduate degree in communications, journalism, or liberal arts; specialized degrees for scientific and technical publications.

Experience—Background as editor and journalist or writer essential

Special Skills—Grammar and editing knowledge; self-motivation; intellectual curiosity; administrative ability

CAREER LADDER

Publisher

Editor

Senior Editor; Associate Editor; Assistant Editor

Position Description

The editor has complete responsibility for the editorial content and production of a magazine. He or she reports to the publisher; in some cases, the editor may be the publisher as well.

Responsibilities depend on the size of publication. On a small magazine, the editor may perform many of the day-to-day editing and production tasks. On a larger publication, those tasks are all delegated, and the editor concentrates on broad administrative duties. Some editors may be in charge of groups of publications under a common ownership.

The typical magazine editor divides working time between editorial, production, and administrative duties. Editorial duties include planning future issues, making assignments to the staff and freelance writers, editing and rewriting manuscripts, and assigning photo coverage. Editors supervise the activities of subordinate editors, as well as monitor work-in-progress against deadlines. They have ultimate approval of all articles and copy.

Production duties include working with a layout editor to decide placement of articles, use of photos, and other artwork, plus final approval of page layouts. On small publications, the editor may have sole responsibility for production; this may entail proofreading galleys and spending time at the typesetter's shop.

Administrative duties include hiring and firing staff members, planning and managing budgets, negotiating freelance contracts, writing reports, answering letters from readers, and other managerial tasks.

In addition, editors may:

- attend trade conventions;
- participate in promotional and publicity activities for the publication;
- write signed or bylined columns or editorials.

Salaries

Editors earn between $20,000 and $38,000 a year. A small, new magazine may pay less. Major consumer magazines pay far more, from $100,000 to $230,000.

Employment Prospects

The market is competitive and characterized by high turnover. The best opportunities will be in business and trade publications, especially those serving growth industries such as executive management, computers, and health. The consumer field is unstable.

Advancement Prospects

Editor is the top position of many magazines, directly under the publisher (who almost always comes from the advertising and marketing side of the business). Since editor usually is the top position, advancement can only be made by moving on to bigger, more prestigious publications. Such advancement opportunities can be slow in coming—turnover is less frequent at higher editorial positions.

Education

As with many writing and editing jobs, there is little agreement as to the preferred major. Many editors have undergraduate degrees in communications or journalism, while others have degrees in liberal arts, history, philosophy, or the social sciences. Some editing jobs require business, economics, science, or engineering degrees.

Experience/Skills

The amount of experience required to be editor depends on the publication. Three to five years may be necessary for some jobs; ten years or more for others. Experience can include work as a journalist, assistant news editor, copy editor, or section editor; work in book publishing as a junior editor or editor; or work on a magazine staff in lower editorial positions.

Editors should have good judgment about what to publish and what to reject; they should have tact and the ability to direct and motivate staff members and freelance writers. They should be creative, highly self-motivated, and have a strong sense of curiosity. They should be able to meet deadlines and manage budgets. Production knowledge is also important.

Unions/Associations

Major professional associations include the American Society of Journalists and Authors, Inc.; American Society of Magazine Editors; and Women In Communications, Inc. Other writer associations as well as trade and industry groups are open to magazine editors. The Newspaper Guild represents some employees on major news and feature magazines.

EXECUTIVE EDITOR

CAREER PROFILE

Duties: Supervise magazine preparation; manage staff; assign stories; rewrite and edit

Alternate Title(s): Editor; Senior Editor; Managing Editor

Salary range: $22,000 to $55,000

Employment Prospects: Fair

Advancement Prospects: Fair

Prerequisites:

Education—Undergraduate degree in journalism, English, communications, or other liberal arts; advanced or specialized degrees for scientific, technical, or specialty publications

Experience—Several years' background as journalist, writer, or editor is essential

Special Skills—Knowledge of editing and grammar; good organization; knowledge of a particular field or specialty; ability to manage and direct people

CAREER LADDER

Editor

Executive Editor

Senior Editor; Associate Editor; Assistant Editor

Position Description

The executive editor is a title more closely associated with larger publications, since smaller magazines allocate the executive editor's duties to senior editors and the top editor. The executive editor may have total responsibility for a particular magazine, reporting to the editor-in-chief in charge of a magazine group under common ownership. The structure of magazine staffs varies greatly from one publication to another.

Like senior editors, executive editors supervise lower-level editors and may take responsibility for freelancers, photographers, and illustrators. Executive editors assign stories, monitor the department or entire magazine's work, and have ultimate responsibility for final editing. They may also write features or articles, but usually they confine their responsibilities to editing. They are responsible for meeting deadlines.

Usually second-in-command to the editor, executive editors delegate authority and story assignments often without prior approval. Should the editor be out of town or ill, the executive editor takes over complete control of the magazine.

In addition, the executive editor may:

- represent the magazine at professional meetings or functions;
- attend workshops, annual meetings, seminars, and trade shows to stay abreast of industry trends;
- work with the editor on budget and give approval for editorial expenses;
- handle production skills, such as page-checking and proofreading.

Salaries

Median salaries are in the mid-thirties. Executive editors at large publications earn $55,000 to $100,000 or more. About 20 to 25 percent of executive editors receive bonus incentive compensation.

Employment Prospects

The best opportunities for an executive editor are with large publications, since smaller magazines often have no executive editorial position. Competition is strong, however. It is less likely that an executive editor will be hired from outside than promoted from within the organization.

Advancement Prospects

Since the executive editor is directly under the editor or editor-in-chief, advancement prospects are less promising than for senior editor. If the editor has been with a publication for many years and has no intention of leaving, an executive editor may have to move to another publication to advance to the editor's slot. Editors do move though, often to start their own magazines.

Education

Any executive editor worth his salt will have an undergraduate degree in journalism, English, communications, or liberal arts. Most have probably acquired advanced degrees in journalism or technical fields along the way as well or, at least, have taken advanced course work. Specialized publications, such as those for medicine, science, law, or high technology require advanced education.

Experience/Skills

Prior experience as a senior editor or editor of a smaller publication is usually necessary for most executive-editor positions. Work as a professor or academic researcher may be sufficient for certain spots, especially if there is more writing and less editing involved. In these cases, the executive editor's title reflects background and expertise more than editing and managerial functions.

Good writing and editing skills, as well as the ability to manage people effectively, are vital to an executive editor. Depending upon the executive editor's level of responsibility, he or she must also deal with the publisher, the advertising department, and the readers.

Unions/Associations

Executive editors, like their counterparts, may belong to the American Society of Magazine Editors or writers' trade organizations.

PUBLICITY/PUBLIC-RELATIONS SPECIALIST

CAREER PROFILE

Duties: Promote the publication to the press and other industry professionals through press releases, interviews, conferences, etc.

Alternate Title(s): Publicity Director; Public-Relations Director or Manager

Salary Range: $14,000 to $50,000

Employment Prospects: Fair

Advancement Prospects: Fair to poor

Prerequisites:

Education—Undergraduate degree in communications, English, or liberal arts

Experience—Previous work for a public-relations firm or other public-relations department; background as writer or journalist

Special Skills—Ability to write and speak clearly and concisely; desire to work with people; enthusiasm

CAREER LADDER

Director of Public Relations

Publicity/Public-Relations Specialist

Assistant Public-Relations Specialist; Writer; College

Position Description

The publicity/public-relations specialist is responsible for making sure the press and other professionals in the industry know about the magazine. If the magazine offers a special editorial or advertising section, breaks a big investigative piece, adds a new writer, or wishes to publicize an event that is newsworthy, the public-relations specialist writes a press release, or other materials, to send to the media and interested parties.

There's more to spreading the word than press releases, although that is the principal writing function of the job. The public-relations specialist organizes press and trade parties, handling everything from invitations to food to entertainment. The most important thing he or she must do is to put together the press kits to be given at such events. All the details about the event are covered in the kit. Such a press kit can be as small as a short press release, or it might include brochures, biographies of the magazine's publisher and/or editor, announcements of advertising-rate increases, or anything else the magazine feels is important. In short, the public-relations specialist should be prepared to write or tell everything about the magazine.

Besides having a daily familiarity with the magazine—knowing what stories are coming up, who's new on staff, how the magazine's ad sales are doing this year—the publicity specialist needs enthusiasm and the drive to get these items into the news. The more the publicity specialist keeps everyone informed of how the publication is doing and what great articles it is providing, the more people will want to read it, the more advertising sales will be generated, and the more important the magazine will be in the community. The publicity person is a support for all other departments, but when it comes to talking and writing about the magazine, he or she should be the front line.

On larger publications, the publicity department can include more than one publicity specialist. Smaller magazines usually have only one public-relations staffer, and he or she may also help the advertising department with sales promotion.

In addition, publicity specialists may:

- handle press inquiries and arrange interviews;
- handle production duties connected with the promotional materials;
- attend seminars, trade shows, and industry functions as a representative of the magazine.

Salaries

Most entry-level publicity specialists start at $14,000 to $16,000. Salaries are higher in the Northeast, even for beginners, than in the Midwest or South. The median is in the high thirties. Top magazine publicists at the largest magazines earn $50,000 or more.

Employment Prospects

Because a public-relations specialist needs no extensive formal training, the job offers a chance to break into the public-relations business. Competition is very stiff, and many magazines are forced to cut promotion expenses—that is, the job of the public-relations person—before cutting any other overhead. The best opportunities are with consumer magazines or trade books that deal with media issues, such as magazines about advertising and television. Trade publications often do not have publicity departments or, if they have them, do not experience much turnover.

Advancement Prospects

Breaking into the public-relations business is the tough part; once a person has served as a publicity specialist, he or she can usually move either to another publication or to a separate public-relations firm. There is not a great deal of turnover, however, and no direct career path within a magazine's organization. Most public-relations specialists end up changing companies rather than waiting long for promotion.

Education

An undergraduate degree in communications, English, or other liberal-arts fields is essential. Knowledge of a particular technical field is also necessary in order to speak with any authority for a magazine specializing in that area.

Experience/Skills

While previous experience in another public-relations department or firm is quite helpful, the biggest asset a public-relations specialist can have is the ability to write good, clear, well-punctuated English. Any background as a writer or journalist is a plus. Some magazines, particularly technical trade journals, hire publicity specialists who come from that industry. A good vocabulary, organizational skills, and a pleasing telephone manner are very important.

Unions/Associations

Professional organizations include the International Association of Business Communicators; American Society of Journalists and Authors, Inc.; and the Public Relations Society of America, Inc.

PROMOTION SPECIALIST

CAREER PROFILE

Duties: Organize, arrange, and handle campaigns and programs which build a magazine's image; write advertisements; help a magazine's ad sales force

Alternate Title(s): Promotion Director; Advertising Promotion Manager; Research Director

Salary Range: $18,000 to $57,000

Employment Prospects: Fair

Advancement Prospects: Fair

Prerequisites:

Education—An undergraduate degree in English, communications, business, marketing, or the liberal arts. Advanced course work in marketing or journalism a plus

Experience—Previous experience as a magazine-ad-sales representative or assistant publisher; promotion work for another magazine or company

Special Skills—Ability to work with the advertising director and ad-sales staff to develop promotional programs and literature; good writing and editing skills; knowledge of the industry; organizational and research skills

CAREER LADDER

Advertising Sales Director

Promotion Specialist

Assistant Promotion Specialist; Writer; Reporter; College

Position Description

The promotion specialist works for the advertising director and sales force. On smaller magazines, promotion specialists handle public relations as well.

Responsibilities of the promotion specialist are varied. He or she may collect extensive marketing data on the magazine's advertising and circulation, then use that information to prepare charts, tables, and graphs. Such data allows the ad-sales people to back up their statements when making a sales pitch, and it lets the circulation department know which segments of readers are getting the magazine—and which ones are not. Often the promotion specialist converts such dry statistics into colorful visual aids, designing the materials and handling their production. Promotion specialists should keep up with demographic and marketing trends, readership studies, reader preferences, and always, the competition.

Promotion specialists try to see how their magazines could benefit by association or sponsorship of certain events or programs. A tennis magazine, for example, might sponsor a tennis clinic or match, while a computer publication could offer a daylong seminar on a new software product. The promotion specialist organizes such programs, handling all the details including writing up the accompanying literature. Such promotions accomplish two things: They keep the magazine's name prominently displayed, and they keep the magazine involved with its readers and therefore knowledgeable about the market.

In addition, promotion specialists may:

- attend seminars, trade shows, and industry functions on behalf of the magazine,
- select premium items, such as coffee cups and T-shirts, with the magazine's logo.

Salaries

Beginning promotion specialists usually start at about $18,000 to $20,000. With advancement, promotion specialists can earn salaries of more than $50,000 a year.

Employment Prospects

As with all other magazine editing and promotion jobs, competition is keen. The best chances for getting a job as a promotion specialist are usually with larger magazines. At the smaller publications, such responsibilities are likely to be handled by the ad director.

Advancement Prospects

The career path for a promotion specialist is rather short, so unless he or she replaces the promotion director or advertising director at a publication, one's best bet is probably to change publications. Such promotional work experience transfers well to public-relations firms.

Education

Undergraduate degrees in English, communications, advertising, or business are preferred choices for a promotion specialist. Courses in marketing and sales are also helpful.

Experience/Skills

For a beginner, emphasis is placed on college course work and his or her natural ability at sales. Promotion is, after all, a selling job for the magazine. Work as a promotion assistant usually suffices to recommend a candidate for advancement to promotion specialist. Any background in sales, marketing, or writing is a plus. Finally, a promotion specialist should enjoy working with people and meeting the public.

Unions/Associations

Promotion specialists may want to join the Public Relations Society of America, Inc., or the International Association of Business Communicators. Women In Communications, Inc., is open to all women who write. The Newspaper Guild represents some employees on major news and feature magazines.

Television

DESK ASSISTANT

CAREER PROFILE

Duties: Provide clerical and general assistance to television newsroom personnel

Alternate Title(s): News Desk Assistant

Salary Range: $10,000 to $15,000

Employment Prospects: Fair

Advancement Prospects: Good

Prerequisites:

Education—High school diploma; some college preferred

Experience—None necessary, but news-related work is helpful

Special Skills—Clerical skills; writing ability; organization skills

CAREER LADDER

News Writer; Reporter; Production Assistant

Desk Assistant

High School; College

Position Description

Persons who are interested in careers in television news often begin as desk assistants, general apprentices who perform routine office and clerical tasks while learning the trade.

Generally this job is found only at medium and large stations and networks, where staffs are large enough to need desk assistants. Desk assistants may work part- or full-time, any hours of the day or night, any days of the week.

Duties include fielding telephone calls, distributing messages and mail, running errands, typing letters, reports, and scripts, and filing them. Desk assistants may be responsible for maintaining office supplies and seeing that equipment such as typewriters and copiers are serviced and repaired.

Duties relating directly to news operations include monitoring and ripping the copy from wire service printer terminals, and disseminating it among reporters and editors, as well as filling requests for information and tapes from the library or videotape storage room. Tapes must be logged in and out. Desk assistants may also handle the sending and receiving of tapes to and from sister stations and affiliates; they themselves may be required to act as couriers.

Desk or production assistants help with script preparation. "Breaking script," as it is called, is done for every news broadcast; this includes typing, updating, and delivering scripts to all appropriate staff persons. It's not unusual for multiple updates to be done for each broadcast, especially when major stories happen.

In addition, desk assistants may:

- do research work for reporters, such as collecting background information and updating facts, sports scores, and weather reports;
- learn production work by assisting in the control room;
- learn reporting by accompanying reporters on assignments.

Salaries

Entry-level jobs in television pay low salaries. Most desk assistants earn between $10,000 and $15,000, even at large stations and networks. Earnings over $15,000 are rare. Desk assistants are paid either a weekly rate or, if part-time, an hourly rate.

Employment Prospects

Most desk-assistant jobs are concentrated in medium to large market cities, including network headquarters and bureaus. Cable is opening more opportunities for desk assistants. Finding a job may be difficult and time-consuming, but once in the field, prospects are good for advancement because of high turnover.

Advancement Prospects

The desk assistant is in an excellent position for internal promotion to production, newswriting, or reporting work. The successful candidate for advancement must demonstrate a knowledge of broadcasting operations, good writing and speaking skills, and good news judgment. He or she should be highly motivated, seeking assignments beyond the normal range of the desk assistant's duties.

Education

A college degree is not necessary for desk-assistant jobs, but it is preferred for higher positions. Some desk assistants work part-time while they attend college. Studies should include communications, liberal arts, history, social sciences, and courses in broadcasting.

Experience/Skills

Any kind of experience in a news-related job is helpful, such as working on a community newspaper, or school publication, radio, or TV station. Clerical and office skills are paramount for desk assistants, who must type and file reports, correspondence,and scripts. Good organization also is important; desk assistants may have to quickly locate or handle information for someone under deadline pressure. Those who aspire to newswriting or reporting jobs should have good journalistic research and writing skills, as well as strong self-motivation.

Unions/Associations

At many major stations and the networks, desk assistants belong to such unions as the National Association of Broadcast Employees and Technicians; American Federation of Television and Radio Artists, or Writers Guild of America.

RESEARCHER

CAREER PROFILE

Duties: Assist television staff with background research for news and other programs

Alternate Title(s): None

Salary Range: $14,300 to $35,000

Employment Prospects: Fair

Advancement Prospects: Good

Prerequisites:

Education—Undergraduate degree in communications or liberal arts

Experience—Any background in the media helpful

Special Skills—Accuracy; good organizational skills; attention to details; good writing ability; curiosity

CAREER LADDER

Reporter; News Writer; Associate Producer

Researcher

College; Desk Assistant; Production Assistant

Position Description

Most researchers employed at television stations work in the news department. The job is an entry-level position, though there may be levels of junior and senior researchers at large stations and networks.

Researchers assist reporters, news writers, and news directors or editors with gathering background information for stories. A half-hour broadcast can contain anywhere from 14 to 30 stories, and a single researcher may be assigned to work on several stories for each broadcast.

They do most of their work by telephone, pre-interviewing sources to find the best ones for the reporter to then interview on tape. They also interview sources in order to gather and check information pertaining to stories, then write summary reports of their findings for reporters or news writers to use. The job is often demanding and pressured, and researchers must be able to absorb a wide range of information quickly, sorting out the most important material.

Researchers also generate ideas for stories. They maintain contact with news sources, and they scan magazines and newspapers. They may be assigned a geographic area of responsibility or to certain topics, such as education, business, or government.

Researchers help reporters assemble audio and visual materials for stories, searching library files or contacting other stations to acquire film or videotape footage.

In addition, researchers may:

- do follow-up work on stories to check for new developments;
- work on other programs or documentaries;
- work in the marketing department, tracking ratings.

Salaries

Researchers are likely to be paid on a weekly or hourly rate, with extra compensation for overtime. Some may work only part-time. Junior researchers earn roughly $14,300 to $16,000 a year, while senior researchers with more than three years of experience can earn up to $35,000, including overtime. The best-paying jobs are at large stations and the networks.

Employment Prospects

Researcher usually is considered an entry-level position in the news department, though large stations and networks may require some experience. Part-time openings, if offered, should be seriously considered; they may lead to full-time work.

Advancement Prospects

It may be difficult to find a job as a researcher but, once established, advancement opportunities are good. Researchers have several avenues open to them: reporting the news; writing scripts for the news; or assisting in the production of news and other programs.

Education

Undergraduate degrees in communications, history, social sciences, or liberal arts are preferred for jobs in the news media. Also acceptable are degrees in political science or business. Courses in broadcasting are helpful.

Experience/Skills

Any experience in the news media is helpful for competing for researcher positions, including school or community publications. Researchers may have previously worked as desk or production assistants, reporters, or news writers for newspapers or radio stations.

Researchers should be adept at quickly gathering information. They should be well organized, detail-oriented, and comfortable with interviewing over the phone. They should be able to handle pressure well, and provide clearly written reports and summaries of their findings. News judgment also is important.

Unions/Associations

Researchers may belong to such unions as the American Federation of Television and Radio Artists; Writers Guild of America; or National Association of Broadcast Employees and Technicians. Some researchers may join professional associations as well, such as the National Academy of Television Arts and Sciences or the Academy of Television Arts and Sciences.

REPORTER

CAREER PROFILE

Duties: Prepare news and feature stories; report on air

Alternate Title(s): Newscaster; Correspondent

Salary Range: $14,500 to $47,000+

Employment Prospects: Fair to good

Advancement Prospects: Poor to fair

Prerequisites:

Education—Undergraduate degree in communications, liberal arts, history, social sciences, or political science

Experience—Work as news writer or researcher helpful

Special Skills—Good reporting, writing, and speaking ability; self-motivation; astute news judgment

CAREER LADDER

Anchorperson; Assistant News Director

Reporter

News Writer; Researcher; Assistant; College

Position Description

The prime responsibility of a television reporter is to gather news and prepare stories for broadcast. The work involves interviewing sources, researching facts, directing a film crew, writing a script, delivering news on the air, and working with film editors.

Time pressures are enormous. Not only do reporters work against the clock for scheduled news programs—they are limited severely in the amount of time they have to present a news story. A major story typically runs about two minutes; many stories run 90 seconds or less. Reporters must strive to summarize highlights, give important information, and make the story visually interesting as well.

Reporters are assigned stories and estimated time allotments by an assignment editor or news director. Editors often rely on a reporter's news judgment to determine the slant and length of a story. Some reporters, especially those at large stations, may specialize in certain areas, such as business or politics, and have more control over the stories they generate.

Gathering information involves interviewing people by phone and in person. Some stations employ researchers and assistants to do background legwork and news writers to write scripts. Otherwise, reporters do those tasks themselves.

Reporters then go on location with a camera crew and direct the shooting. Their on-air report may include portions of a taped interview, a voice-over of the visuals, and a stand-up summary. Live reports have gained increasing popularity as new technology has made smaller, more portable cameras available.

Stories can run the gamut from city council meetings to major disasters. They can be features or investigative pieces. Some reporters occasionally prepare special series.

Salaries

Market size has a great deal of influence on salaries in television. The larger the market and the size of news staff, the higher are the salaries. Typical salaries range from $14,500 to $26,000. Top reporters in major metropolitan areas are likely to earn $21,500 to $47,000. According to the Radio-Television News Directors Association, the median salary paid to reporters in 1989 was $19,240. A small percentage of experienced, prestigious reporters or network correspondents earns from

$50,000 to $300,000 or more. Salaries are highest in the East and lowest in the Midwest.

TV news operations have been expanding, and cable is opening more job opportunities. Also, turnover is high in this field. At very small stations and cable operations, it is possible to get a reporting job right out of college; however, most reporters have had prior experience as assistants, researchers, or news writers before going on camera.

Advancement Prospects

Many reporters aspire to be anchorpersons, jobs that are seen to have semi-celebrity status, high salaries, and much glamour. The prospects for attaining such positions are poor. There is intense competition for limited openings. Turnover is better in smaller markets, but in large cities it is not unusual for anchors to keep their jobs for many years.

Two other avenues of advancement are possible for reporters: to larger stations, thus to higher pay and more prestige; or to off-camera jobs as assistant news directors or news directors. Some reporters, especially those who are correspondents or have special "beats" for networks, want no change to other types of jobs.

Education

An undergraduate degree in communications, liberal arts, history, social sciences, or political science is preferred for TV reporting jobs. Specialized degrees in business, health, or law may be advantageous. Communications courses should include study in broadcasting.

Experience/Skills

At some stations, reporter is an entry-level job; others may require the applicant have one or more years of experience as an assistant, researcher, or news writer. Some newspaper reporters are able to switch to television. Experience on college publications or college-operated radio and television stations also is helpful.

TV reporters should possess the same skills as all journalists—accuracy, astute news judgment, ability to work under pressure, and strong self-motivation. In addition to good writing skills, they should be good speakers who are comfortable ad libbing before cameras.

Unions/Associations

The Writers Guild of America; National Association of Broadcast Employees and Technicians; and American Federation of Television and Radio Artists are major unions representing many TV reporters. Small stations may not be unionized. Professional associations include Radio-Television News Directors Association; International Radio and Television Society; Radio and Television Correspondents Association (for Congressional reporters); National Academy of Television Arts and Sciences; Women in Communications, Inc.; Academy of Television Arts and Sciences; and Society of Professional Journalists, Sigma Delta Chi.

ANCHOR

CAREER PROFILE

Duties: Host news or other shows; read the news or other copy on air; interview guests; may also go on location for coverage of major events

Alternate Title(s): Anchorperson

Salary Range: $14,980 to $400,000+

Employment Prospects: Poor

Advancement Prospects: Poor

Prerequisites:

Education—Undergraduate degree in communications or political science with emphasis on liberal arts; graduate degree may be preferred

Experience—Many years as reporter, correspondent, or other television positions

Special Skills/Attributes—Pleasing appearance on camera; good voice; competitiveness; ability to work under pressure; ability to be spontaneous

CAREER LADDER

Major market anchor

Anchor

Reporter, Correspondent

Position Description

The anchor job is the brass ring sought by many who start careers in television reporting. Competition for these coveted jobs is fierce. Anchors earn their jobs by putting in years of hard work as reporters or correspondents, and by becoming well-versed in politics and other issues of high public concern.

The anchor serves as host to a news or entertainment show and reads the news, introduces the stories and interviews the guests who appear on the show. Essentially, the entire show revolves around the anchor or anchors. These individuals become public personalities and celebrities.

In small markets, anchors do their own research, writing and work with production on editing videotape for broadcast. In larger markets, these functions are performed by supporting staff, and the anchor's primary job is to read the copy and perhaps interview guests. Prior to broadcast time, all anchors review the contents of the broadcast with staff. The anchor has a say in determining the content and in giving time priority to various stories. Increasingly, news and entertainment shows provide time for anchors to question reporters and exchange conversation and banter. Some of this is orchestrated and some is spontaneous.

In addition to the regular show, anchors may go on location for major events, such as conferences and conventions, and may work on documentaries or specials to be broadcast at different times.

Salary Range

Anchors in small markets can start at under $20,000 a year, while large markets offer salaries of $80,000–$100,000 or more. According to the Radio-Television News Directors Association (RTNDA), the typical 1989 salaries for anchors were $33,800 at network affiliates and $36,450 at independent stations. In the top 25 markets, typical salaries are closer to $100,000, except at the independents, which typically offer about $40,000. In smaller markets, typical salaries depend on geographic area and station size, and range from a low of less than $15,000 to a high of about $34,000. High anchor salaries—for those who have track records and demonstrated ratings pull—range from about $29,000 to $200,000. A small number of star personalities at networks and major market stations earn up to $400,000; a handful earn $1 million or more.

Employment Prospects

Only a small percentage of television reporters ever become anchors. The typical station hires two or more anchors, while major stations and networks have numerous anchors. The constant emphasis on ratings creates high turnover as anchors don't make the grade or are picked off by competing stations or higher-paying stations in larger markets. The expansion of cable television news programs is likely to increase employment opportunities in the future. Job openings are somewhat better for women and minorities, as stations seek to provide a balance in highly visible positions.

Advancement Prospects

The anchor job is the highest position for a reporter or correspondent, and the only advancement then can be achieved by moving up to larger markets or the networks.

Education

Virtually all jobs in television news require an undergraduate degree in communications or one of the liberal arts; some posts may require a graduate degree. Other fields of study can include political science.

Experience/Skills

Reporters typically spend many years in the field before becoming eligible for promotion to anchor. Grooming is of paramount importance. Anchors must have a pleasing on-camera appearance and personality and a good, clear voice. They must convey authority to the viewer. They also must be able to ad-lib and think on their feet in the event something unexpected happens live on the air. When major stories break, they must be able to react quickly. Because competition for these jobs is keen, anchors must be tough and stay on their toes.

Unions/Associations

Anchors may belong to the Writers Guild of America, the American Federation of Television and Radio Artists, the RTNDA, and the Society of Professional Journalists.

NEWS WRITER

CAREER PROFILE

Duties: Write scripts for news programs

Alternate Title(s): Senior Editor

Salary Range: $18,000 to $50,000+

Employment Prospects: Fair to good

Advancement Prospects: Fair to good

Prerequisites:

Education—Undergraduate degree in liberal arts, history, social sciences, or communications

Experience—None to several years in similar or related position

Special Skills—Good news judgment; script-writing ability; speed

CAREER LADDER

News Editor; Reporter; Producer

News Writer

College; Desk Assistant; Researcher

Position Description

News writer is a fast-pace, high-pressure job in television news departments. It requires quick, sound news judgment, good reportorial skills, and the ability to write for the ear rather than the eye.

News writers may be assigned any shift around the clock, any day of the week, depending on the station's needs. They usually begin their workday by reviewing wire copy, newspapers, and stories aired on previous newscasts. They attend one or more editorial meetings each day; decisions at these meetings are made on what stories to cover and who will be responsible for tracking and updating breaking stories.

A single news writer may be responsible for writing copy for a major newscast and one or more regularly scheduled news breaks or digests (which typically include about 30 seconds of news). News writers often do their own research, corroborating other news sources and checking out conflicting reports, such as differences in the number of fatalities in a disaster or accident. They interview sources by phone and research information in the station's library. Often they are aided by researchers and desk assistants. They also coordinate graphics and tapes to be used during newscasts, working with artists, producers, and representatives of other television stations.

News writers must be able to write tight scripts that are easy to read and easy for listeners to understand—and also fit a teleprompter screen. They are restricted by time—news stories seldom run over 90 seconds and may be as short as 10 seconds for news breaks—and their scripts must match what viewers see on their sets. News writers either preview tapes or receive "shot sheets" that describe visuals and time lengths. Scripts are written down to the second, a skill that can only be developed over time, with experience.

The daily workload for news writers often varies. Reporters write their own scripts, and anchors often write scripts for the lead stories. The workload also depends on the day's news—a news writer may work on a few big stories or on many small ones.

News writers work under the supervision of an editor, assistant news director, or news director. Overtime is often required, and shifts of 10 to 11 hours are not uncommon.

In addition, news writers may:

- produce news digests, documentaries, or other programs;
- supervise tape editing for news reports;
- write promotional scripts to publicize upcoming broadcasts.

Salaries

News writers at entry level in small, nonunion stations can expect to start at about $18,000 a year. Comparable salaries are higher by several thousand dollars at large, unionized stations. News writers at top local market stations earn between $35,000 and $40,000, including overtime. Some of the best earn more than $50,000.

Employment Prospects

Job prospects for news writers are fair to good, though beginners usually will have to go to small stations. Networks and large stations hire only seasoned news writers who've worked their way up the markets. Cable and independent stations may offer the best prospects for beginners.

Advancement Prospects

News writers have fair to good chances for advancement, either as news editors, news directors, or as producers. Some experienced news writers take on production assignments as part of their development.

Education

News writers must be able to handle wide ranges of topics and need some historical perspective of news events. A broad education in liberal arts, social sciences, history, or political science can be better preparation than a degree in communications or broadcasting. Broadcasting courses are helpful for learning the technical end of the business.

Experience/Skills

At small stations, news writer is often an entry-level position. Large stations and networks require experience and proven skills. Candidates typically work as desk assistants or researchers before becoming news writers.

News writers must be able to condense important information into scripts written for the ear. They seldom have time to revise. They must be good, accurate, detail-oriented researchers. News writers also must be adaptable and versatile, able to understand many different topics and issues.

Unions/Associations

News writers in large markets usually are members of a union, such as Writers Guild of America; National Association of Broadcast Employees and Technicians; or American Federation of Television and Radio Artists. Major professional associations are the National Academy of Television Arts and Sciences; Academy of Television Arts and Sciences; Radio-Television News Directors Association; and Society of Professional Journalists, Sigma Delta Chi.

ASSISTANT NEWS DIRECTOR

CAREER PROFILE

Duties: Assign news coverage; manage news operations

Alternate Title(s): Assistant News Editor; Assignment Editor; Managing Editor; City Editor

Salary Range: $22,100 to $65,000

Employment Prospects: Poor

Advancement Prospects: Good

Prerequisites:

Education—Undergraduate degree in communications, liberal arts, history, social sciences, or political science

Experience—Several years' experience as reporter

Special Skills—Good news judgment; managerial ability; organizational skills

CAREER LADDER

News Director

Assistant News Director

Reporter

Position Description

Assistant news directors are middle managers responsible for the day-to-day supervision of television station newsrooms. They work under the supervision of a news director, executing the director's decisions. Depending on the size of staff, they have a certain amount of their own decision-making authority for assigning reporters and crews to stories. They evaluate suggestions for stories and monitor the reports made by reporters.

Assistant news directors are responsible for many of the nuts and bolts of daily operations. They may make up work schedules so that the newsroom has adequate personnel at all times and complies with any union regulations concerning varying shifts in a given period of time. They also monitor assignments and work-in-progress. They may assume complete responsibility for fast-breaking stories.

Managerial responsibilities include coordinating the work of various departments, solving problems, and handling complaints. Assistant news directors are in complete charge of the newsroom in the absence of the news directors.

At some small stations, assistant news directors may do some of the writing, editing, and reporting for newscasts.

Salaries

Salaries for assistant news directors at major stations can range from a low of about $22,100 to a high of $65,000 or more. The 1989 median salary was $36,920, according to the Radio-Television News Directors Association.

Employment Prospects

Job turnover is high, but candidates for assistant news director have poor employment prospects due to keen competition. Small stations may not have this middle-management position, but large stations or networks may have several. Assistant news directors usually are promoted within, from the ranks of reporters. More opportunities are becoming available in the rapidly growing cable industry.

Advancement Prospects

Assistant news directors are directly in line for news-director positions, which undergo high turnover. The best opportunities are in commercial and cable television; public television staffs are shrinking due to cutbacks in federal support. Assistant news directors may also advance their careers by switching to a related field, such as newspapers, wire services, or government.

Education

An undergraduate degree in communications, English, liberal arts, history, or social sciences is considered the minimum educational requirement. Other degrees include political science, economics, or business.

Experience/Skills

Assistant news directors typically have worked for several years as reporters, researchers, or news desk assistants. They may also have had experience in radio or print journalism. They should be familiar with video and studio operations.

Sound news judgment and leadership qualities are important for this job. Decisions must be made quickly and often under pressure. Assistant news directors need to be able to edit, write, and even report, as needed. They should have managerial and leadership qualities. In addition, they should understand Federal Communications Commission regulations governing fairness and equal-use time, as well as laws concerning copyright and libel.

Unions/Associations

Major professional association is the Radio-Television News Directors Association, National Academy of Television Arts and Sciences and Academy of Television Arts and Sciences. Women may join Women in Communications, Inc. Assistant news directors who write or report on air may belong to such unions as the American Federation of Television and Radio Artists; Writers Guild of America; or National Association of Broadcast Employees and Technicians. In addition, some assistant news directors may belong to the Society of Professional Journalists, Sigma Delta Chi.

NEWS DIRECTOR

CAREER PROFILE

Duties: Assign news coverage; manage entire news operations of a TV station; determine policy

Alternate Title(s): News Editor

Salary Range: $26,000 to $150,000

Employment Prospects: Poor

Advancement Prospects: Poor

Prerequisites:

Education—Undergraduate or graduate degree in communications, liberal arts, history, social sciences, or political science

Experience—Several years in TV or radio news work

Special Skills—Good news judgment; managerial and administrative ability

CAREER LADDER

General Manager; News Vice President

News Director

Assistant News Director; Reporter

Position Description

Television news directors have overall responsibility for stations' news operations. They decide and coordinate the content of news programs, including what will be covered, how the stories will be presented, and which reporters will be assigned to them. They edit and review scripts and file reports. Ultimate responsibility for and authority over what appears on the air is theirs.

An average station has a news staff of about 10; larger stations typically have 40 or more. In addition, news directors coordinate the technical operations of news production. This involves assigning camera crews to stories and camera operators to work in the studio.

News directors report to station general managers or, in the case of large stations, to vice president of news. They often work long hours under great pressure, and their jobs are heavily dependent on ratings. In breaking major stories, they must make quick decisions.

News directors hire and promote news staffs. They are involved in determining budgets, and they handle many administrative responsibilities. At small stations, news directors may also take part in news gathering and reporting, or they may act as talk show hosts.

In addition, news directors may:

- supervise public-affairs programs;
- coordinate news activities with programming and other departments.

Salaries

The median annual salary for TV news directors was $42,485 in 1989, according to the Radio-Television News Directors Association. Most news directors earn between $30,000 and $45,000.

Employment Prospects

Though the federal government projects moderate overall growth in TV jobs during the next decade, competition will remain strong for news-director positions, particularly in major cities. Turnover is high, especially at large stations where news directors seldom stay more than two to three years. Aggressive job candidates, however, are many. More opportunities are available in the rapidly growing cable industry.

Advancement Prospects

News directors face limited opportunities for advancement; at many stations their job is the highest on the news side. Some may be promoted to general managers, though sales managers are the most likely candidates for that position. Large stations and networks offer vice president and assistant vice president positions in news.

Education

An undergraduate degree in communications, liberal arts, history, English, or social sciences is considered the minimum educational requirement. Many news directors have degrees in political science. A master's degree may be helpful for employment and advancement.

Experience/Skills

Television news directors generally have had at least several years' seasoning as reporters or assistant news directors in TV or radio. Large stations require more experience than small stations. News directors need sound news judgment and the ability to make quick decisions. They should understand Federal Communications Commission regulations governing fairness and equal-use time, as well as laws concerning copyright and libel.

Unions/Associations

The major professional associations are the Radio-Television News Directors Association, National Academy of Television Arts and Sciences, and Academy of Television Arts and Sciences. Women may join Women In Communications, Inc. Since news directors are managers, they generally do not belong to unions.

PUBLICITY/PROMOTION ASSISTANT

CAREER PROFILE

Duties: Write copy for and coordinate activities relating to public relations, publicity, and/or promotion

Alternate Title(s): Publicity/Promotion Specialist; Assistant Director of Information; Assistant Director of Public Relations

Salary Range: $10,000 to $30,000+

Employment Prospects: Good

Advancement Prospects: Good

Prerequisites:

Education—Undergraduate degree in public relations, communications, or advertising

Experience—Background in public relations, promotion, or advertising helpful

Special Skills—Creativity; salesmanship; good writing ability; interpersonal skills

CAREER LADDER

Publicity/Promotion Director or Manager

Publicity/Promotion Assistant

Other Public-Relations Position; College

Position Description

Publicity/promotion assistants handle much of the detail work delegated to them by publicity/promotion directors. Their duties support the publicity and promotion campaigns that are planned to boost viewer and advertiser awareness of the station, its programs, and its talent. A station may have one or more assistants, depending on its size.

The assistants may write material for press and sales kits, assemble the kits, and handle their distribution and mailing. They write scripts and help produce on-air promotion spots as well as print (newspapers and magazines) and outdoor-media (billboards) ads. They know the difference between press-release copy and ad copy, and have knowledge of layout and graphic arts. They also update, type, and distribute program schedules, listings, and changes.

Publicity/promotion assistants are good coordinators and work well with others. They are able to manage several projects at once, reporting on the status of each. They keep mailing lists and media-contact lists up to date.

Much of their work involves scheduling and arranging, such as setting up tours of the station or confirming speaking engagements and public appearances for station talent and executives.

In addition, publicity/promotion assistants may:

- handle and route correspondence, including viewer and press inquiries;
- maintain and update all publicity and promotion files, including print material, scripts, and videotapes;
- make public appearances on behalf of the station.

Salaries

Salaries depend on station, market size, and individual experience. They can range from $10,000 to $30,000 or more. Commercial stations pay more than public stations.

Employment Prospects

Many good job opportunities exist in lower-level publicity/promotion work at small to medium-size television stations. A moderate rate of turnover opens entry-level jobs to college graduates and candidates with minimal experience. Jobs at large stations and networks often require experience at other stations and are more difficult to get.

Advancement Prospects

Chances of advancement are fair to good either by promotion from within to a more senior position or by movement to a larger market. However, the larger the market, the tougher the competition—and the lower the rate of turnover. Job candidates shouldn't overlook cable television, a promising job field. Others can find advancement by moving out of television, into other media, agencies, or businesses.

Education

Undergraduate degrees in communications, public relations, or advertising are preferred for publicity/promotion work. A degree in liberal arts is also acceptable. Courses in broadcasting are helpful.

Experience/Skills

Some experience in public relations, promotion, advertising, or in other media is desirable for television publicity/promotion assistants. Job candidates should be imaginative and creative, commanding a range of good writing and editing skills for print or broadcast. They also should be personable and persuasive. Knowledge of layout and graphic arts is helpful. Typing usually is a necessary skill.

Unions/Associations

The major professional organization is the Broadcasters' Promotion Association. Publicity/promotion assistants also may belong to other professional or trade associations, such as the National Academy of Television Arts and Sciences; Academy of Television Arts and Sciences; Public Relations Society of America, Inc.; American Advertising Federation; and Women In Communications, Inc.

PUBLICITY/PROMOTION DIRECTOR

CAREER PROFILE

DUTIES: Direct a television station's public relations, publicity, and/or promotion activities

Alternate Title(s): Publicity/Promotion Manager; Director of Information; Director of Public Relations

Salary Range: $14,000 to $50,000+

Employment Prospects: Fair

Advancement Prospects: Poor

Prerequisites:

Education—Undergraduate degree in public relations, communications, or advertising

Experience—Background in public relations, promotion, or advertising required

Special Skills—Salesmanship; good writing ability; interpersonal skills

CAREER LADDER

Director or Vice President of Public Relations, Publicity, Promotion, or Information

Publicity/Promotion Director

Publicity/Promotion Assistant

Position Description

A television station's talent, programming, and image are shaped by a wide range of public relations, publicity, and promotion activities. At many stations, all these responsibilities are handled by a director and perhaps one or more assistants; at large stations and networks, publicity and public relations may be handled separately from promotion, which is more sales-oriented.

Publicity/promotion directors report to either stations' program directors or general managers. They coordinate their activities with community-relations directors, sales directors, and sometimes fundraising directors (in the case of public television).

Responsibilities include developing public-relations campaigns to boost a station's image with viewers and advertisers. A campaign may be ongoing or may be focused around the start of a new season, a special series, an event, or the hiring of new talent.

A campaign can include press kits (releases, photographs, background sheets, talent biographies, etc.); on-air ads, newspaper, magazine, and billboard ads; posters, buttons, flyers, and other specialty advertising items; contests and special events; sales kits (ad rate sheets, audience ratings, demographics, upcoming special programs, other material aimed at potential advertisers); and brochures. All pieces of a campaign must be carefully coordinated and scheduled.

Publicity/promotion directors supervise the writing and production of campaign materials and, in many cases, do much of the work themselves. In developing and producing campaigns, they work with graphic artists, type and print shops, and outside ad agencies. They must see that production schedules and budgets are met.

If their station is a network affiliate, publicity/promotion directors coordinate their efforts with network campaigns. At public stations, publicity and promotion often are coordinated with fundraising activities.

In addition, publicity/promotion directors may:

- coordinate special appearances and speeches of station personnel at public events;
- arrange special screenings for the media;
- make public appearances on behalf of the station.

Salaries

Salaries range from $14,000 in small public-television markets, to $50,000 and up, for experienced persons in larger commercial markets and networks.

Employment Prospects

There is little turnover in the top publicity/promotion positions in television. Opportunities are decreasing in public television due to federal budget cuts. But the growth of cable TV is creating new job openings, though pay may be lower than at many commercial stations.

Advancement Prospects

Prospects for advancement in this field in television are poor. Publicity/promotion director is often the top such position in a station's organization and therefore offers no path to higher station management. Advancement can be achieved by moving to a similar position at a larger station or network, or by moving out of television to other public-relations fields. Those in public television may advance to supervisory fundraising or development positions.

Education

The minimum and preferred requirement is an undergraduate degree in communications, public relations, or advertising. A degree in liberal arts is also acceptable. Courses in broadcasting are helpful.

Experience/Skills

Publicity/promotion directors should have at least two to three years of experience in other positions in public relations, advertising, or promotion. The experience may be as a publicity/promotion assistant in television, other media, public relations, or advertising. Some supervisory experience is desirable.

Creativity and a range of good writing and editing skills are necessary. For example, job candidates should understand the differences between writing press-release copy versus sales-promotion copy. Salesmanship and ability to persuade are also important. Publicity/promotion professionals should be personable and outgoing.

Unions/Associations

The Broadcasters' Promotion Association is the major professional organization serving this field. Publicity/promotion directors may belong to other professional or trade associations, such as the National Academy of Television Arts and Sciences; Academy of Television Arts and Sciences; Public Relations Society of America, Inc.; American Advertising Federation; and Women in Communications, Inc.

COMMUNITY AFFAIRS DIRECTOR

CAREER PROFILE

Duties: Write and produce public-service announcements and programs; meet with community groups

Alternate Title(s): Community-Relations Director; Public-Service Director

Salary Range: $15,000 to $30,000+

Employment Prospects: Poor

Advancement Prospects: Fair

Prerequisites:

Education—Undergraduate degree in social sciences, liberal arts, or communications

Experience—Background in nonprofit or service organizations

Special Skills—Good writing ability; interpersonal skills

CAREER LADDER

Program Director; Producer

Community-Affairs Director

Nonprofit-Organization Director

Position Description

The Federal Communications Commission (FCC) requires all licensed commercial and public television stations to devote a certain amount of air time to community affairs and public-service announcements (PSAs). At many stations, the responsibility for managing and coordinating these operations is given to community-affairs directors.

Community-affairs directors plan—and in many cases write and produce—public-affairs programs on local news and issues. These may include talk and panel shows or documentaries. Sometimes the community-affairs directors work on-air as hosts, moderators, or narrators, of programs. In addition, they develop, prepare, and supervise the production of public-service announcements—short spots that feature upcoming community events or highlight the services of particular groups. The station's public-service activities and feedback from the community are documented for the FCC.

Community-affairs directors spend much of their time meeting with local nonprofit and service groups to discuss proposals and concerns, which they then evaluate for air time. They also represent the station at group meetings, sometimes as featured speakers. They may also plan special public-service events sponsored by their stations.

Community-affairs directors generally work regular business hours, though evening and weekend work is often required for organization meetings. They report either to program directors or general managers.

In addition, community affairs directors may:

- perform publicity and promotion duties;
- conduct station tours for the public;
- coordinate speaking engagements for other station personnel.

Salaries

Community-affairs directors earn moderate salaries, averaging about $20,000 to $25,000. Small stations pay considerably less, as low as $15,000, while large stations pay up to $30,000 or more.

Employment Prospects

Job opportunities are poor, due to limited job openings in commercial television and budget cutbacks in public television. Opportunities may be further limited by locale. Stations frequently select candidates who already are familiar with local community groups and concerns.

Many small stations do not have designated positions for community affairs.

Advancement Prospects

Prospects are fair for advancement into programming or producing; these jobs, however, require additional skills. Community-affairs directors may also advance by moving to positions in other fields, such as nonprofit organizations or the federal government.

Education

A broad education in liberal arts or social sciences is ideal for service work. The minimum requirement is an undergraduate degree. Other areas of emphasis include urban affairs, government, public relations, and communications.

Experience/Skills

Most community-affairs directors enter television with at least two years of experience in a nonprofit organization, as director or as manager of public information. They are familiar with local businesses and government units. They understand local social issues and concerns.

Community-affairs directors are personable and sensitive in their relationships with the community. They also must be good writers and speakers, and understand television production.

Unions/Associations

Community-affairs directors may belong to a variety of associations, depending on their communities and major interests. They may also belong to the Public Relations Society of America, Inc.; Women In Communications, Inc.; National Academy of Television Arts and Sciences; or Academy of Television Arts and Sciences.

REPORTER

CAREER PROFILE

Duties: News gathering, rewriting, and editing; announcing

Alternate Title(s): Newscaster

Salary Range: $10,450 to $50,000+

Employment Prospects: Good

Advancement Prospects: Good

Prerequisites:

Education—High school diploma sufficient for some entry-level jobs; undergraduate degree in communications, broadcasting, or liberal arts necessary for most positions

Experience—None to one or more years

Special Skills—Sound news judgment; concise writing; good speaking ability; tape editing skills

CAREER LADDER

News Director; Air Personality; Announcer

Newscaster

Continuity Writer; College; High School

Position Description

Radio reporters generally have two primary responsibilities: to collect and prepare news stories for broadcast, and to read their copy on the air. At large stations, these responsibilities may be divided into two jobs held by different persons—one who collects, writes, and edits; and one who announces.

Reporters do most of their work in the studio, where they monitor incoming wire-service copy and other news sources. They select stories for the newscasts, they rewrite and edit the copy to fit time limitations and the interests of their audiences. Some reporters may do their own news gathering, by taping interviews over the phone or in person. Some may actually be sent out of the studio to cover disasters or major news events. The tapes, called "actualities," are edited for quotes to be aired. It's not uncommon to have to rewrite copy just before airtime.

Most radio stations air news breaks on the hour, giving shorter, periodic updates as well, especially for major, breaking stories. Many AM radio stations are all news/talk, a format that has gained considerable popularity in recent years. The news/talk format allows longer and more in-depth stories, providing more opportunities for feature stories and personality interviews as well.

Reporters work under the direction of a news director who assigns coverage and responsibilities. Working hours can range anywhere around the clock, seven days a week; most beginners usually draw evening, night, and weekend shifts. Overtime is often required.

Most radio stations have small facilities and staffs. At smaller stations, reporters are more likely to either work part-time or share other duties, such as ad copywriting or programming.

In addition, reporters may:

- prepare and read news analyses or editorials;
- research stories for major air personalities.

Salaries

Beginners are likely to earn as little as $10,000 a year in small markets, and $18,000 to $20,000 in large markets. Top newscasters with several years' experience can earn $50,000 or more, depending on the station and size of market. Median salaries range between $10,450 and $18,100.

Employment Prospects

Most of the nation's 4,500 AM radio stations and 4,000 FM stations have at least one full-time newsperson. Most have more than one, and medium to large stations have news staffs of 10 to 40 persons or more. Other broadcast news jobs are available at the major networks and news wire services. Beginners will find their best opportunities at small stations. Competition is keen.

Advancement Prospects

Turnover in radio jobs in general is high. In addition, according to industry sources, openings occur more frequently in news and clerical positions than in such other areas as programming and ad copywriting. A reporter can advance to news director, or build an audience to become an air personality or announcer.

Education

A high school diploma is the minimum requirement for many entry-level jobs. A college degree in broadcasting or mass communications is strongly recommended to be competitive for more prestigious, higher paying positions.

Experience/Skills

Beginners who've had experience at school newspapers or radio or TV stations have significant advantages for acquiring reporter jobs. Most large radio stations, however, hire experienced newscasters from smaller stations rather than novices fresh from college. Continuity writing, which is writing advertising copy for broadcast, is excellent experience.

Reporters should have good news judgment and be able to work quickly under deadline pressure. They should be able to write "for the ear" and know how to handle studio taping and broadcasting equipment. Good speaking ability is essential—clear enunciation and correct grammar.

Unions/Associations

Many broadcast professionals are represented by unions, such as the American Federation of Television and Radio Artists; National Association of Broadcast Employees and Technicians; or Writers Guild of America. Other major professional associations include American Women in Radio and Television, Inc.; Radio-Television News Directors Association; National Association of Educational Broadcasters; National Association of Broadcasters; and Women In Communications, Inc.

NEWS DIRECTOR

CAREER PROFILE

Duties: Supervise content of newscasts; report, write, edit, and deliver news as needed

Alternate Title(s): News Editor

Salary Range: $15,000 to $65,000+

Employment Prospects: Fair to good

Advancement Prospects: Fair

Prerequisites:

Education—Undergraduate degree in communications, English, history, or liberal arts

Experience—Several years in broadcast journalism

Special Skills—Decision-making; managerial ability; sound news judgment

CAREER LADDER

Program Director; General Manager

News Director

Reporter; College

Position Description

Radio news directors are in charge of their station's news operation. They supervise other newscasters or news writers, assign coverage of stories, and make decisions concerning the content of news broadcasts. They set news-gathering and writing policies. They are often called upon to make quick decisions on breaking news stories. Many news directors have production responsibilities as well, which include tape editing and overall supervision of a program.

At large stations, radio news directors may be in charge of staffs of 30 to 40 persons. Most stations have much smaller staffs; at some stations, the news director is the entire staff—reporter, editor, director, and newscaster all rolled into one.

News directors have hiring and firing responsibility. They report to general managers or station managers. Their responsibilities also include administrative tasks, correspondence, reports, and paperwork.

In addition, radio news directors may also:

- act as working reporters—gathering, editing, and rewriting news stories;
- deliver the news on the air.

Salaries

Radio news directors earn median salaries of $15,000 to $29,000, depending on the size of the market and staff. News directors of large staffs can earn $65,000 or more. The news directors on very small stations may be one-person staffs, doing all jobs from reporting to editing to delivering the news. These positions are usually low-paying and are likely to be filled by persons with little or no experience.

Employment Prospects

Small and medium markets offer the best job prospects for persons seeking news-director positions. Turnover in radio is high, and news directors average one to two years in a particular job. Competition is tougher for jobs at stations and networks that have large news staffs.

Advancement Prospects

The increasing importance and profitability of news operations in recent years has greatly enhanced opportunities for advancement for radio news directors. Most general managers of stations typically have come from the sales and programming operations, but more and more are coming from the news department. Ambitious news directors should become familiar with all station operations, including sales, programming, engineering, and production.

Education

An undergraduate degree in communications, liberal arts, or other fields is preferred. Some broadcast journalists have graduate degrees in communications.

Experience/Skills

Most radio news directors have had several years' experience as radio newscasters or news writers; some start their careers as directors at very small stations that have one-person news operations. In addition to newswriting, some also have experience in production.

Skills for this job include the ability to supervise others, make decisions and assignments, and have good news judgment. News directors should be good writers and editors, with good speaking skills. A familiarity with other station operations is advantageous.

Unions/Associations

Many broadcast professionals are represented by such unions as the American Federation of Television and Radio Artists; National Association of Broadcast Employees and Technicians; or Writers Guild of America. Other major professional associations include American Women in Radio and Television, Inc.; Radio-Television News Directors Association; National Association of Educational Broadcasters; National Association of Broadcasters; and Women in Communications, Inc.

PROMOTION MANAGER

CAREER PROFILE

Duties: Stimulate audience and advertiser interest in station

Alternate Title(s): Promotion Director

Salary Range: $15,000 to $50,000+

Employment Prospects: Fair

Advancement Prospects: Fair

Prerequisites:

Education—Undergraduate degree in advertising, communications, or liberal arts

Experience—None to several years

Special Skills—Creativity; knowledge of advertising; salesmanship; outgoing personality

CAREER LADDER

Sales Manager

Promotion Manager

Continuity Writer; Production Assistant; College

Position Description

Promotion managers work on the sales side of broadcasting, usually under the supervision of sales managers or directors. Their primary responsibility is to generate audience and advertiser interest, which will help raise rating points and bring in greater ad revenues.

Promotion managers stimulate audience interest with press releases, commercials, and other ads about air personalities, upcoming celebrity guests, or special programs. At small stations, the promotion manager may handle all aspects of the job, from writing all press and ad copy to producing air commercials. At large stations, the promotion manager may supervise the work done by continuity writers and production assistants, and may also work with an outside ad agency to develop promotion and publicity campaigns.

Promotion managers are responsible for developing such materials as brochures and biographical information on air personalities. They arrange for photographs to be taken, which can be used for publicity purposes—for example, a portrait of a popular air host may be printed on a postcard for answering fan mail.

Promotion managers also schedule public appearances by station personalities, as well as handle special events, such as contests. They order and distribute giveaway items printed with their station's logo or ad slogan, such as T-shirts, mugs, buttons, hats, bumper stickers, and posters.

The job is demanding and often high pressure. Promotion managers generally work regular weekday schedules, but overtime, weekend, or evening work is often required for special promotion events and activities. In addition to coordinating a wide range of tasks, promotion managers must be able to manage budgets.

Promotion managers may also:

- work with the sales department to develop materials and campaigns for advertisers;
- combine their job with another, most likely sales;
- handle community relations;
- do research for advertising and sales.

Salaries

Most promotion manager salaries range from about $18,000 to $30,000. Men tend to earn more, in the twenties and thirties, while women and minorities hold most of the lower-paying positions. A very small percentage earns $50,000 or more.

Employment Prospects

Not every radio station has a position devoted solely to promotion. Job candidates may begin as sales representatives whose duties include promotion work. Promotion jobs at large stations are highly competitive.

Advancement Prospects

The person who manages or directs promotion is at the top in that line of work. A promotion manager with sales experience may aspire to advance to sales manager or director, heading the entire sales operation.

Education

An undergraduate degree in advertising, communications, or liberal arts is preferred. Degrees in other fields are acceptable.

Experience/Skills

Promotion managers generally have had several years of experience in sales, advertising, continuity writing, or production work. Stations with very small staffs may employ someone with little or no experience to handle promotion, sales, and other duties. Sales or copywriting experience is beneficial. Some promotion professionals have backgrounds as journalists.

Promotion managers should be creative, able to write good ad and news copy, and work well under pressure. They should understand sales persuasion, be able to supervise many different tasks, and be able to manage budgets. Persons who do well in this line of work tend to have outgoing personalities and be at ease in demanding social situations and at public appearances.

Unions/Associations

Major professional associations include the Broadcasters' Promotion Association; American Women in Radio and Television, Inc.; and Women In Communications, Inc.

BOOK PUBLISHING

EDITORIAL ASSISTANT

CAREER PROFILE

Duties: Clerical, secretarial, and minor editorial tasks

Alternate Title(s): Editorial Secretary; Editorial Trainee

Salary Range: $15,000 to $20,000

Employment Prospects: Fair

Advancement Prospects: Good

Prerequisites:

Education—Undergraduate degree in liberal arts, English, history, or communications
Experience—Secretarial training helpful
Special Skills—Organizational ability; office skills; knowledge of grammar

CAREER LADDER

Assistant Editor

Editorial Assistant

College; Secretary

Position Description

Editorial assistant is the entry-level editorial job in a publishing house. It is largely a training position for more advanced editorial posts. Most of the duties revolve around office tasks, such as receptionist duties, filing, typing, and running errands. Editorial assistants usually work for one or more editors, such as an editorial director and assistant or associate editors, depending on the size of the publishing house.

Publishing houses receive thousands of manuscripts every year. Most are unsolicited and relegated to what is called the "slush pile." In some major publishing houses, the slush pile can fill an entire storage room. Editorial assistants usually are responsible for the initial handling of all incoming manuscripts, directing some to the appropriate editors and assigning the rest to the slush pile.

Reading the slush to search for publishable manuscripts is a job often shared by editorial assistants as well as lower-level editors. In some houses, editorial assistants may not be allowed to read the slush, while in others they may have the entire responsibility for it. First readings of most manuscripts are quick and partial, due to limited time. Rejected manuscripts are returned, usually with form letters. For manuscripts that look promising, editorial assistants write summary reports on the plots, including their opinions and recommendations. They then pass the manuscripts and reports to the appropriate higher editors for evaluation.

Editorial assistants also act as coordinators and liaisons for a variety of functions. For example, they work with copy editors and proofreaders, who may either be on staff or be hired freelancers. They monitor production schedules for editors—researching and relaying information on cost estimates for design work and typesetting, as well as giving the status of production work for various manuscripts. They may also act as liaisons with authors, handling phone calls and correspondence, and typing book contracts.

In addition, editorial assistants may:

- have responsibility for copyright applications;
- route requisitions for author advances, editorial expenses, freelancer invoices, and other bills.

Salaries

Editorial assistants earn an average salary of about $18,000. Salaries not only depend on the size of the publishing house but also on the type of books it publishes—a technical or medical publisher who requires more specialized job skills may pay more than a small trade publisher, for example. The highest paying jobs are in the Middle Atlantic region—New York, New

Jersey and Pennsylvania—while the lowest are in the Midwest.

Employment Prospects

Publishing is a glamour industry and attracts many job applicants. Competition is fierce, however, because jobs are limited and the industry has suffered a downturn in recent years. Most jobs are in the New York City area, the center of publishing.

Advancement Prospects

Job turnover in publishing is high, especially at the lower editorial levels. Editorial assistants have good chances of moving up to assistant or associate editors.

Education

Persons interested in careers as book editors should have well-rounded undergraduate educations in liberal arts, English, history, or communications, including publishing courses. Some universities have specialized publishing curricula. A number of summer institutes offer intensive publishing programs. For work in educational publishing, a degree in education is desirable but not necessary.

Experience/Skills

Any kind of editing experience, such as working on school publications or taking summer jobs on local magazines or newspapers, is helpful. Working in a bookstore also provides excellent experience and understanding of the marketing end of publishing, as well as a sense of what type of books sell well.

Editorial assistants should have good office skills and be well organized, able to monitor many projects at once. They should possess a thorough understanding of grammar and use of the English language.

Unions/Associations

District 65 of the United Auto Workers represents editors of some large book publishers. Major professional associations include the Women's National Book Association, Inc.; P.E.N. American Center; Manhattan Publishing Group; and Women In Communications, Inc. Editors may also belong to a variety of authors' groups.

ADMINISTRATIVE ASSISTANT

CAREER PROFILE

Duties: Assist publicity, promotion, or advertising managers with routine tasks and minor writing activities

Alternate Title(s): Executive Assistant; Publicity Assistant; Promotion Assistant; Advertising Assistant; Marketing Assistant

Salary Range: $14,000 to $22,500

Employment Prospects: Fair

Advancement Prospects: Fair

Prerequisites:

Education—Undergraduate degree in communications, liberal arts, advertising, or marketing

Experience—Background in publishing, media, advertising, or public relations helpful

Special Skills—Writing; organization; clerical skills

CAREER LADDER

Publicity Specialist; Promotion Specialist; Advertising Specialist; Marketing Specialist

Administrative Assistant

College

Position Description

Administrative assistant is an entry-level position found in almost all publishing departments. Many of the duties usually are low-level, routine clerical and secretarial tasks, although they can involve higher responsibilities. The job does provide one with an excellent background and training in how books are publicized, advertised, and marketed. With experience, one's responsibilities increase; this can lead to more interesting work and, in some cases, direct contact with prominent authors.

Administrative assistants may be assigned to one department and limited to tasks in a particular function, such as publicity, advertising, or promotion. Some assistants work in the sales and marketing department. Other assistants may be shared by several departments and have broader, more versatile responsibilities.

Routine tasks common to all departments include typing, filing, answering the telephone, placing calls, running errands, and performing general office duties.

Administrative assistants also maintain mailing lists, updating and cleaning them as necessary; handle correspondence, including routing letters and writing letters for their supervisors to sign; stuff envelopes, press and sales kits; and prepare materials for meetings and conferences.

They also maintain records, such as sales figures, price changes, as well as ad and publicity campaign results. They distribute review copies and press releases.

Writing duties may include departmental reports; material for press kits; promotional or advertising copy; and copy for sales catalogs, which describes books, gives the track records and expertise of authors, and the commitment the publisher expects to make for advertising, publicity, and promotion.

In many cases, administrative assistants act as liaisons between departments, helping coordinate various activities that support the marketing of books. Administrative assistants often work long hours and have many deadline pressures. They must be flexible and able to accommodate last-minute changes. Travel is seldom required.

In addition, administrative assistants may:

- help organize sales conferences, publicity, and promotional events;
- work with film and television contacts concerning movie and TV tie-ins;

- assist in the booking of author tours and speaking engagements

Salaries

Administrative assistant salaries vary from department to department within a publisher, and also depend on the size of the publishing house and the geographic location. Average salaries are in the $17,000 to $18,000 range in the editorial and art departments, while advertising and publicity departments pay an average of about $20,000. Salaries can start as low as $14,000, even in advertising/publicity.

Employment Prospects

Job candidates have a fair chance of finding entry-level assistant positions. In some publishing houses, the job may be limited to publicity functions, while in others it may cover other departments as well, such as advertising and promotion.

Advancement Prospects

Administrative assistants have few opportunities to advance in publicity, due to the limited number of managerial positions in the industry. Some may find more opportunities in the sales promotion and advertising departments in publishing. Advancement may also be achieved with lateral moves to other fields, such as magazines, news media, or corporations.

Education

An undergraduate degree in communications, especially journalism, or liberal arts provides a good background for publicity work. Publishing courses are not as helpful as media courses. Familiarity with advertising and public relations is advantageous.

Experience/Skills

Most administrative-assistant jobs are entry-level positions and require no experience. Candidates who've had college internships, summer jobs, or experience on school publications have significant competitive advantages. Some assistant jobs—particularly at major publishers—are more advanced, carrying greater responsibilities. One or two years' experience at another publisher is often required for such positions.

Publicity assistants should be able to juggle many projects at the same time, paying close attention to detail and follow-through. They should have good written and oral communications skills, and be self-motivated and disciplined.

Unions/Associations

Among major professional organizations are the Publishers' Ad Club; Public Relations Society of America, Inc.; Publishers' Publicity Association, Inc.; American Publicists Guild; and Women In Communications, Inc. District 65 of the United Auto Workers represents some employees at major publishers.

COPY EDITOR

CAREER PROFILE

Duties: Edit manuscripts for grammar, style, and consistency; proofread

Alternate Title(s): None

Salary Range: $18,000 to $25,000

Employment Prospects: Fair

Advancement Prospects: Fair

Prerequisites:

Education—Undergraduate degree in liberal arts or communications preferred

Experience—Background as editorial or production assistant preferred

Special Skills—Thorough knowledge of grammar and style; attention to detail; production knowledge

CAREER LADDER

Production Editor; Managing Editor

Copy Editor

Editorial Assistant; Production Assistant; College

Position Description

Once book manuscripts have been accepted, edited, and revised to the satisfaction of authors and editors, they are turned over to copy editors for final editing and checking. This vital part of the editing process protects both authors and publishers by ensuring the accuracy and quality of the final end product.

Much of the copy editors' work is meticulous and detail-oriented. They carefully go over each manuscript (including indexes, glossaries, and bibliographies), correcting spelling, punctuation, and other points of grammatical style. Each publishing house has its own internal style for such things as abbreviations, titles, capitalizations, use of italics, etc., and copy editors must make certain all manuscripts conform to that style.

Copy editors may also check for inconsistencies in fact and logic, a time-consuming process that is not always possible at many publishing houses. Copy editors consult reference sources and may even contact authors to verify information in question. They may also consult with other editors over questions about the manuscript.

Copy editors do not change the substance of a manuscript or alter an author's style or "voice." Revisions or rewrites are the prerogative of the authors and their "line" editors—assistant, associate, or senior editors.

While copy editors must be thorough in their editing, they also must adhere to production schedules, delivering manuscripts on time for typesetting. In other stages of production, copy editors usually proofread galleys for typographical errors and check to see that typesetting instructions have been followed. They also proofread mechanicals and check any layouts, such as artwork and captions.

Copy editors work under the direction of a production editor or managing editor, and may themselves supervise production assistants and freelance copy editors and proofreaders. They are a liaison between editorial and production functions. Their work can be tedious, requiring patience and great attention to detail. Errors should be caught early in the production process to avoid delays and costly corrections.

Publishers have begun to experiment with editing manuscripts on computer terminals. In the future, manuscripts are likely to be transmitted electronically from one department to another, and perhaps outside—to author and typesetter—as well. Ambitious copy editors would be wise to learn how to use computer technology.

Salaries

Most copy editors earn between $18,000 and $25,000, depending on their experience and the size of the publishing house. Salaries can start as low as $15,000.

Employment Prospects

Most publishers employ copy editors. Many copy editors start as production assistants. The greatest job opportunities are in New York City, the center of the publishing industry, although the rise of small and moderate-sized publishers throughout the country offer prospects elsewhere, albeit usually at lower pay.

Advancement Prospects

The most likely advancement opportunities for copy editors are on the production side of publishing—to production or managing editors. Computer technology is creating new growth in production-oriented jobs, and copy editors who have experience in using computer systems will have an advantage for advancement. It is possible, but difficult, to switch to the editorial side and become an assistant editor.

Education

Copy editors should have a minimum of three years of college, though preference is given to those who have earned undergraduate degrees. Areas of study include liberal arts, communications, and publishing. Additional training in editing and production is valuable.

Experience/Skills

A production background is preferred for copy-editing positions. Work as a production assistant, or any editing and production work done in college, is helpful for getting a job.

Copy editors must be familiar with production stages and with typesetting symbols and terminology. They should be excellent spellers and know rules of grammar and style. Also, they should have a high tolerance for detail work. Copy editors who can work with computer systems will be more in demand as publishers increasingly computerize their operations.

Unions/Associations

Industry associations include the Manhattan Publishing Group; Women's National Book Association; and Women In Communications, Inc. Copy editors who freelance on the side may belong to the Editorial Freelancers Association. Some at large publishing houses may be represented by a union, District 65 of the United Auto Workers.

ASSISTANT EDITOR

CAREER PROFILE

Duties: Screen, edit, and occasionally acquire manuscripts; monitor production

Alternate Title(s): Editorial Assistant

Salary Range: $16,000 to $20,000

Employment Prospects: Fair

Advancement Prospects: Fair

Prerequisites:

Education—Undergraduate degree in liberal arts, English, history, or communications; publishing courses
Experience—Work as editorial assistant or trainee
Special Skills—Editing; organization

CAREER LADDER

Associate Editor

Assistant Editor

Editorial Assistant; Editorial Trainee; College

Position Description

The assistant editor position usually is one step above editorial assistant, who is little more than a clerk and secretary. In large publishing houses with big and highly structured staffs, assistant editor may be the equivalent of editorial assistant.

Most assistant editors have learned the editorial process, know how to screen manuscripts and can edit them according to the in-house style of the publisher. They assume more responsibilities than editorial assistants.

Typical duties include reading queries and proposals submitted by authors through agents, and screening unsolicited manuscripts for publishable material. Assistant editors are responsible for helping publish a specified number of books a month or year; this means shepherding the product from manuscript to finished book. The work involves editing and coordinating proofreading and production. Much of the work is routine. Editing is done under the supervision of a higher-level editor. Assistant editors may or may not have direct contact with authors concerning revisions and rewrites. If a staff is small, job duties may be broad enough to include writing jacket copy, as well as proposing publicity and promotion ideas.

Assistant editors report to associate editors, senior editors, managing editors, or editorial directors, depending on the size of the house. They help plan deadlines and production schedules, and they may delegate work to editorial assistants.

In many cases, assistant editors recommend manuscripts for acquisition, and they may even make the initial offer to the author. Actual contract negotiation usually is done by more experienced editors. Assistant editors generally do not work on the most important books.

In addition, assistant editors may:

- write reports and make presentations to recommend manuscripts for purchase;
- attend trade and professional meetings.

Salaries

Salaries for assistant editors range from $16,000 to $20,000, depending on their experience, responsibilities, and employer.

Employment Prospects

Job applicants have a fair chance of getting low-level editing jobs. The best opportunities are at small publishing houses. Employment agencies which specialize in publishing can be helpful in a job search. Employment prospects in educational publishing are decreasing due to school budget cutbacks.

Advancement Prospects

Assistant editors have a good chance of being promoted in-house, due to the high turnover typical of the publishing industry.

Education

An undergraduate degree in liberal arts, history, English, or communications is preferred, though virtually any degree is acceptable. Job candidates benefit from courses in book publishing.

Experience/Skills

Prior experience as an editorial assistant, trainee, editor, or writer in another field is necessary for many assistant-editor jobs. Some positions, however, are entry-level for persons right out of college.

Assistant editors should have good editorial and grammatical skills, and understand the entire editorial process. They should have a good sense of the book marketplace and know what has sales potential. Oral presentation skills are advantageous for editorial and sales meetings.

Unions/Associations

Major professional associations include the Women's National Book Association, Inc.; Women In Communications, Inc.; Manhattan Publishing Group; and various authors' organizations. Editorial employees at some large publishers are members of District 65 of the United Auto Workers.

ASSOCIATE EDITOR

CAREER PROFILE

Duties: Screen, edit, and rewrite manuscripts; manage projects; recommend acquisitions

Alternate Title(s): Editor; Project Editor

Salary Range: $18,000 to $25,000

Employment Prospects: Fair

Advancement Prospects: Poor

Prerequisites:

Education—Undergraduate degree in communications, liberal arts, English, or history

Experience—One to two years in editorial work

Special Skills—Good editing and organization; supervisory ability; business knowledge; presentation skills

CAREER LADDER

Editor

Associate Editor

Assistant Editor; Editorial Assistant

Position Description

Associate editors may delegate much of the routine work in a publishing house to subordinates, concentrating more on the screening, acquisition, and editing of manuscripts. Their responsibilities are likely to include screening the slush pile of unsolicited manuscripts and evaluating manuscripts that have passed a first screening by a lower level editor or assistant. Associate editors are not likely to do the actual acquiring and contract negotiating, but they do make acquisition recommendations to the editorial board. They must have a clear sense of the needs of the publisher as well as the conditions in the book marketplace. If a publisher is seeking an author to write a book, they may recommend or search for candidates.

Associate editors usually work under the direction of senior editors or editorial directors. They may help plan long-range projects for series of books; this involves scheduling deadlines for acquisitions, editing, production, and promotion, and working within a budget.

They also edit manuscripts and work directly with authors concerning revisions and rewrites (subject to the approval of a superior editor). They may oversee the work done by copy editors.

Associate editors attend regular in-house editorial meetings, during which potential books are discussed and decisions made. They may be asked to make informal or formal presentations explaining why particular manuscripts should be purchased. They make periodical progress reports.

On large staffs, associate editors are likely to have one or more subordinates who help with routine work and correspondence.

In addition, associate editors may:

- maintain contact with literary agents;
- supervise special editorial projects;
- write jacket copy;
- help plan publicity and promotion.

Salaries

Associate editors are paid modest salaries for work that often involves long hours. Most salaries range from $18,000 to $25,000.

Employment Prospects

Turnover is high in publishing. Most low and middle positions, including associate editor, are filled from within. Though much smaller publishing "centers" exist in the areas around Chicago, Boston, San Francisco, Los Angeles, the Pacific Northwest, and Florida, most publishers are located in the New York City area.

Advancement Prospects

Competition is very keen for editorial positions above associate editor. At higher levels, many jobs are filled by outside candidates rather than those promoted within.

Education

Most associate editors have undergraduate degrees in communications, liberal arts, English, or history. Additional courses in publishing are desirable.

Experience/Skills

Most associate editors have had at least one or two years of experience in lower editorial positions; some have worked as editors of magazines and newspapers. Associate editors should have strong editing skills and a good business sense of a book's potential commercial appeal. They should be able to work within budgets and supervise others. Oral presentation skills and the ability to persuade are invaluable.

Unions/Associations

Major professional associations include Women In Communications, Inc.; Manhattan Publishing Group; Women's National Book Association, Inc.; and authors' groups. District 65 of the United Auto Workers represents employees of some large publishers.

EDITOR

CAREER PROFILE

Duties: Develop ideas for books, recommend books for acquisition, negotiate deals, work with authors, supervise staff

Alternate Title(s): Developmental Editor

Salary Range: $23,000 to $40,000

Employment Prospects: Poor to Fair

Advancement Prospects: Poor to Fair

Prerequisites:

Education—Undergraduate degree in communications, publishing English, liberal arts, humanities; special publishing courses advantageous

Experience—Work as editorial assistant, assistant editor or associate editor

Special Skills—Creativity; organization; knowledge of all phases of publishing process; ability to work well with others and to work under pressure

CAREER LADDER

Senior Editor

Editor

Associate Editor

Position Description

Editors perform may of the same duties as associate editors, but have more responsibility and work on more important books. Editors read manuscripts and proposals submitted by authors and agents, and make presentations to the editorial board to recommend acquisitions. When they receive the green light to proceed, editors negotiate the terms. Editors also generate book ideas, and then work with agents and authors to develop them into acceptable proposals.

Once a proposal or manuscript is acquired, editors shepherd it through the editing and production process. Editing responsibilities vary considerably according to publishing house. At a large house, an editor does a general edit and asks for revisions if they are necessary. Once the manuscript is acceptable, it is turned over to line and copy editors who read for consistency, grammar and style. At a small house, the editor may do all of those functions.

The editor coordinates with art, production, marketing and publicity departments to help meet their needs and deadlines, and contributes information and ideas that will help the success of the book.

Editors talk and meet with agents frequently to discuss ideas and potential book projects. They work closely with authors. They supervise other editors and delegate tasks, and report to a senior editor, editorial director or executive editor. They attend staff meetings, and spend a certain amount of time reading the "slush," or unsolicited manuscripts and proposals. At a large house, an editor may be responsible for dozens of books a year, requiring constant juggling and attention to detail. Publishing is fraught with delays—especially from authors—and editors must work under pressure.

Salary Range

The average editor's salary is about $33,000. The lowest salaries, starting at about $23,000, are in the Midwest, while the highest, at about $40,000, are in the Middle Atlantic region.

Employment Prospects

Major publishing houses, most of which are concentrated in Middle Atlantic and Northeastern United States, are expected to remain under financial pressure throughout the 1990s, thus limiting job opportunities.

Many jobs have been lost due to mergers, acquisitions and consolidations, and also to ill-conceived spending that has left some houses with piles of debt. The best opportunities may be in the lower end of the market, the small presses and moderately sized independent presses, though pay is lower.

Advancement Prospects

Promotion opportunities are limited for the same reasons.

Education

Most editors have an undergraduate degree in communications, publishing, liberal arts, English or humanities. Many have taken additional courses in publishing and marketing.

Experience/Skills

The editor's job requires prior experience as an editorial assistant, assistant editor or associate editor—or two of those positions, depending on the house and the nature of the editor's job.

Editors must be able to work well with a wide variety of people and temperaments. They must be able to supervise, delegate and work under pressure. They are creative and intuitive when it comes to anticipating trends and interests in the marketplace. They are well organized and able to work with budgets and deadlines.

Unions/Associations

Editors may belong to the Women's National Book Association, the Manhattan Publishing Group, Women In Communications, Inc., or other groups related to publishing. Some may belong to a labor union.

SENIOR EDITOR

CAREER PROFILE

Duties: Acquire and develop major books and authors; supervise other editors; plan and execute editorial policies

Alternate Title(s): Acquisitions Editor; Project Editor

Salary Range: $25,000 to $60,000

Employment Prospects: Poor

Advancement Prospects: Poor

Prerequisites:

Education—Undergraduate degree in liberal arts, communications, English, or history

Experience—Three to five years or more in editing

Special Skills—Negotiation and supervisory ability; business and decision-making skills

CAREER LADDER

Editorial Director; Executive Editor

Senior Editor

Associate Editor

Position Description

Senior editors play influential roles in the editorial policies, directions, and products of publishing houses. They are heavily involved in the marketing and business aspects of publishing, and they usually handle the most prestigious books.

Senior editors work under the direction of editorial directors or publishers. They help develop comprehensive, long-range publishing plans, which include acquisition and publishing schedules, budgetary analyses, and sales projections. They have overall responsibility for the completion of book projects, including supervision of editing done by other editors, production work, adherence to schedules and deadlines, and use of freelance and consultant help.

Most senior editors are also responsible for acquisitions, though some large houses may delegate this task to specialized acquisitions editors. Acquisition involves deciding which manuscripts should be purchased, then negotiating the contracts with authors and agents. Each publisher has a standard contract, and senior editors must know the limits of negotiable points. Senior editors often work closely with in-house legal staff and subsidiary-rights editors in contract negotiations. The actual sale of a book's subsidiary rights to foreign publishers, magazines, or paperback publishers may be handled by a senior editor.

Senior editors also work with marketing and publicity/promotion staff to persuade them which titles deserve the most sales, advertising, and publicity support. They make many presentations, some informal at weekly editorial and sales meetings, and others formal, at major sales conferences.

In addition, senior editors may:

- accompany sales representatives on sales calls;
- represent their publisher at major industry conventions.

Salaries

Most senior editors earn in the low to mid-thirties. Senior editors at small houses may earn as little as $25,000, while those at major publishers may earn $60,000 or more.

Employment Prospects

Senior-editor positions are highly competitive and require years of experience in the publishing industry. It is often necessary to change employers in order to get a job at this level.

Advancement Prospects

A tight job market in publishing makes advancement to editorial director or executive editor very difficult. There is much less turnover at this level than at lower editorial levels. Advancement usually is made by changing employers.

Education

Senior editors are expected to have undergraduate degrees, most preferably in liberal arts, English, history, or communications. Education ideally should include publishing courses. Additional study at a publishing summer institute is advantageous.

Experience/Skills

Three to five years' experience in editing is required for most senior-editor posts; large publishers may require more experience. A background at one or more publishers is advantageous. Most publishers do not fill senior- editor positions from within but instead hire from the outside.

Senior editors should understand publishing contracts and be able to negotiate them. They should have a good grasp of the business and financial side of publishing, be able to develop budget plans, and know how to supervise other employees.

Unions/Associations

Women In Communications, Inc. and Women's National Book Association are among the principal professional groups for book editors. In addition, senior editors may belong to authors' organizations, or, at some major publishers, to District 65 of the United Auto Workers.

COPYWRITER

CAREER PROFILE

Duties: Write copy for advertising, promotion, and direct-mail campaigns; flap copy; and press releases

Alternate Title(s): None

Salary Range: $16,000 to $35,000

Employment Prospects: Fair

Advancement Prospects: Fair

Prerequisites:

Education—Undergraduate degree in communications, advertising, or liberal arts
Experience—Background in advertising or marketing
Special Skills—Sales orientation; graphic-arts knowledge

CAREER LADDER

Promotion Manager; Advertising Manager; Sales Manager

Copywriter

Administrative Assistant

Position Description

Copywriters create many of the materials that help sell books, not only to the public but to booksellers, wholesalers, and the media as well. They usually work under the direction of managers of advertising, sales, or promotion. They write copy for print ads and book catalogs, and scripts for radio commercials. Television ads are uncommon for books but may be required for special, major campaigns or for lines of books. Some romance publishers, for example, advertise their lines in TV commercials. Other sales-oriented material includes literature for the sales force (such as information on discounts to booksellers, sales records of authors' previous books; special displays available; and advertising and publicity plans) plus posters, flyers, and displays for use in bookstores.

In some highly structured publishing houses, copywriters also handle certain editorial copy tasks that might otherwise be done by junior editors. These include press releases for the media and book reviewers, material for press kits, and jacket copy. Jacket copy consists of a synopsis of a book's plot, and it is intended to entice customers into a purchase. Sometimes information on the author and his or her previous books is included as well.

Copywriters coordinate their work with others, such as advertising and promotion representatives as well as editors. They may do their own research for projects or may delegate the work to assistants. They often work with graphic artists in designing and laying out ads, brochures, and catalogs. They must be able to work with space limitations. For example, jacket copy for paperback books must fit the space allowed by the illustration, type, and universal price code. Some copywriters may specialize in certain areas, such as direct mail.

Salaries

Most copywriters earn in the low to mid-twenties, though salaries can range from $16,000 to $35,000, depending on experience, responsibilities,and employer. On the average, copywriting jobs at publishing houses do not pay as well as those at ad agencies or businesses.

Employment Prospects

Copywriting jobs aren't as glamorous as editorial jobs in publishing. However, they may be easier to get, due to the increasing importance of effective book marketing.

Advancement Prospects

Skilled copywriters can advance to managerial positions in sales, advertising, or promotion. Some publishers have direct-mail specialists as well. These business-oriented jobs also lead to higher executive positions overall in publishing houses.

Education

An undergraduate degree in communications or advertising is preferred for copywriting jobs. A degree in liberal arts also is acceptable.

Experience/Skills

A background in advertising or sales-promotion work is usually required for this type of job. Some copywriters come from jobs in advertising agencies, while others start as entry-level assistants.

Copywriters should be able to write crisp, persuasive sales copy. They should also have some knowledge of graphic arts—layout and production.

Unions/Associations

Major professional organizations include the American Advertising Federation; Publishers' Ad Club; the Direct Mail/Marketing Association, Inc.; Copywriters Council of America; and Women In Communications, Inc. Employees of some major publishers belong to District 65 of the United Auto Workers.

PUBLICITY MANAGER

CAREER PROFILE

Duties: Generate publicity for books and authors; arrange for book reviews and author tours

Alternate Title(s): Publicist

Salary Range: $20,000 to $36,000

Employment Prospects: Fair

Advancement Prospects: Poor

Prerequisites:

Education—Undergraduate degree in communications, English, or liberal arts

Experience—Background as publicity assistant or journalist essential

Special Skills—Good writing and organizational skills; salesmanship

CAREER LADDER

Director of Publicity

Publicity Manager

Publicity Assistant

Position Description

Publicity managers have highly visible jobs in publishing houses. They represent their publishing houses to the media, and they are responsible for generating favorable press coverage of books and authors.

Most books receive minimal publicity support, but a certain few are identified for receiving special effort. The amount of publicity can vary from a mailing of review copies with press releases to a full-blown campaign that includes an author tour, as well as advertising and sales promotion.

Planning for publicity begins long before a book is finished and ready to be delivered to the stores. Publicity managers coordinate their plans with editorial, advertising, sales, and promotion staffs. Budgets and deadlines are set for materials, mailings, travel, and other expenses.

For a major campaign, the publicity manager works with the author to develop press-kit material, such as author's biography and photograph, questions for interviewers to ask, press releases, and clips of early reviews or other notable news coverage an author may have received previously.

Review copies and press releases are mailed to book reviewers in advance of publication. Publicity managers are responsible for maintaining up-to-date lists and for seeing that books are sent to appropriate reviewers. A technical book, for example, would require a different mailing list than a novel.

In addition to reviews, publicity managers try to generate news or feature stories in the media. They send press releases and follow up with phone calls to arrange interviews for the authors. They also book speaking engagements and autograph signings at bookstores, libraries, and other places.

For author tours, publicity managers may do the bookings themselves or may hire freelance publicists to make all arrangements. Tasks include deciding tour cities; contacting the media for interviews; setting up schedules; arranging for transportation, accommodations, and travel advances for authors' out-of-pocket expenses. Tours are complicated, time-consuming, and involve a great many last-minute changes.

Publicity managers may be in charge of their publishers' entire publicity operation, or they may report to directors of publicity. They are likely to supervise assistants who handle much of the routine writing, stuffing, and mailing jobs.

In addition, publicity managers may:

- be responsible for maintaining clipping files on all authors and books;
- maintain good relations with the media through regular contact;

- plan and direct company publicity functions, such as dinner and cocktail parties.

Salaries

Salaries range from about $20,000 to $36,000. Most publicity managers earn in the low to mid-twenties.

Employment Prospects

The job market in this field is very tight, due to the competitive nature of such desirable jobs and the fact that publicity is one of the first areas to be cut back in bad economic times. Many openings at this level are not openly advertised. The best bet is to start as a publicity assistant and make industry contacts.

Advancement Prospects

Opportunities for promotion are limited in this field. At some publishing houses, publicity manager is the top position, supervised by a director or vice president of sales and/or advertising. In others, the next highest position is director of publicity. Advancement is usually achieved by changing employers rather than being promoted from within. Competition is strong.

Education

An undergraduate degree in communications or journalism is preferred for publicity jobs in publishing. Also acceptable are degrees in liberal arts and social science.

Experience/Skills

Three to five years of experience usually is required for publicity-manager positions, either as a publicity assistant or journalist for a newspaper or magazine. Publicity managers should understand the needs of the media and know what constitutes good publicity material. They should have good newswriting skills, and be outgoing and personable in their relations with the media. Publicity managers also should be persuasive, as they must "sell" their ideas to the press.

Unions/Associations

Major professional organizations include the American Publicists Guild; Publishers' Ad Club; Public Relations Society of America, Inc.; Publishers' Publicity Association, Inc.; and Women In Communications, Inc. District 65 of the United Auto Workers represents some employees of large publishing houses.

PROMOTION MANAGER

CAREER PROFILE

Duties: Supervise promotional projects to help book sales

Alternate Title(s): Sales Promotion Manager

Salary Range: $18,000 to $50,000

Employment Prospects: Poor

Advancement Prospects: Poor

Prerequisites:

Education—Undergraduate degree in advertising or marketing preferred

Experience—Two to five years in copywriting, promotion, or marketing

Special Skills—Sales orientation; copywriting ability; marketing knowledge; supervisory skills

CAREER LADDER

Director of Marketing or Sales

Promotion Manager

Copywriter; Researcher; Publicity Assistant

Position Description

Promotion is an important part of the overall marketing support given books once they are published. Other elements of support include media advertising, publicity, and direct-sales efforts. The most visible work of the promotion department can be seen in bookstores, where certain titles are out in special floor displays or emphasized by shelf tags, wall posters, buttons, and bookmarks at the cash register.

Other promotion products include direct-mail brochures and order blanks, sales literature, exhibits at industry conventions, and tie-ins such as T-shirts, tote bags, caps, key rings, and other items that are given away to the public.

Promotion managers work with editorial, advertising, and sales staffs to identify the books that will be supported. They develop and coordinate promotion plans, including scheduling, deadlines, and budgets. They then delegate work to copywriters, researchers, and assistants, and approve the final products. If specialty items such as T-shirts and note pads are to be used, they supervise their purchase and distribution.

Promotion managers often play an instrumental role in determining whether certain manuscripts are purchased by publishers. If a book is not promotable, in terms of getting attention and attracting a big enough audience, it may be rejected. Promotion managers sometimes sit in on editorial meetings at which buying decisions are made.

Promotion managers usually report to directors or vice presidents of marketing or sales. They may work with outside advertising agencies, if their publishers use such agencies, in the development of copy and materials. They may also supervise freelance copywriters in addition to their own staff.

In addition, promotion managers may:

- supervise publicity efforts;
- supervise jacket copywriting;
- assist in the preparation of sales catalogs.

Salaries

Most salaries for this middle-management position are in the upper twenties to mid-thirties. Some promotion managers earn as little as $18,000, while others earn well over $40,000.

Employment Prospects

Not all publishing houses have separate job positions for promotional work. Duties may be folded into another job, such as advertising manager.

Advancement Prospects

Promotion managers face stiff competition from their peers in sales and advertising for promotion to director or vice president of sales/marketing. Sales experience is an asset for advancement.

Education

An education in marketing or advertising is preferred for sales-promotion work. Also acceptable are undergraduate degrees in communications, liberal arts, or social sciences.

Experience/Skills

Two years of experience in copywriting, market research, publicity, or sales is considered the minimum for sales-promotion manager; ideally, job candidates should have at least five years of experience.

Sales-promotion managers should be knowledgeable in advertising and marketing techniques, and should be skilled copywriters themselves. Managerial skills include preparing budgets and long-range plans, and hiring, training, and supervising staff.

Unions/Associations

Major organizations include the Publishers' Ad Club; Publishers' Publicity Association, Inc.; American Publicists Guild; American Advertising Federation; and Women In Communications, Inc.

ARTS AND ENTERTAINMENT

AUTHOR

CAREER PROFILE

Duties: Research and write nonfiction or fiction books and articles

Alternate Title(s): Writer; Novelist

Income Potential: $0 to no limit

Work Prospects: Fair

Prerequisites:

Education—None required; undergraduate or advanced degrees in specialized fields desirable for nonfiction credentials

Experience—Background as a journalist or professional writer helpful

Special Skills—Creativity; self-motivation; persistence; good writing ability

Position Description

Authors enjoy an envied, glamorous image. Many people think they don't really "work" for a living, merely spending a few hours a day at their typewriters composing whatever strikes their fancy.

In truth, most authors work hard, spending long hours researching, writing, editing, and rewriting. A good portion of their work is done on speculation—that is, they don't get paid unless their finished work is accepted—and rejections are far more common than acceptances.

Most professional authors work on nonfiction books and articles, which in general earn more money than fiction. Nonfiction includes textbooks, encyclopedias, and academic works as well as topical books. Some authors also write novels, and a very few write nothing but novels.

The author's work is a solitary pursuit requiring strong self-discipline and motivation. Authors treat their writing like any other job—it must be done daily, and deadlines must be met. Authors do have an advantage in being able to choose their working hours. Some authors gauge their work by hours per day, while others measure it by numbers of pages or words written. They spend a great deal of time searching for ideas by reading periodicals and books, as well as by being naturally curious and observant.

Established authors seldom complete manuscripts before trying to sell them. They make a sale based on a proposal, which consists of an introductory pitch, an outline and sometimes a sample chapter, or a partial, which is generally three or more chapters, a synopsis and an outline. Beginners may be asked by publishers to complete their manuscripts before they are purchased, especially in fiction.

Most authors prefer to have agents handle their material. The agent sends manuscripts or proposals, called properties, to publishers. Agents also negotiate contracts, collect payments on behalf of the author, and often mediate in any problems that arise. Agents also find work for their clients by being aware of editors' interests.

The author's work is not done once a book is written and sold. Revisions must be completed and galleys proofread. Authors often spend their own time and money in helping publishers promote and advertise their books.

Authors may work on more than one project at a time, including developing ideas for sale while working on books under contract. Authors essentially run a small business, and must keep track of tax deductible expenses.

In addition, authors may:

- supplement book income with freelance writing or part- or full-time jobs.
- speak or teach at writers' conferences, colleges, and universities.

Income Potential

According to an Authors Guild survey of 2,239 authors, only 5 percent are able to support themselves with their writing; the rest write part-time. Of the full-time authors, fewer than half earn more than $20,000 a year, and the average author earns about $5,000.

Advances for beginning novelists can range from $500 to $10,000, but few novels earn royalties (a percentage of the retail price) beyond the advance. Authors of genre novels—mysteries, science fiction, romances, and westerns—fare the best, with some earning up to $50,000 a year or more.

Nonfiction books, especially if they are "hot" topics, can bring high advances and earn royalties over a long period of time. Most books in general, however, are out of print within a year of publication. Scientific and technical authors are able to earn more money than many other nonfiction authors.

Work Prospects

More than 40,000 books are published every year in the U.S., but that number represents only a fraction of the total number of manuscripts, proposals, and queries submitted by authors. Most ideas are rejected. Authors can wait months, even years, to sell their books. It's not uncommon to collect dozens of rejections before making a sale, even with the help of an agent.

Education

For nonfiction, an undergraduate degree of any kind is helpful. If the author is writing as an expert in a specialized field, an advanced degree is helpful. Fiction depends more on creativity and imagination than education.

Experience/Skills

Any kind of writing experience, such as school newspaper, a creative-writing class, or a media job, is good training. Professional writing experience as a news journalist or magazine staff writer is an asset for nonfiction credentials.

Authors must be imaginative, very self-disciplined, and able to spend long periods of time alone. They must possess a high degree of perseverance, both in perfection of craft and against the odds of rejection. They cannot afford to be easily discouraged.

Knowledge of publicity and promotion is helpful in aiding publishers in selling published books.

Unions/Associations

Major national authors' associations include the Authors Guild; P.E.N. American Center; American Society of Journalists and Authors, Inc.; National Writers Union; Authors League of America, Inc.; and National Writers Club, Inc. Other organizations serve a wide range of specialized interests. Major women's groups include the International Women's Writing Guild and National League of American Pen Women. The Writers Guild of America is a union representing radio, TV, and film scriptwriters.

GHOSTWRITER/COLLABORATOR

CAREER PROFILE

Duties: Work with others to write, rewrite, and edit books and articles

Alternate Title(s): None

Income Potential: $250 + for trade articles; $200 + per day or percentage of advance and royalties for books; $15 to $50 per hour

Work Prospects: Fair

Prerequisites:

Education—High school diploma or undergraduate degree in communications, journalism, English, or liberal arts

Experience—Background as an author, journalist, or novelist helpful

Special Skills—Good organization and research; editing skill; ability to imitate another's style or "voice"

Position Description

Ghostwriting carries little glamour but can be very lucrative. Many books and articles that appear under celebrities' or experts' names are in fact written, rewritten, or edited by professional writers who receive little or no credit for their role. The celebrity or expert provides the raw material; the writer molds it into a salable work.

The amount of work performed by ghostwriters varies. They may do all the researching, interviewing, writing, and editing, or they may write only a first draft. Some ghostwriters are hired to fix manuscripts by rewriting and editing.

The job of the ghostwriter is to become the voice of the subject. Thorough research is required in order to become familiar with the subject's manner of expression.

Most ghostwriting is nonfiction, such as articles or papers written for business officials, politicians, professionals, or scientific and academic leaders who wish to gain prestige through authorship. Many celebrities hire ghostwriters to write their first-person autobiographies. The ghostwriter may also write a textbook and nonfiction book for publication under an expert's name.

Some ghostwriters write novels for well-known authors. This is much more difficult than nonfiction.

Ghostwriters may be acknowledged in the introduction for "help in preparing the manuscript," or receive credit on the cover and title page under the guise of "with" or "as told to." Many ghostwriters prefer to remain invisible or are required to do so by their contracts. While they receive scant public recognition for their work, they can build reputations within publishing circles.

Collaboration is a more visible form of ghostwriting, often involving working in a partnership with another writer or celebrity. Collaborators usually share the research, writing, and revising.

Ghostwriting or collaboration can be an excellent way for writers to break into publishing and earn book credentials. Some ghostwriters build big reputations and do no other kind of writing.

In addition, ghostwriters and collaborators may:

- write their their own books and novels;
- write magazine articles, short stories, scripts, screenplays, or other freelance material;
- work as a freelance editor.

Income Potential

Income varies greatly, depending on the project, the celebrity or expert, and the experience of the ghostwriter or collaborator. In publishing, ghostwriters generally are able to earn more for a celebrity's book than they would writing under their own name. Business articles can earn $250 and up, or fees of more than $200 per day. Some ghostwriters charge by the hour, with rates ranging from about $15 to $50 an hour or more.

For books, some ghostwriters charge flat fees and some take a percentage of the advance, royalties, and all other income. Flat fees can be as low as $1,000 or as high as $100,000. Percentages vary from about 15 to 50 percent. A celebrity book may command an advance of several hundred thousand dollars, and it may become a bestseller. Some ghostwriters or collaborators may work on a cents-per-word basis.

Work Prospects

The ongoing popularity of celebrity books, plus the increasing number of specialized and trade publications that require expertise, provide a fair number of opportunities for ghostwriters and collaborators. Most of these writers tend to live in major cities near publishing and entertainment centers.

Education

There are no minimum education requirements unless a writer is working in business, professional, or technical fields.

Experience/Skills

Most ghostwriters and collaborators are experienced journalists, freelance business and magazine article writers, or novelists. Even with a writing background, it can be difficult to get one's own book published. Many writers break into publishing by ghosting or collaborating, and then use the credentials to help sell their own books.

Good interviewing, researching, writing, and editing skills are necessary. Above all, collaborators and ghostwriters are able to mimic others.

Unions/Associations

Major national authors' associations include the Authors Guild; American Society of Journalists and Authors, Inc.; National Writers Union; Authors League of America, Inc.; and National Writers Club, Inc. Other organizations serve a wide range of specialized interests. Major women's groups include the International Women's Writing Guild and National League of American Pen Women.

SCRIPTWRITER/SCREENWRITER

CAREER PROFILE

Duties: Write scripts and screenplays for film, television, and radio

Alternate Title(s): None

Income Potential: $9,000 to $100,000+ a year

Work Prospects: Poor

Prerequisites:

Education—Undergraduate degree in fine arts, English, or communications

Experience—Writing for any medium helpful

Special Skills—Creativity; writing talent; production knowledge

Position Description

Writing scripts and screenplays for the entertainment industries, particularly for film and television, is prestigious and glamorous—and can be quite lucrative. The business also is extremely unpredictable, high-pressure, and intensely competitive. Many scripts and screenplays that are commissioned are killed before production, which means lower fees for writers, if any at all. And many scripts that are produced undergo so many changes by so many writers that the original writer may not be credited with the final product. (Some even request no credit, if they dislike the alterations.)

In the golden days of Hollywood, most screenwriters worked under contract to the big studios. Today, most screenwriters and scriptwriters are freelance. They may work on a project-by-project basis, trying to interest producers in ideas for series or one-shot programs. Or, they may work under short contracts—13 weeks is standard for most serial shows on television, such as soap operas or comedy/variety programs.

A beginner usually must write an entire script or screenplay before a producer will consider it for option. Writers with more experience and good track records may be commissioned on the basis of less—a "treatment" or "story," which is an outline. According to Guild rules, writers are paid for all work, even outlines and the polishing of someone else's work, though rates are less than if a writer does all the work alone. Not every producer, however, recognizes Guild agreements. It's not uncommon, especially for beginners, to work on speculation.

Most scriptwriters and screenwriters employ agents to help them find work and negotiate contracts. They may attend special screenings of pilots for new television shows, at which networks solicit script ideas. They may meet with production executives to discuss ideas, a process called "pitching" or "spitballing." Such a session can lead to an assignment for a treatment.

Scriptwriters and screenwriters often work in stages, with many projects never seeing completion. Some projects never go beyond treatments; others are killed after a first draft is written. Frequently other writers are called in to rewrite and polish someone else's work. Payments are negotiated for each step.

It's difficult to write full-time for the entertainment industry without living in its capital, Los Angeles. Day-to-day contacts and proximity to producers and studios are vitally important. Many writers also live in New York City.

Income Potential

The Writers Guild of America sets a minimum scale for work by scriptwriters and screenwriters. Income varies according to the medium (TV, film, or radio), the length and type of script, and other services such as narrations, treatments, rewrites, and polishing. Income also depends on whether or not a writer is under contract to a network or studio to produce multiple scripts. According to the Writers Guild of America's 1988 Theatrical and Television Basic Agreement, some of the minimum pay ranges were as follows: screenplay with treatment—$28,110 to $52,274; rewrite of a screenplay—$10,540 to $16,144; polish of a screenplay—$5,297 to $8,033; 60-minute other than network prime-time telepay and story—$11,468 to $12,583. In addition, writers receive additional pay for reruns and foreing sales.

Week-to-week and term employment for theatrical and television writers ranges from $2,142 to $2,745 per week, depending upon the number of weeks employed in a given period of time.

Radio scriptwriters are paid according to the number and length of programs. For example, a writer earns a minium of $154 for one five-minute program. The same writer earns progressively higher fees for successive five-minute programs, up to a minimum of $510 for the sixth program. There is a minimum fee of $1,283 for a single 60-minute program. For a sixth 60-minute program the writer earns $3,386.

Work Prospects

In spite of the large number of films, television, cable TV, and radio programs produced every year, breaking into the business is very difficult—particularly in film or commercial television. An agent in Los Angeles is almost mandatory for most film and television work. Most scriptwriters and screenwriters live in Los Angeles or New York City. Steady work is unpredictable and highly competitive.

Education

Most scriptwriters and screenwriters have broad educations, such as undergraduate degrees in fine arts, English, or communications. Some have degrees in advertising and start their careers as ad copywriters.

Experience/Skills

It is possible for someone with little previous writing experience to write salable scripts and screenplays. Most scriptwriters and screenwriters have had seasoning in some medium, such as print or broadcast. Experience matters less than talent, creativity, and ability to write good dialogue. Scriptwriters and screenwriters have an ear for how people talk. They also understand the visual aspects of their work—how their ideas will translate to the screen.

Minorities/Women's Opportunities

Most scriptwriters and screenwriters in the entertainment industry are white males; women far outnumber minorities. Since this is largely a freelance field, there are no affirmative-action policies. Opportunities depend on talent, contacts, and luck.

Unions/Associations

Writers who work for most major film studios and television networks are required to join the Writers Guild of America. Salaried writers for radio and television stations may belong to the WGA; American Federation of Radio and Television Artists; or National Association of Broadcast Employees and Technicians. Scriptwriters and screenwriters may belong to other professional writing groups as well.

PLAYWRIGHT

CAREER PROFILE

Duties: Write dramatic and comedic scripts for public performance

Alternate Title(s): Dramatist

Income Potential: Quite variable; $75 to $2,000 for a radio script; $1,000 and up (often including royalties, percentages of gross receipts, and/or expenses) for a stage production

Work Prospects: Fair to poor

Prerequisites:

Education—Undergraduate degree in drama, writing, English, communications, or other liberal or fine arts; advanced course work in drama and writing beneficial

Experience—None necessary to break in; acting experience considered a must by some

Special Skills—Excellent command of English; writing skills, particularly in dialogue; self-motivation; ability to withstand repeated rejection before finally achieving success

Position Description

Like working on a novel, writing a play is a labor of love. Unless commissioned to create a particular story, playwrights usually develop their plays in their spare time. Few can devote all their energies to playwriting unless receiving income from another source. Writing a play may be something that many writers dream of doing, but it is more hard work than glamour.

Formerly, a playwright knew his audience: a congregation of interested (he or she hoped) individuals enjoying the action at the time it was performed. The playwright received instant feedback about the play's success or failure. Now, however, playwrights may write initially for the stage, but the play may also appear as a TV movie, a miniseries, a film, or even on radio.

A play written for the stage is much less susceptible to change by directors, actors, or producers. If the playwright's work is covered by a contract approved by industry organizations such as the Dramatists Guild, no changes at all may be made in the script without the author's consent. He or she, along with the producer, also have approval of cast and director, full ownership of copyright and all other rights, and the right to formulate contracts for all other uses of the play. Works for TV or the movies may be rewritten, according to the dictates of commercial and moral standards.

On radio, playwrights must create "movies" of the imagination and are expected to be familiar with sound effects, music, narration, and dialogue. As on the stage, the power of the author's written word is so important that few producers choose to change it.

In addition, playwrights may be called upon to:

- act as agent to sell the play;
- perform in the production, either on stage or behind the scenes;
- represent the play at industry functions and be responsible for talking with the press.

Income Potential

Since writing a play is quite different from regular employment, payment is not so much a salary as consideration for a finished work. Radio scripts can bring from $75 to $900 for a half-hour, and from $1,000 to $2,000 for a full hour. Regional theater groups may pay a playwright a flat $500 to $2,000 for a play, or negotiate a variety of payment schedules. Some theaters pay $50 a week against a percentage of the box office receipts; some offer $35 for the first performance and $15 for every performance thereafter; some offer a percentage of the receipts only; and some generously pay a flat rate, a percentage, and travel and/or living expenses for the playwright. Payment depends entirely on the size of the theater company, the support of the community, and the previous success or "bankability" of the playwright.

Work Prospects

Playwrights do not apply for jobs in the same manner as magazine editors, although there are established channels for getting a play published and performed. Contrary to popular belief, publishers and theater groups are seeking new works all the time; the best chances are with small and regional theaters. Another "given" that is no longer true: Playwrights do not have to live in New York (or Los Angeles).

The prospects of making a career out of playwriting can be quite good if the playwright enjoys a successful first play—or better yet, a successful second or third effort. Advancement is based on luck and skill; there is no established career path.

Education

While an undergraduate degree in English, drama, writing, or other liberal or fine arts field is preferable, there is no set educational requirement for playwriting. Course work in writing or acting is a plus. Sometimes education in the "school of hard knocks" gives a playwright as much fodder for drama as college might.

Experience/Skills

It is difficult to pinpoint exactly what experience a playwright should possess. Some authorities feel that work as an actor is almost a necessity in order to know how actors transmit words to an audience. Others merely want proof that the playwright can write plays—sort of a chicken-and-the-egg situation, but usually borne out by work for small, regional theaters or academic productions. A good knowledge of English is essential; so is the ability to write dialogue and visualize how the actor will express the playwright's words. One successful play does not guarantee a playwright a career in drama, but it does make him or her more likely to receive attention upon completion of the second effort.

Unions/Associations

Playwrights for radio join the Writers Guild of America—the union for TV, motion picture, and radio writers—upon selling a script. There is no union for stage dramatists, but most usually join the Dramatists Guild to protect their rights to a play, to stay informed of standard business practices, and to learn who's looking for scripts. Guild membership also offers members use of the Members' Hotline for emergency problems, access to health insurance, subscriptions to Guild publications, and participation in Guild workshops and symposia. The Dramatists Guild is part of the Authors League of America. Playwrights may also join the National Writers Union.

LYRICIST/JINGLE WRITER

CAREER PROFILE

Duties: Write lyrics for musical compositions, whether for popular distribution or as commercial advertising vehicles

Alternate Title(s): Songwriter

Income Potential: $0 to no limit

Work Prospects: Fair to poor

Prerequisites:

Education—An undergraduate degree in music, writing, English, or other liberal or fine arts field is preferable but not required; knowledge of music theory, harmony, counterpoint, standard, and popular songs is necessary

Experience—Previous work as a lyricist; no experience necessarily required

Special Skills—Ability to write "singable" words; skill to take a commercial idea or motto and create singing verse around it; attentiveness; ability to take directions and compromise; business and public-relations skills; self-discipline; versatility; feel for current trends; poise and stamina

Position Description

As with playwright, employment as a lyricist or jingle writer is not quite definable. Fitting words to music is not a science or learned skill so much as a talent. Lyricists are employed by stage producers, record producers, movie companies, and struggling composers.

The life-style is anything but "normal." Lyricists keep no regular hours, have little or no job security, and can count on night and weekend work. Few lyricists become famous, but some achieve modest recognition after receiving industry awards.

For jingle writing, the important thing is to make sure the product's name and motto or slogan are incorporated prominently into the song. Being able to write jingles or little songs quickly is definitely a plus, as advertisers may request almost immediate turnaround.

Most jingle writers work for music production houses, although some may work for advertising agencies. Some freelance. Jingle writing is considered less "important" work than writing legitimate lyrics, yet a jingle is heard instantly by millions on television and may accompany a really catchy tune. Some jingles become part of American popular culture, such as "Join the Pepsi generation," "Have it your way" or "It's the real thing."

Most jingle writers also write song lyrics, and some see their jingles expanded into full-length songs. Many lyricists began their careers as jingle writers. Once a lyricist has sold a song lyric successfully, he or she is more likely to be called upon to write the words for other pieces of music. Occasionally a composer and lyricist work so well together that they collaborate on all future work.

Income Potential

Lyricists can sell songs for one-time flat fees, or on a royalty basis. The average advance against royalties is $5,000 to $6,500. According to the American Guild of Authors and Composers, a good minimum contract should pay the songwriter 50 percent of the gross receipts earned from mechanical reproduction (royalties from sale of records, tapes, or sheet music), electrical transcriptions, and synchronization.

The three performing-rights organizations—American Society of Composers, Authors and Playwrights (ASCAP); Broadcast Music Inc. (BMI); and SESAC Inc.—monitor the performances of all members' music and handle payment of royalties. ASCAP uses a formula based on the number of performances within each media group (radio, TV, concert, restaurant music, etc.) and weights the performance by factors accounting for that medium's share of income among all media and the possibility of performances not accounted for. This formula yields "credits," which are then multiplied by a standard figure. ASCAP then distributes the member lyricist's royalties based on the fee negotiated in his contract. Both BMI, which is the largest performing-arts organization in America, and SESAC, which is the smallest, operate similarly.

If the lyricist is not the composer, his or her 50-percent share will be divided between the two songwriting partners. The more popular and successful a lyricist becomes, the higher a percentage he or she may negotiate, and the more money he or she earns. Successful songwriters earn $500,000 or more a year. A few earn more than $1 million a year.

Work Prospects

Breaking into the field is quite difficult. Many people want to write song lyrics. The field is highly competitive, but there are opportunities for talented people. As more television and film projects use music, whether for title songs or as background, the need for lyricists will grow. Check the business trade weekly magazines and newspapers such as Songwriter magazine, for the names of publishers interested in songs.

Becoming a jingle writer is most likely an intermediate stop for a serious lyricist; the best opportunities are in New York or Los Angeles, with the major advertising and music production companies. Getting your foot in the door usually works best through personal connections, individual contractors, studios, music reps, and your own sterling reputation. Other opportunities exist as staff writers for music publishing companies, or lyricists for TV or movie soundtracks.

There is no set career path. Once a lyricist has had success with a producer or advertiser, he or she is likely to continue. Good jingle writers can count on more and more work as companies put catchy words and tunes on television. Industry recognition, such as a Clio award in advertising, an Oscar, an Emmy, or a Grammy, help assure the lyricist of continued success and financial reward.

Education

There are no educational prerequisites for work as a lyricist or jingle writer, but a background in music or writing is definitely a plus. Undergraduate degrees in music, English, or other liberal or fine arts are the norm. One source believes that jingle writers must have a complete musical education, with a working knowledge of theory, harmony, and counterpoint. Talent alone is not quite enough. It is also important for any lyricist or jingle writer to remain familiar with the old standards and keep abreast of current pop tunes.

Experience/Skills

As with playwriting, success at writing song lyrics depends on the success of earlier efforts, but the trick is getting the first one accepted. Most producers of songs, movies, and television shows prefer previous work on other songs or productions. Spending time in a music or recording studio as an observer will give you a good grounding in how the system operates.

The best skills to have for this business are the abilities to write clearly, to work well with the music's composer, and to be willing to compromise. Jingle writers often begin with copy provided by the advertising agency or client, so he or she needs to be flexible. The ability to work fast, sometimes producing immediate turnaround, is also important. Business and public-relations skills, self-discipline, versatility, stamina, and poise help as well.

Unions/Associations

Most lyricists join one of the performing-rights organizations—ASCAP, BMI and SESAC—and/or guilds. Both the American Guild of Authors and Composers/the songwriters' guild and the Dramatists Guild are open to lyricists. Guild membership entitles members to review of contracts, health insurance, and participation in seminars and workshops. Membership in a performing-rights organization provides the lyricist with a valid tally of performances and distribution of royalties. Other groups include the National Association of Composers, USA, and Songwriters Resources and Services.

POET

CAREER PROFILE

Duties: Compose various forms of verse and poems for magazines, books, and greeting cards

Alternate Title(s): None

Income Potential: Up to $1.50 per line, sometimes more

Work Prospects: Poor

Prerequisites:

Education—Undergraduate degree in English or liberal arts

Experience—Background in creative writing helpful

Special Skills—Thorough understanding of grammar and English language; knowledge of disciplines of poetry

Position Description

Poetry is an artistic form of expression of emotions, ideas, and visual images. There are three basic types of poetry: dramatic, which is action-oriented; narrative, which tells a story; and lyric, which describes first-person emotions and also includes verses for songs. Each of those types is broken down into specific forms. Free verse, for example, follows no meter but allows the poet to compose in lines of any length. A haiku poem has a rigid form of three lines with five, seven, and five syllables per line, respectively.

Many persons write poetry as a hobby. Professional poets publish their work in literary, academic, and a few general-circulation magazines, and occasionally in books, such as poetry anthologies.

Some write traditional, humorous, and inspirational verses for greeting-card publishers, while still others take their talent to music, writing lyrics for songs and plays (see "Lyricist," page 106). Whatever market is sought, a poet should be thoroughly familiar with the work being published and produced.

Most poets earn their livings teaching English, literature, creative writing, or poetry, or by freelance writing.

Income

All but a handful of poets earn little or nothing for their work. Literary and academic magazines, even small book presses, often pay in free copies rather than money. Some magazines pay from $1 to $15 per poem, while others pay per line. A good rate range is $1 to $1.50 per line. Prestigious magazines pay up to $10 a line.

Books of poems do not sell well—a few hundred copies is considered excellent. Advances are negligible, perhaps several hundred dollars, or nonexistent. Many poets resort to self-publishing in order to see their works in print, or enter into cooperative arrangements with publishers to share production and distribution costs.

Greeting-card publishers pay about $15 to $80 per verse, gag, or idea, which may be used for cards, posters, buttons, plaques, calendars, etc.

Typical advance pay for the lyrics to a song ranges from several hundred dollars to $1,000, plus royalties. Many music publishers pay no advance but will underwrite the costs of a demonstration tape.

Some poets can obtain foundation grants to subsidize their work.

Work Prospects

Selling poetry is hard work. Markets include literary and academic magazines, as well as general interest magazines and some newspapers. Poets in search of a book publisher will find their best chances with small presses or in self-publishing.

Songwriting and selling poems, gags, and ideas to greeting-card publishers are more lucrative areas for the poet but very competitive.

Education

Most accomplished poets have had extensive educations in English, poetry, literature, and creative writing. An undergraduate degree in English or liberal arts is good preparation. Graduate degrees—preferably a

Ph.D.—are required for college-level teaching positions. Lyricists should have an educational background in music.

Experience/Skills

Many poets begin by joining writing groups and reading their work aloud for critiques. Command of the English language—a good vocabulary and grammar skills—is essential.

Unions/Associations

The American Guild of Authors and Composers and the American Society of Composers, Authors and Publishers represent music publishers, composers, and lyricists. Other associations for poets include the Academy of American Poets; P.E.N. American Center; Poetry Society of America; and National Writers Union. The National Society of State Poetry Associations can provide contacts for state poetry affiliates. The National Association of Greeting Card Publishers has an industry market list for artists and writers.

BUSINESS COMMUNICATIONS AND PUBLIC RELATIONS

PUBLIC-RELATIONS ASSISTANT

CAREER PROFILE

Duties: Assist public-relations manager, director, editor, and others with public-relations activities

Alternate Title(s): Editorial Assistant; Publicity Assistant

Salary Range: Under $20,000 to $25,000

Employment Prospects: Good

Advancement Prospects: Good

Prerequisites:

Education—Undergraduate degree in communications, journalism, liberal arts, or English

Experience—School journalism experience helpful

Special Skills—Good writing and editing skills; knowledge of graphics; ability to work as part of team or independently; outgoing personality; secretarial skills

CAREER LADDER

Communications Specialist

Public-Relations Assistant

College; Journalist

Position Description

The role of the public-relations professional is to present a favorable image of the employer to its audience, which could include the general public, the investment community, lawmakers, or clients.

Public relations encompasses many image-building tasks, and the public-relations assistant gets exposure to all or nearly all of them. The job is entry-level and can be found in private business and industry, government, nonprofit associations, and education. Many of the job duties are menial, such as typing, filing, running errands, and taking telephone calls. Most public-relations assistants get opportunities to work in a variety of public-relations functions. For example, they may contribute short articles to an internal newsletter or magazine, called the "house organ," or write and distribute bulletin board notices and paycheck stuffers.

They may also help develop and update mailing lists for news releases, write simple news releases for executive approval, assemble press kits and stuff envelopes. They may handle certain media queries themselves.

In addition, a public-relations assistant may:

- update biographies of key company executives and photo files;
- help arrange speaking engagements;
- assist in community activities and fundraising drives;
- assist internal publication editors on production work.

Salaries

A beginner with no experience may receive a starting salary under $20,000. Salaries range up to about $25,000.

Employment Prospects

More than 140,000 persons are employed in public relations, and job opportunities are expected to remain good throughout the 1990s. The profession can be greatly affected by cyclical swings in the economy. The best job opportunities are in major cities, in private business and industry.

Advancement Prospects

Public-relations assistants who perform well can expect good chances of advancement. The exposure to a wide range of activities is helpful for targeting a career path.

Education

Most public-relations professionals have undergraduate degrees in communications, journalism, liberal arts, or English. Journalism graduates are often preferred for their writing skills and knowledge of the media.

Experience/Skills

No experience is necessary for entry-level positions, though internships or college newspaper experience is advantageous. Public-relations professionals should be creative, outgoing, and able to motivate and persuade others. They should be good writers and editors, understand the needs of the media, and be knowledgeable in graphics and layout. Experience with video display terminals is helpful.

Unions/Associations

Major professional associations include the International Association Of Business Communicators; the Public Relations Society of America, Inc.; and Women In Communications, Inc.

INTERNAL PUBLICATIONS EDITOR

CAREER PROFILE

Duties: Write, edit, and produce employee magazine or newsletter

Alternate Title(s): Communications Specialist; Editor

Salary Range: $20,000 to $40,000+

Employment Prospects: Good

Advancement Prospects: Good

Prerequisites:

Education—Undergraduate degree in communications, journalism, public relations, liberal arts, or English

Experience—Background as news reporter or editor helpful

Special Skills—Good writing and editing ability; photography and graphics skills; self-motivation; organizational skills

CAREER LADDER

Manager of Editorial Services

Internal Publications Editor

Journalist; News Editor; Public-Relations Assistant; College

Position Description

Rare is the company, association, or organization that does not produce and distribute an employee newsletter or magazine. Management views internal publications as a pipeline for communication and a means to foster goodwill and boost morale. A publication may be a mere two-sided single sheet of paper or a slick, four-color magazine. Many employers have more than one internal publication; a slick magazine may come out quarterly, supplemented by monthly newsletters. Most publications, however, are monthly magazines.

The job of internal publications editor encompasses planning, writing, editing, editorial decision-making, photography, layout, and production. Most editors are able to put their personal stamp on their publications.

The editors usually work under the supervision of communications coordinators or managers of editorial services. The editors must plan issues in advance and submit outlines for managerial review and approval, then arrange for interviews and photographs. Editors must be able to meet deadlines and stay within their production budgets.

Some editors produce a publication alone, doing all the work or hiring freelancers to assist them. Some may have an assistant, and others may have a staff.

Editors are responsible for clearing all material for publication through management channels. They also spec type (decide typeface style and point size), do page layouts, or work with graphic artists. In addition, they instruct typesetters and printers.

Content depends on the nature of the publication. Articles usually include profiles of employees or departments; new hires and promotions; messages from senior executives; community projects; and other news and features.

In addition, an internal publications editor may:

- write occasional press releases and speeches;
- produce slide shows and films for internal audiences.

Salaries

An entry-level internal publications editor is generally paid between $20,000 and $40,000.

Employment Prospects

The job of internal publications editor is one of the most common public-relations positions, and is often the easiest way to break into a public-relations department. Turnover in this type of job is steady.

Advancement Prospects

An employee publication provides a good showcase for talent, skill, and visibility. Prospects for advancement to higher-level positions are good.

Education

The minimum requirement is an undergraduate degree in communications, journalism, public relations, liberal arts, or English.

Experience/Skills

Some internal-publications-editor positions are entry-level, filled by college graduates. Others require several years of experience, preferably as a news reporter or editor, or in another aspect of public relations.

Excellent writing and editing skills plus leadership qualities are essential for any editing job. Editors should have good news judgment and organizational skills as well. They also must be able to work well with others and be able to take direction. Corporate editors have much less latitude than news media editors in determining content. Corporate interests are served first, and negative news is often downplayed or ignored.

Unions/Associations

Major professional associations include the Public Relations Society of America, Inc.; International Association of Business Communicators; and Women In Communications, Inc.

EXTERNAL PUBLICATIONS EDITOR

CAREER PROFILE

Duties: Write news releases, articles, informational brochures, speeches, slide scripts, and letters for an external audience

Alternate Title(s): Communications Specialist; Communications Associate; Information Representative; Public Information Officer

Salary Range: $20,000 to $40,000

Employment Prospects: Good

Advancement Prospects: Good

Prerequisites:

Education—Undergraduate degree in public relations, communications, journalism, liberal arts, or English

Experience—Background in news reporting helpful

Special Skills—Strong newswriting ability; organizational and analytic skills

CAREER LADDER

Communications Coordinator; Public-Relations Manager

External Publications Editor

Public-Relations Assistant; Journalist; News Editor

Position Description

External publications editor is a job that specializes in promoting the interests of the employer with the general public, media, or special-interest groups. In some cases, particularly small companies and organizations, job duties may be combined with others for more generalized job descriptions.

The external publications editor is responsible for educating and informing external audiences, such as the general public, stockholders, the news media, or special-interest groups. The job involves producing news releases, feature articles for the business and trade press, brochures, slide scripts, and speeches.

The communications could concern the announcement of new products; how ongoing programs are benefiting the economy or community; or the appointment of new executives. Feature articles are written for trade, industry, and professional publications. For example, a bank may describe a program to serve customers more quickly at teller windows, or a trucking firm might put together an article about how a computerized maintenance system has cut repair bills by a significant percentage.

External publications editors may also develop informational material, such as booklets that answer common questions for stockholders, or pamphlets that tell the histories of their companies or organizations.

In addition, external publications editors may:

- write articles for internal publications;
- write community-relations letters for an executive officer's signature.

Salaries

An external publications editor with some experience either in public relations or journalism can expect to earn about $20,000 to $40,000 a year. Salaries can go as high as $50,000—and more—after several years of experience, depending on the level of the job.

Employment Prospects

Job opportunities in public relations are expected to be good throughout the 1990s, though the profession is subject to cutbacks in economic downturns and recessions.

Advancement Prospects

External publications editors are in good positions to move into managerial jobs. They often work directly with upper management, which gives them visibility that helps them move through the ranks.

Education

An undergraduate degree in communications, public relations, journalism, liberal arts, or English is the minimum requirement. Degrees in finance or business can be advantageous, as can advanced degrees.

Experience/Skills

A journalism background is the best preparation for this type of public-relations work. An external publications editor must be able to write not only many types of material but for different audiences as well.

Good writing and editing skills are important, as is an understanding of the needs of the news media. A background in graphics is useful.

Unions/Associations

Major professional associations include the Public Relations Society of America, Inc.; International Association Of Business Communicators; and Women In Communications, Inc.

PUBLIC INFORMATION OFFICER

CAREER PROFILE

Duties: Handle media relations for company or organization; write and distribute news releases; place articles in news media

Alternate Title(s): Public-Relations Manager; Public Affairs Practitioner

Salary Range: $25,000 to $45,000+

Employment Prospects: Good

Advancement Prospects: Good

Prerequisites:

Education—Undergraduate degree in communications, journalism, English, or liberal arts

Experience—Newswriting, wire service, or previous communications experience essential

Special Skills—Newswriting; organizational ability; outgoing personality

CAREER LADDER

Director of Communications

Public Information Officer

Communications Coordinator

Position Description

Public information officers act as liaison between the news media and the company or organization they represent. They answer questions from the news media; generate favorable news stories about the company or organization, then try to place these stories in newspapers, with the wire services, or on television and radio; keep management informed of issues that might result in media inquiries, and prepare in advance management's responses to anticipated questions.

A large part of the public information officer's job is to maintain regular contact and establish a relationship of trust with the news media. Trust is very important in getting a message or image across to the public. The public information officer also must be able to answer press questions immediately or within a set deadline. Other duties include coaching company executives on how to handle media interviews.

Public information officers must stay informed of all news developments that affect their employers so that they can act quickly to shield executives from unfavorable publicity or seize opportunities for favorable publicity. They may be responsible for providing daily news digests and clips to management.

Most supervise a staff or one or more assistants; some may have only secretarial help. Depending on the employer, the public-information-officer position can be a mid-level position or a top position.

In addition, a public information officer may:

- write speeches and slide show scripts;
- produce informational brochures.

Salaries

Salaries vary greatly according to professional experience, geographic location, type of employer, and where the public information officer fits into the hierarchy. Average salaries are in the thirties; nearly half of the professionals earn more than $45,000, depending on their expertise, special skills and employer.

Employment Prospects

Public information officers have become increasingly important in recent years to many businesses, organizations, and government agencies, due largely to more aggressive reporting by the news media. Job opportunities are expected to be good throughout the 1990s, especially in private industry. Job openings in education—school districts, colleges and universities—will be limited due to staff cutbacks.

Advancement Prospects

The public information officer is a front-line position with high visibility. Chances are good for promotion to higher-level, more responsible positions.

Education

Most public information officers have undergraduate degrees in communications, journalism, English, or liberal arts. Some have undergraduate or graduate degrees in business, economics, or political science.

Experience/Skills

Public information officers generally have previous experience working in the news media as well as in other public-relations positions. Some employers may require several years' experience.

Public information officers should have sound news judgment, as well as good writing and editing skills. They should be outgoing and able to mix well with a wide variety of people. In addition, they should be well organized and responsive to requests made on deadline.

Unions/Associations

Major professional associations include the Public Relations Society of America, Inc.; International Association of Business Communicators; American Business Communication Association; and Women In Communications, Inc.

GOVERNMENT AFFAIRS SPECIALIST

CAREER PROFILE

Duties: Monitor government and public-affairs issues of concern to employer; prepare position papers for management; oversee company's political action committee

Alternate Title(s): Public Affairs Specialist

Salary Range: $30,000 to $50,000

Employment Prospects: Good

Advancement Prospects: Good

Prerequisites:

Education—Undergraduate degree in communications, journalism, public relations, liberal arts, political science, or history; graduate degree helpful

Experience—Background in journalism, politics, or public relations essential

Special Skills—Strong analytical skills; good organizational ability; understanding of political process; speaking ability; salesmanship

CAREER LADDER

Manager of Government Affairs

Government Affairs Specialist

Communications Specialist

Position Description

The government affairs specialist plays a very important role in many large companies and corporations, by monitoring the activities of various local, state, and federal government bodies and agencies whose activities might affect a company's business and operations. He or she may be part of a large public-relations department and assigned specific areas of responsibility, or else be the company's sole legislative watchdog.

Government affairs specialists keep track of such things as tax legislation, labor regulations, consumer rights regulations and legislation, and other related issues. They keep management apprised of pending issues that are of immediate or long-term concern. They often prepare position papers outlining the effect of proposed laws or regulations on a company's business.

Government affairs specialists also act as spokespersons for their companies when the media calls for information about their companies' stands on certain issues, such as proposed tax increase or regulations governing minority hiring. Occasionally, they testify on behalf of their employers at government hearings; they may also lobby lawmakers and members of government agencies.

A government affairs specialist may also coordinate a company's political action committee, or PAC—the arm of the company that is allowed to contribute to political campaigns. As part of the job, a government affairs specialist may develop dossiers on various candidates for public office, evaluating which deserve support by his or her company; write letters or prepare newsletters for other PAC members to update them on pending issues; and answer queries from governmental agencies seeking information to help them formulate legislation or regulations.

In addition, a government affairs specialist may:

- prepare speeches or testimony for management on a variety of issues.

Salaries

A government affairs position carries a great deal of responsibility in most companies and is not an entry-level job. Salaries typically begin in the low thirties and climb according to a person's experience and the size of the employer.

Employment Prospects

This is a crucial position for many companies because of the proliferation of governmental agencies, the activities of which need to be monitored, as well as ever-changing and complex regulations. Employment prospects are good for qualified individuals.

Advancement Prospects

A government affairs specialist has a high-visibility job and often works closely with upper management, which enhances opportunities for advancement.

Education

An undergraduate degree in communications, journalism, public relations, liberal arts, political science, or history is the best preparation for this type of work. Advanced degrees may be advantageous.

Experience/Skills

Experience as political journalists or legislative assistants or aides on the state or federal level are ideal backgrounds for government affairs specialists. A background in public-relations work is also good.

Government affairs specialists must be able to analyze complex information and explain it clearly to others. They should be well organized, personable, and outgoing. In addition, they should be persuasive and comfortable making speeches.

Unions/Associations

Major professional associations include the Public Relations Society of America, Inc.; International Association of Business Communicators; and Women In Communications, Inc.

SPEECHWRITER

CAREER PROFILE

Duties: Write speeches for company executives on a variety of topics and for a variety of audiences

Alternate Title(s): Management Communications Specialist

Salary Range: $30,000 to $100,000+

Employment Prospects: Good

Advancement Prospects: Good

Prerequisites:

Education—Undergraduate degree in communications, journalism, liberal arts, English, or business

Experience—Background in journalism or public relations essential

Special Skills—Excellent writing ability; creativity; good research and organizational skills; persuasiveness

CAREER LADDER

Director of Management Communications

Speechwriter

Public Information Officer; Publications Editor

Position Description

Speechwriting jobs are found mainly in larger corporations with highly structured communications staffs and in companies whose executives make frequent public appearances. Speechwriters are responsible for developing speeches for corporate executives on a wide range of subjects and for a wide range of audiences. For example, an executive might address a group of Wall Street analysts one week and a community-fundraising organization the next.

Some executives work closely with speechwriters to develop content and tone, but in many cases, the speechwriter must research and write alone. Before beginning a draft, the speechwriter usually meets with the executive or his or her assistant to get preliminary information: the audience, topic, length of speech, and general content; whether anyone from the company has addressed this audience before and on what topic; who else is on the roster; whether the speeches will be before or after a meal; whether or not questions will be allowed; and the possibility of media coverage.

In some cases, the speechwriter may be able to rewrite or update a previously delivered speech. In most cases, he or she will write from scratch, going through many drafts and revisions. There is little pride in authorship in speechwriting.

The speechwriter does extensive reading to stay abreast of news and trends that relate to his or her employer.

In addition, a speechwriter may:

- write slide scripts and video tape presentations;
- write articles for industry or business publications, which will carry an executive byline.

Salaries

Speechwriters are paid according to experience and talent. A beginning speechwriter can expect to earn about $30,000; experience can bring salaries up to $100,000 or more. Some freelance speechwriters earn well over $200,000 a year.

Employment Prospects

Speechwriters are always in demand. The profession is noted for its high turnover, because of the pressure of the job and also because speechwriters tend to move from company to company. The best job opportunities are in private industry and business.

Advancement Prospects

Speechwriter is a highly visible position, and those who do well in the job have a good chance of being promoted to management.

Education

An undergraduate degree in communications, journalism, English, or liberal arts is essential. Some speechwriters have undergraduate or advanced degrees in business, economics, or political science.

Experience/Skills

Speechwriters come from all backgrounds. Many started in the news business; others have come from other public-relations jobs.

Speechwriters should have a flair for writing the spoken word. They should be able to easily mimic an individual's style of speaking. In addition, they need strong research skills and patience in dealing with extensive revisions.

Unions/Associations

Major professional associations include the Public Relations Society of America, Inc.; International Association of Business Communicators; and Women In Communications, Inc.

COMMUNICATIONS COORDINATOR

CAREER PROFILE

Duties: Coordinate internal/external public-and community-relations activities

Alternate Title(s): Public-Relations Specialist; Communications Specialist

Salary Range: $20,000 to $45,000

Employment Prospects: Good

Advancement Prospects: Good

Prerequisites:

Education—Undergraduate degree in public relations, communications, journalism, liberal arts, or English

Experience—Background in public relations or journalism essential

Special Skills—Strong writing and organizational skills; creativity; administrative ability

CAREER LADDER

Public-Relations Manager

Communications Coordinator

Internal Publications Editor; Journalist

Position Description

Communications coordinator is a position usually found in a company or organization with three to four communications professionals reporting to a manager or director. The coordinator generally has decision-making authority and may supervise lower level employees, such as public-relations assistants or publications editors.

The communications coordinator has a broad range of responsibilities, almost all of which are writing-related. Duties fall into three categories: internal communications; external communications; and community relations.

Internal communications account for the greater share of the communications coordinator's workload. He or she might be responsible for editing or supervising the editing and production of the employer's newsletter, magazine, company notices for the bulletin board or paycheck stuffers, and/or informational brochures on company benefits and programs. Other internal responsibilities might include managing an employee feedback program or assisting the personnel department in a recruiting program.

External communications include quarterly and annual stockholder reports; financial statements for the federal government; mailings to stockholders and the public; and all press materials and inquiries.

Community-relations activities might include coordinating a speakers' bureau or representing the company on communications committees of allied industry groups or trade associations.

In addition, a communications coordinator may:

- write speeches for executives;
- write or supervise the writing and production of scripts for slide shows and films.

Salaries

This is not an entry-level position in most companies. Depending on previous experience, employer, and geographic location, salaries can range from $20,000 to $45,000 or more.

Employment Prospects

Employment opportunities for all public-relations jobs are expected to be good throughout the 1990s, according to the federal government. The best prospects for communications coordinator are in private business and industry, especially with large corporations that have big public-relations departments.

Advancement Prospects

A communications coordinator has a good chance of advancing to a higher managerial or supervisory position within the communications department.

Education

Most public-relations workers have undergraduate degrees in public relations, communications, journalism, liberal arts, or English. A degree or advanced degree in business or economics may be advantageous for employment and advancement.

Experience/Skills

A background in public-relations work is desirable for communications coordinator, though some persons may come directly from a journalism background.

Strong writing skills are a must, as is the ability to handle a diverse number of projects simultaneously with minimum supervision. Communications coordinators should be creative and able to direct and motivate others.

Unions/Associations

Major professional associations include the Public Relations Society of America, Inc.; International Association Of Business Communicators; and Women In Communications, Inc.

PUBLIC-RELATIONS ACCOUNT EXECUTIVE

CAREER PROFILE

Duties: Perform public-relations functions for, and advise clients

Alternate Title(s): Consultant

Salary Range: $18,000 to $40,000

Employment Prospects: Good

Advancement Prospects: Good

Prerequisites:

Education—Undergraduate degree in communications, public relations, journalism, liberal arts, or English

Experience—Three to five years in public relations, journalism, or as assistant account executive

Special Skills—Outgoing personality; salesmanship; good writing and organizational skills

CAREER LADDER

Account Supervisor

Account Executive

Assistant Account Executive; Journalist; News Editor; Public-Relations Professional

Position Description

A large percentage of public-relations professionals work for agencies or consulting firms. These businesses function the same way as advertising agencies—they perform public-relations services for clients, create publicity campaigns and strategies, and advise clients on public-relations matters, for all of which they charge fees or commissions. Some clients have little or no public-relations staff, while others use agencies to handle projects that would be too big or time-consuming for their own staff.

The account executive is the liaison between the agency and client. He or she works under the supervision of an accounts supervisor or senior consultant. Beginners are usually called assistant account executives, and they perform mostly routine tasks.

Duties depend on the types of services requested by the client. These may include preparing and mailing press kits; conducting press conferences; arranging media interviews and tours for client executives; placing favorable news or feature stories in the media; handling arrangements for promotional luncheons and dinners as well as trade shows; and conducting opinion surveys.

Advisory duties concern planning publicity campaigns; setting up a public-relations department or program; evaluating such a program; and establishing a lobbying platform. Account executives are likely to coordinate their work with advertising and marketing activities.

Many agencies or consultants specialize in certain areas, such as entertainment or government regulations.

In addition, public-relations account executives may:

- canvass for new clients;
- write reports for senior staff.

Salaries

Most account executives who have at least three years' professional experience are paid between $18,000 and $40,000; assistants with no experience are paid less. Median salaries range from the low to high twenties.

Employment Prospects

The best job prospects are in large cities, which have the greatest number of agencies and big businesses.

Advancement Prospects

The account executive is in a good position for advancement, either in the agency or by moving to a corporation or association. Some account executives become self-employed consultants.

Education

An undergraduate degree in communications, journalism, public relations, liberal arts, or English is the minimum requirement. For consulting, a graduate degree in business or finance is advantageous.

Experience/Skills

Most account executives have backgrounds in public-relations work or in the news media—as journalists or news editors. Skills include ability to work well with others; salesmanship; good writing; creativity; and self-motivation.

Unions/Associations

Major professional associations include the Public Relations Society of America, Inc.; International Association of Business Communicators; and Women In Communications, Inc.

TECHNICAL COMMUNICATOR

CAREER PROFILE

Duties: Write and/or edit technical materials for technical and lay audiences

Alternate Title(s): Technical Writer; Technical Editor

Salary Range: $16,000 to $55,000+

Employment Prospects: Excellent

Advancement Prospects: Fair

Prerequisites:

Education—Undergraduate degree in English, technical communications, science, engineering, computer science, journalism, liberal arts

Experience—Previous work as writer or in some capacity in a technical or scientific field advantageous

Special Skills—Comprehension of field being served; ability to work with engineers, technicians and scientists; ability to rewrite technical material for lay audiences

CAREER LADDER

Technical Communications or Publications Manager

Technical Communicator

Writer

Position Description

Technical communicators write and edit a wide range of technical material for a variety of audiences. Depending on the industry in which they work, they might write software manuals for the lay computer user, technical manuals for the computer programmer; sales materials that will be aimed at engineers and technicians; repair manuals; inhouse communications; specifications sheets; inserts for pharmaceutical products; speeches for industry conferences and meetings; scripts for slides and films, etc.

Their duties may extend into production, for which they work with graphic artists and oversee galleys, proofs and mechanicals. They may supervise other writers, assistants and freelancers. Some technical communicators work in education, preparing information and training materials.

Technical communicators often have prior experience in journalism or corporate communications, or in technical fields.

The typical member of the Society for Technical Communications (STC), the leading professional organization, has seven years' experience, lives in a major metropolitan area and works for private industry. More than half are writers, and slightly less than half are editors. Most say they have a high level of job satisfaction and stress creativity, pay, freedom and professional development among the major benefits of this career.

Salary Range

Pay is influenced by job responsibilities, experience, industry and geographic location. The median salary for technical communicators is about $34,000. Private industry and the federal government offer the highest-paying jobs, while education pays the lowest. By region, the highest-paying jobs are in the Northeast and the lowest in the Midwest.

Employment Prospects

Job opportunities for technical communicators should be excellent throughout the 1990s, due to the growth of technology and the increasing emphasis on technical communications. Most technical communicators are employed in the computer industry in software. Other primary employers are research and development, computer manufacturing, electronics, aerospace and aircraft, engineering and construction, science and telecommunications.

Advancement Prospects

Technical communicators can advance in responsibility, but respondents to an STC survey rated managerial responsibility and promotion potential as among the least important factors in their jobs. Instead, they value autonomy and creativity.

Education

Most technical communicators have undergraduate degrees in English, technical communications or journalism. Others have degrees in science, engineering, computer science, graphic arts and education. Many have master's degrees or some graduate education.

Experience/Skills

Prior experience as a writer, journalist or editor is advantageous prior to becoming a technical communicator. Some jobs require little technical training or background, while others require degrees. Technical communicators must be able to understand technical language and, when necessary, rewrite it in terms the lay person can understand. Many technical communicators have experience using desktop publishing systems. Other skills are attention to detail, precision, creativity, organization and self-discipline.

Unions/Associations

The Society for Technical Communication is the primary professional association. Technical communicators also may belong to organizations in their areas of expertise, such as the American Medical Writers Association and National Association of Science Writers, Inc.

ASSISTANT ACCOUNT EXECUTIVE

CAREER PROFILE

Duties: Research and prepare materials pertaining to advertising agency account management

Alternate Title(s): Account Executive Trainee

Salary Range: $15,000 to $30,000

Employment Prospects: Fair

Advancement Prospects: Good

Prerequisites:

Education—Undergraduate degree in advertising, liberal arts, journalism, business

Experience—None

Special Skills—Grasp of advertising and marketing; organization; salesmanship

CAREER LADDER

Account Executive

Assistant Account Executive

Trainee; College

Position Description

Assistant account executive is generally an entry-level position, though in some agencies it may be a step up from trainee, which is essentially a clerical and secretarial job.

Assistant account executives learn the advertising business by performing routine and low-level tasks for the account service department. They may work for one account executive on one or two accounts, or they may work for an entire department of account executives. In the process, they learn how to look after a client's interests, coordinate creative and production work, plan campaigns, and do market analyses.

Duties include research for client proposals and advertising campaigns; assistance in preparing reports and proposals, including writing and graphics; typing; proofreading; and errands. Assistant account executives may occasionally take part in meetings with clients or in presentations.

Assistant account executives often shoulder the bulk of the legwork on projects but share very little of the credit. Work hours are regular business hours, but overtime is not uncommon, especially on short notice.

Some public-relations agencies may also employ assistant account executives to work on public relations and publicity campaigns.

Salaries

Assistant account executives earn a median salary of $21,100. Those at large agencies can earn up to $30,000.

Employment Prospects

Mergers and consolidations of agencies make the field very competitive (see introduction).

Advancement Prospects

An assistant account executive who is willing to work hard has a good chance of being promoted to a full-fledged account executive. Often promotion comes through turnover, which is high in the advertising industry.

Education

Assistant account executives generally have undergraduate degrees in advertising, business, journalism, or liberal arts. The work is marketing-and sales-oriented, so an educational emphasis on business and economic studies is helpful. Advanced degrees in business or advertising can give job candidates the competitive edge with many employers.

Experience/Skills

Some assistant account executives begin their careers as trainees, little more than clerical and secretarial assistants. Others come straight from college or from entry-level work in a related field, such as sales, public relations, or journalism. Writing and selling experience is helpful.

Skills include a flair for making favorable impressions and getting along well with others; clear writing ability; salesmanship; good organization; persistence.

Unions/Associations

Major associations for advertising professionals include the American Advertising Federation; Business/Professional Advertising Association; American Marketing Association; and Women In Communications, Inc.

ACCOUNT EXECUTIVE

CAREER PROFILE

Duties: Coordinate all advertising activities for advertising agency clients; maintain good client relations

Alternate Title(s): None

Salary Range: $25,000 to $40,000+

Employment Prospects: Fair

Advancement Prospects: Fair

Prerequisites:

Education—Undergraduate degree in advertising, business, liberal arts, journalism, or communications

Experience—One to three years as trainee or assistant account executive helpful

Special Skills—Leadership and salesmanship; copy judgment; knowledge of graphics, media, and marketing

CAREER LADDER

Accounts Manager; Accounts Supervisor

Account Executive

Assistant Account Executive; Trainee

Position Description

Most account executives work for advertising agencies; others work in the advertising or sales departments of businesses and media. The account executive is in charge of the advertising for one or more of an ad agency's clients (usually one large account or several small accounts). He or she determines and plans the nature of the advertising to be produced, relaying the client's expectations and needs to the agency's creative and media buying departments. The account executive coordinates the agency's activities and reviews the creative work produced, before presenting it to the client. He or she is the agency's liaison with clients, and must work to maintain good communication and a good relationship.

Account executives must have a thorough knowledge of all operations within an agency, and understand their clients' businesses, marketing, and competition. They must be able to judge whether or not creative copy and proposed ad campaigns are on target. They must be able to understand market analyses and have a thorough understanding of all media, in order to plan the most effective ad campaigns. When campaigns are developed, account executives make formal presentations to the clients or management.

Account executives report to an account supervisor or account manager, who in turn reports to a director or vice president of account services. In large agencies, account executives may delegate research and clerical functions to assistants; in small agencies, they may do everything themselves.

Public-relations agencies also employ account executives, who are responsible for publicity campaigns and press relations.

Additionally, account executives may:

- participate in campaigns and presentations to win new clients;
- coordinate publicity and promotional activities along with advertising.

Salaries

Account executives generally earn between $25,000 and $40,000, depending on the agency's size and location, plus their own prior experience. The median salary is $31,400. Persons who hold graduate degrees in business, finance, or advertising command salaries at the high end of the scale. Bonuses and perquisites are common for high performers. Experienced and skilled professionals can earn $40,000 to $60,000 or more.

Employment Prospects

The 1980s witnessed major changes in the advertising field that continue to reshape job opportunities. Numerous large agencies have merged and consolidated operations; foreign agencies, most notably Saatchi & Saatchi of Great Britain, own much of the American ad business. Many smaller agencies likewise have disappeared into mergers and acquisitions. The emphasis is on global marketing. While competition for jobs is keen, small agencies continue to thrive and fill local and regional needs.

Advancement Prospects

Account executives who excel at their jobs can advance rapidly in responsibility and pay. The top executives of most advertising agencies came up through the ranks of account executives. Competition is fierce, however, and job security is low—it is not uncommon to be fired if an agency loses an account or if the economy is in recession.

Education

Most account executives have undergraduate degrees in advertising, business, liberal arts, or journalism. A graduate degree in advertising, business, or economics is not necessary but works to the candidate's advantage.

Experience/Skills

In most cases, account executives work as assistant account executives or trainees before being given full responsibility for clients. Some account executives have worked previously as journalists or in advertising sales.

Account executives must understand all aspects of an advertising campaign, from judging creative copy to coordinating the purchase of media space and time. Since they have highly visible positions as their agencies' representatives, they must be skilled in salesmanship and demonstrate leadership.

Unions/Associations

Associations include the American Advertising Federation; Business/Professional Advertising Association; and Women In Communications, Inc.

ASSISTANT COPYWRITER

CAREER PROFILE

Duties: Assist in development and execution of creative ad copy; clerical tasks

Alternate Title(s): None

Salary Range: $18,000 to $30,000

Employment Prospects: Fair

Advancement Prospects: Good

Prerequisites:

Education—Undergraduate degree in advertising, liberal arts, journalism, communications, or art

Experience—None

Special Skills—Imagination; creativity; command of English

CAREER LADDER

Copywriter

Assistant Copywriter

Trainee; College

Position Description

Assistant copywriter is an entry-level position, usually at an advertising agency, sometimes in the advertising or marketing department of a business. An assistant copywriter may be fresh out of college or may still be enrolled, working during summers or through class internships.

The position involves routine work assisting copywriters, as well as limited opportunities to handle creative projects. Routine work includes researching a client, product, service, or industry that will be used by the copywriter in developing an ad; proofreading copy; trafficking copy among departments; and running errands.

Assistant copywriters also may be assigned creative projects of their own. They work under the supervision of a copywriter or senior copywriter, sometimes the copy supervisor. Their position may enable them to receive career counseling or training. Opportunities to learn other aspects of the advertising business, such as production, media buying, or account services, may be offered them.

Salaries

Most salaries for such entry-level/training positions fall in the $18,000 to $25,000 range, depending on an individual's previous experience or education.

Employment Prospects

Competition is keen for limited openings. Many employers believe the ability to create ideas for effective ads cannot be taught, and so they give preference to applicants who have had actual experience, including internships, in addition to education.

Advancement Prospects

Once hired, advancement opportunities in the creative department can be good for those with talent and initiative. New and fresh ideas are always encouraged, and successful ideas are well rewarded in salary, bonuses, and other peaks.

Education

An undergraduate degree in advertising, liberal arts, communications, or art is the minimum requirement. Education should include courses in writing and creative writing. Advanced degrees are not all that helpful for the creative side of the advertising business.

Experience/Skills

Any kind of writing experience, especially advertising-related, is advantageous for copywriting jobs. Aspiring copywriters should work on school publications, community projects, or for agencies or the media part-time. Some journalists make the transition to advertising copywriting.

Copywriters should excel in command of English and have a flair for persuasion. They should be able to write for different media.

Unions/Associations

Associations open to advertising professionals include the American Advertising Federation; Direct Marketing Creative Guild; American Marketing Association; Business/Professional Advertising Association; and Women In Communications, Inc. The Writers Guild of America, a union, includes many copywriters who also write scripts and screenplays for television and film.

COPYWRITER

CAREER PROFILE

Duties: Develop ideas and write ad copy and scripts for media, sales campaigns and direct marketing

Alternate Title(s): None

Salary Range: $25,000 to $60,000+

Employment Prospects: Fair

Advancement Prospects: Fair

Prerequisites:

Education—Undergraduate degree in communications, liberal arts, art, advertising, or business

Experience—Background as a professional writer or journalist helpful

Special Skills—Creativity, imagination, salesmanship, command of English

CAREER LADDER

Copy Supervisor

Copywriter

Assistant Copywriter; Journalist; College

Position Description

Copywriters write the text of print ads for radio and television ads, as well as text for promotional material, sales campaigns and direct marketing campaigns.

Many copywriters work for advertising agencies, while others work for the in-house advertising departments or marketing departments of companies and corporations. Their jobs are highly demanding, because the success of the advertising depends greatly on the creativity and sales stimulus of the copy. Working hours generally are regular weekday hours, but overtime is often required to meet deadline pressures.

In a large agency or department, copywriters report to a senior copywriter or copy supervisor, who in turn reports to a creative director or advertising director. In a smaller environment, copywriters may report directly to the creative or advertising director.

The creation of an advertising campaign is a team effort. The creative staff works with the account service or marketing staff to execute an overall strategy or theme that will accomplish the client's goals. Any combination of media may be used: print, broadcast, point-of-sale, direct mail, billboards, transit, or specialty (giveaway premiums imprinted with the client's name).

In a small agency or department, one copywriter may do all the media copy for a particular client; in a large agency, the client's work may be divided among several copywriters who each specialize in one or two media, such as billboards or broadcast. Copy and scripts must convey information and persuade others to buy products or services, or accept ideas. Radio and television scripts must also include instructions for voice-overs and special effects.

In addition, copywriters may:

- research information for ads;
- edit and rewrite copy;
- be responsible for production and distribution of ad materials.

Salaries

Copywriters can expect to start at around $25,000 to $30,000, though some who work for small agencies may be paid less. Experienced copywriters, including senior copywriters with five to ten years on the job, earn up to $60,000 or more. In ad agencies, salaries also depend on agency size in terms of billings (revenue). A large agency has annual billings of $100 million or more.

Employment Prospects

Most copywriters work for ad agencies, most of which are located in major cities, especially in the East. Job opportunities are competitive due to the mergers and consolidations that have taken place in the industry.

Advancement Prospects

Advertising is a highly competitive field, but those with initiative, fresh ideas, and talent advance rapidly and are well rewarded. Good copywriters are given increasing supervisory responsibility and more prestigious accounts. Advertising is characterized by high turnover, and advancement often comes by moving to another agency or company.

Education

The minimum requirement is an undergraduate degree in communications, liberal arts, art, business, or advertising. Advanced degrees are of less value for copywriting than for account service. Education should include courses in copywriting or creative writing.

Experience/Skills

Education should be supplemented with writing experience, such as working on school or community publications. Part-time advertising jobs or advertising-related extracurricular work is helpful. Previous experience in journalism also is useful for copywriting.

The copywriter must have an excellent command of language and be able to visualize ad ideas. One should have a good knowledge of production, including typography and layout. Above all, he or she should be inventive and willing to experiment with unusual approaches or ideas.

Unions/Associations

The American Advertising Federation, Direct Marketing Creative Guild, and American Marketing Association are principal associations of interest to copywriters. Many women in the field belong to Women In Communications, Inc. Some copywriters are members of the Writers Guild of America, a union for television, film, and radio scriptwriters and screenwriters.

PROMOTION SPECIALIST

CAREER PROFILE

Duties: Prepare sales material and advertising literature; work with sales and marketing staff; clerical duties

Alternate Title(s): Merchandising Assistant; Merchandising Specialist

Salary Range: $12,000 to $50,000+

Employment Prospects: Good

Advancement Prospects: Fair

Prerequisites:

Education—Undergraduate degree in advertising, liberal arts, social sciences, communications, or business

Experience—Advertising or sales background helpful

Special Skills—Creativity; sales orientation; organization; writing

CAREER LADDER

Promotion Manager

Promotion Specialist

Promotion Assistant; College

Position Description

Promotion is an important part of an overall advertising campaign for a business, service, or product. Its purpose is to enhance sales or visibility. Many promotion professionals work for advertising agencies. Others work for advertising departments of businesses and media. Some may work for sales promotion houses, which do nothing but promotion campaigns for a variety of clients.

Sales promotion includes anything except media advertising that is used to promote sales. Included are in-store displays, special packaging, promotional events, direct-mail campaigns, sales and advertising literature, coupon offers and sweepstakes, free samples, trade-show exhibits, and novelty items.

Promotion may be brand-oriented or image-oriented. Publicity, such as news releases, press kits, and media events, may also be part of a promotion campaign. The job of the promotion specialist is to identify the customer's goals, develop a campaign, and measure its results.

Promotion specialists work with direct-mail specialists, account executives, creative staffs, and sales and marketing staffs. They are supervised by senior members of their promotion staffs or by promotion managers or directors.

The work involves a high level of creativity, an understanding of advertising and marketing, and the ability to work on multiple projects at the same time. Copy written for promotions is sales-oriented, intended to stimulate a buying response from consumers. Promotion specialists may also work with graphic artists on the design and production of materials.

In addition, beginning promotion specialists or assistants are likely to:

- handle clerical tasks such as filing;
- be assigned telephone duty;
- proofread copy.

Salaries

Beginners can expect to earn in the teens to low twenties. Experienced promotion specialists earn about $38,000 to $40,000. Sales promotion executives can earn $34,000 to $50,000 a year or more.

Employment Prospects

Sales promotion has become increasingly important as a marketing and advertising tool. However, candidates can expect to find limited job opportunities due to the overall consolidation of the advertising agency industry. Opportunities also will be limited by economic downturns that cause clients to cut back on their advertising budgets.

Advancement Prospects

Advancement opportunities are fair, once experience has been established. Often advancement is made through turnover.

Education

Promotion professionals should have undergraduate degrees, preferably in advertising, marketing, business administration, or communications; degrees in liberal arts or the social sciences are also acceptable. Courses in psychology and merchandising are helpful. Graduate degrees in advertising, business administration, or marketing may help advancement.

Experience/Skills

No experience is necessary for many entry-level jobs. Some employers require one to two years' experience for entry-level jobs. Work in sales or advertising is helpful.

Promotion professionals should be highly creative, sales-oriented, and have a flair for merchandising. They should be able to write crisp copy capable of eliciting a positive response from the buying public.

Unions/Associations

Major associations that provide professional support include the American Advertising Federation; American Marketing Association; Sales and Marketing Executives International; Business/Professional Advertising Association; Direct Mail/Marketing Association, Inc.; Direct Marketing Creative Guild; and International Association of Business Communicators. Women In Communications, Inc., and the National Association of Media Women are open to women in the field.

PUBLIC-RELATIONS/PUBLICITY ASSISTANT

CAREER PROFILE

Duties: Research and write publicity material; develop image-building campaigns

Alternate Title(s): Public-Relations/Publicity Associate

Salary Range: $12,000 to $16,000

Employment Prospects: Fair

Advancement Prospects: Good

Prerequisites:

Education—Undergraduate degree in advertising, public relations, communications, journalism, liberal arts

Experience—None

Special Skills—Creativity; ability to write news-oriented copy; understanding of the media

CAREER LADDER

Public-Relations/ Publicity Account Executive

Public-Relations/Publicity Assistant

College

Position Description

Most advertising agencies provide public-relations services for their clients as well as advertising, and maintain a staff to perform these services. Public relations and publicity may be separate job functions in a large agency but combined in a small one.

Duties include working with the clients and account executives to determine newsworthy announcements or events, then write news releases and press kits to be distributed to the media. The public-relations/publicity staff acts as a liaison between the clients and media, answering press inquiries, arranging interviews, and setting up press conferences.

Some clients hire agencies to develop long-range campaigns designed to boost visibility with the public or enhance a company's reputation. Such campaigns may involve press releases, interviews, speaking engagements, advertisements, and public-service projects. The campaigns must be carefully coordinated with advertising and promotional activities done by other departments in an agency.

The assistant is an entry-level position that initially involves routine and low-level assignments such as research, copy editing, proofreading, errands, telephone duty, and envelope stuffing. Assistants are supervised by a department account executive, specialist, or director. Eventually they may be assigned their own projects.

In addition, public-relations/publicity assistants may:

- develop material to promote advertising agency activities and news;
- assist in presentations to clients;
- work to build good relations with key reporters and editors.

Salaries

A typical starting salary for beginners is about $12,000 a year. Those with graduate degrees can command more. Experienced public-relations/publicity professionals at ad agencies earn salaries comparable to those of account executives.

Employment Prospects

Job opportunities are fair at ad agencies, where public relations portions of account service are secondary in importance to advertising.

Advancement Prospects

Experienced public-relations/publicity workers face keen competition for higher level jobs. A graduate degree in public relations or advertising is advantageous.

Advancement is often accomplished through turnover or moves into related fields, such as media or corporate communications.

Education

Most beginners in public relations and publicity have undergraduate degrees in public relations, advertising, journalism, communications, or liberal arts. Courses in creative writing, psychology, and business are helpful. Graduate degrees can help advancement.

Experience/Skills

Work on a school publication or previous experience as a journalist are good backgrounds for those interested in public-relations and publicity work. Broadcast journalism is also helpful.

Public-relations/publicity professionals should be creative, resourceful, and able to write clear, tight news copy. They also should be able to produce speeches and scripts for slide shows and films. They should be well organized and highly motivated.

Unions/Associations

Major associations include the American Advertising Federation; Public Relations Society of America, Inc.; Business/Professional Advertising Association; International Association of Business Communicators; American Marketing Association; National Association of Media Women; and Women In Communications, Inc.

FEDERAL GOVERNMENT

EDITORIAL ASSISTANT AND CLERK

CAREER PROFILE

Duties: Edit and handle production of manuscripts; secretarial tasks

Alternate Title(s): None

Salary Range: $14,573 to $26,252

Employment Prospects: Fair

Advancement Prospects: Good

Prerequisites:

Education—High school diploma minimum
Experience—General office, clerical, or editorial support work required
Special Skills—Knowledge of grammar, editorial production; clerical skills

CAREER LADDER

Supervisory Editorial Assistant
or
Clerk

Editorial Assistant
or
Clerk

High School or College

Position Description

Editorial clerks and assistants perform a wide range of clerical and editorial support work, in preparing manuscripts for publication and in verifying information in copy. Basic duties include proofreading final copy, galleys, and page proofs against the original manuscripts; specifying formats, type, and styles; editing for basic grammatical accuracy and structural clarity; and verifying references, footnotes, and tabular material.

Specific duties vary according to federal agency and grade level. Some editorial clerks and assistants work in groups under the direction of a supervisory editorial clerk or assistant. Others work directly for writers, editors, or subject matter specialists. Regardless of the work setting, editorial clerks and assistants usually all perform the same types of work. Most of their editing jobs concern accuracy and grammar, though they may suggest to editors changes to reorganize material.

They prepare the layout, including placement of graphics, and give typesetting and printing instructions. High-level clerks and assistants may perform more writing, as well as substantive editing tasks similar to those expected of writers and editors.

Special knowledge of subject matter isn't necessary, except for certain specialized and technical subjects. Editorial clerks and assistants should be thoroughly familiar with grammatical rules and production procedures.

Employees frequently work under rigid deadlines, high pressure, and last-minute rushes. Accuracy is all-important. The editorial assistant/clerk also must have the ability to handle a high volume of work independently, follow detailed instructions, and interpret policies and regulations.

Salaries

Editorial assistant and clerk positions are among the few in the federal government in which women tend to earn more than men. Overall, salaries can range from $14,573 to $26,252, according to the 1990 federal general schedule pay scale. Most positions fall within the G54 to G57 range.

Employment Prospects

Federal jobs are highly competitive. Growth in new positions has been slow and is expected to remain so due to budget cutbacks. Nearly 80 percent of all federal employees work outside of Washington, D.C., throughout the United States.

Advancement Prospects

Advancement by grade level brings additional responsibilities and pay. Editorial clerks and assistants may also move up to writer or editor positions, or other posts in communications.

Education

A high school diploma is the minimum education requirement for editorial assistant and clerk positions.

Experience/Skills

Two to five years of clerical or editorial support experience is considered minimal. College education may be substituted for experience in order to qualify. Experience includes responsibilities for grammatical editing, reviewing, and screening; fact-checking; research; proofreading; and editorial production.

Because of the detail of their work, editorial assistants and clerks must be meticulous, dependable, and accurate to a very high degree. The work also requires an unusual degree of patience and a liking for close and exacting work.

Unions/Associations

Major unions and associations that represent federal white collar employees are the National Association of Government Employees; American Federation of Government Employees; National Federation of Federal Employees; National Association of Government Communicators; American Federation of State, County and Municipal Employees; and Federally Employed Women, Inc. Editorial assistants and clerks may also belong to related professional associations outside of government.

WRITER AND EDITOR

CAREER PROFILE

Duties: Write and edit articles, news releases, publications, and scripts

Alternate Title(s): None

Salary Range: $16,305 to $55,381

Employment Prospects: Fair

Advancement Prospects: Good

Prerequisites:

Education—High school diploma minimum; college degree preferred

Experience—Two to six years' writing or editing experience for most positions

Special Skills—Good writing, editing skills; originality; initiative

CAREER LADDER

Supervisory Writer or Editor

Writer or Editor

Editorial Assistant or Clerk; High School or College

Position Description

Writers and editors communicate information for several purposes: to report research and investigations carried on by federal agencies; to explain laws and regulations, as well as changes in them; and to make public reports on the activities and plans of agencies. The forms of communication include articles, press releases, pamphlets, brochures, speeches, and radio, television, and film scripts.

Some writing and editing positions do not require substantial subject-matter knowledge; all positions, however, require the ability to adapt information to a particular style, format, or audience. Most positions do not involve formulating the policy or philosophy behind the content of the information.

Writers collect information through library research, reading, and interviewing subject specialists, policy officials, and others. They turn their manuscripts over to editors, who review, rewrite, and edit as necessary and in consultation with writers. Editors may supervise editorial assistants and clerks to do routine checking and editing.

Most positions are either wholly writing or editing, but some combine the two functions. Those employees are called writer-editors. Writers and editors may specialize according to media, working predominantly in print, radio, film, or television.

The overall scope of a writer or editor's responsibilities depends on the grade level of the job. At lower grade levels, assignments are specific, and detailed instructions cover scope and content. There is limited opportunity for creativity. At higher levels, the writer or editor has greater opportunity to influence the scope of the assignment.

Salaries

Salaries for federally employed writers and editors depend on the job grade and years of experience. Most fall between the pay scales GS5 and GS12 or GS13, with pay ranging from $16,305 at entry level to $55,381 at the top. The highest-paying positions may require ten or more years of experience.

Employment Prospects

The chances of getting a federal writing or editing job are only fair, due to budget cutbacks and lack of growth.

Advancement Prospects

Writers and editors have a good chance of advancing to more responsible grade classification positions or to supervisory jobs. Other communications jobs exist outside of writing and editing.

Education

The minimum requirement is a high school diploma. Undergraduate degrees in English, journalism, or communications may be preferred for many higher level posts. College study may be substituted for job experience in meeting minimum hiring qualifications.

Experience/Skills

Persons without college degrees must be experienced in professional, administrative, technical, or other work that requires the ability to analyze information and present it in written form. Specialized experience in writing or editing jobs in a particular medium may also be required.

Basic skills include researching, analyzing, and organizing information; good writing and knowledge of grammar; editing ability; self- motivation; and the ability to work independently and, at times, under deadline pressure.

Unions/Associations

The National Association of Government Employees; National Association of Government Communicators; American Federation of Government Employees; National Federation of Federal Employees; American Federation of State, County and Municipal Employees; and Federally Employed Women, Inc., are the major unions and associations for federal white collar workers. Employees may also belong to related professional organizations outside of federal government.

TECHNICAL WRITER AND EDITOR

CAREER PROFILE

Duties: Write and edit technical manuals, specifications, and publications for federal agencies

Alternate Title(s): Technical Publications Writer or Editor; Technical Manuals Writer or Editor; Specifications Writer or Editor

Salary Range: $16,305 to $55,381

Employment Prospects: Poor

Advancement Prospects: Fair

Prerequisites:

Education—Undergraduate college degree preferred

Experience—Two to six years' writing or degree with courses in science, engineering, or computer science

Experience—None to several years in technical writing or editing

Special Skills—Understanding of and ability to explain technical subjects; writing and editing skills; self-motivation

CAREER LADDER

Supervisory Technical Writer or Editor

Technical Writer or Editor

College; Other Technical Writing or Editing Job

Position Description

There are three general categories of technical writers and editors in the federal government: publications, specifications, and manuals.

Technical publications writers and editors are involved in government activities that carry on programs of research, investigations, or operation in natural and social sciences, engineering, medicine, law, and the like. They are responsible for disseminating findings and information to the general public as well as to scientific and administrative communities. Their work involves preparation of papers, articles, reports, summaries, and digests based on interviews, research reports, and their own reading.

Many agencies combine technical writing and editing assignments. Some editors may be assigned to groups or committees, and be responsible for assembling individual reports into a single document reflecting the total viewpoint of the group.

Both technical manual and specifications positions are found in federal activities that carry on programs of applied scientific research and development of weapons, communications systems, equipment, and devices. Job duties include writing, editing, and disseminating basic instruction materials, maintenance and operation instructions, design information, and training guides. Equipment specifications are used for purchasing and inventory control.

Most technical writing and editing jobs require substantial knowledge of a particular subject or field. Those technical writers and editors who have educations or specializations in journalism or English usually have had additional training or education in technical subjects.

About three-fourths of the technical writers and editors work for the Department of Defense, writing manuals on weapons and instruments for military personnel. The departments of Agriculture, Interior, and Health and Human Services, as well as the National Aeronautics and Space Administration, also employ many technical writers and editors.

Salaries

Beginning technical writers with undergraduate degrees, including 15 semester hours in science, engineering, or computer science, earn about $16,305; those beginners with superior academic records or one year of experience earn more.

Employment Prospects

Few federal job openings are expected through the 1990s. Most vacancies will occur due to retirements or transfers to other jobs.

Advancement Prospects

Chances of advancement are limited, due to the small number of openings that occur every year. Rising in job grade classification levels brings increasing responsibilities and salaries. Other advancement may be possible by moving to related communications jobs.

Education

Job candidates should have undergraduate degrees, preferably in a science. Those with nonscience degrees should have had studies in science, engineering, or computer science. In this field, a graduate degree in a science is likely to be very advantageous.

Experience/Skills

Job experience is not necessary for some entry-level positions; a year or more of experience can qualify a candidate for a higher level job with more pay.

Technical writers and editors must be able to understand complex subjects and be able to write clearly about them. They are often required to write for different audiences, explaining the same topic to a sophisticated professional group and to the general public, for example. Their job requires accuracy and an orientation to detail. Editing, production, and supervisory skills may be necessary for many positions.

Unions/Associations

Major unions and associations include the American Federation of Government Employees; National Association of Government Communicators; National Association of Government Employees; American Federation of State, County and Municipal Employees; National Federation of Federal Employees; and Federally Employed Women, Inc. Technical writers and editors may also belong to the Society for Technical Communications, as well as to related writing or scientific professional associations.

PUBLIC-AFFAIRS SPECIALIST

CAREER PROFILE

Duties: Create and disseminate information on federal agencies and programs; help formulate policies

Alternate Title(s): None

Salary Range: $16,305 to $55,381

Employment Prospects: Fair

Advancement Prospects: Good

Prerequisites:

Education—Undergraduate degree in communications, public relations, or English advantageous

Experience—Background in communications, public relations, or journalism helpful

Special Skills—Strong written and oral communication skills; interpersonal relations skills; analytical skills; leadership ability

CAREER LADDER

Supervisory Public-Affairs Specialist

Public-Affairs Specialist

College

Position Description

Public-affairs jobs exist throughout the federal government at all major organizational levels, including headquarters, agency, region, command, district, and local installations both in the U.S. and abroad. Public-affairs specialists deal with a wide range of subjects and tasks, and are not necessarily required to be experts in any one particular area. They do, however, understand concepts and programs enough to communicate them in a variety of ways to management, the press, and the public.

Public-affairs specialists advise agency management on the formulation of policies and of potential public reaction to those policies. They develop and administer communications programs to disseminate information about policies, programs, services, and activities, and evaluate the effectiveness of the communications.

The communications are likely to include many forms, such as press releases, brochures, and audio-visual productions. Work may be done in foreign languages as well as English.

In addition, public-affairs specialists may be responsible for maintaining relationships with the news media, and for arranging and conducting workshops and seminars with various organizations. They work closely with senior agency management.

Internal communications can be just as important to the job as external communications. In such cases, public-affairs specialists are responsible for employee newsletters, opinion surveys, and recognition and awards programs. They may also conduct tours of an agency for new employees and the general public.

Salaries

Public-affairs positions pay salaries ranging from $16,305 to $55,381, which represents the starting pay for GS5 to the top pay for GS13, according to the 1990 pay schedule. Each level has ten time-in-grade step increases, requiring usually a year minimum at each step.

Employment Prospects

Public affairs accounts for the highest number of employees engaged in communications-related jobs for the federal government. Employment prospects are only fair, however, due to competition and relatively no growth in new openings.

Advancement Prospects

The wide range of public-affairs jobs and different classification grades afford good advancement opportunities.

Education

Applicants who have undergraduate degrees in communications, journalism, English, or even liberal arts have an advantage over high school graduates. Those with only high school educations may qualify for certain positions if they've had enough prior work experience in public relations, public affairs, or related fields.

Experience/Skills

A background in public relations or public affairs is helpful. Work should include dealing with the media and community organizations, and handling a wide range of media tasks.

Creativity, good writing skills, interpersonal relations skills, and leadership abilities are important for success in this field. Public-affairs specialists should be adept at researching, interviewing, and interpreting data, as well as skillful in clear writing and editing. They should be able to communicate well orally as well as in writing.

Unions/Associations

Major unions and associations include the National Association of Government Employees; American Federation of Government Employees; National Federation of Federal Employees; National Association of Government Communicators; American Federation of State, County and Municipal Employees; and Federally Employed Women, Inc. Public-affairs specialists may also belong to other professional organizations.

AUDIOVISUAL PRODUCTION SPECIALIST

CAREER PROFILE

Duties: Plan, direct, and edit production for radio, television, or film

Alternate Title(s): None

Salary Range: $16,305 to $55,381

Employment Prospects: Poor

Advancement Prospects: Fair

Prerequisites:

Education—High school diploma minimum; undergraduate degree in audiovisual studies helpful

Experience—In lieu of college degree, three to six years' work in audiovisual production for most jobs

Special Skills—Creativity; leadership qualities; audiovisual knowledge

CAREER LADDER

Supervisory Audiovisual Production Specialist

Audiovisual Production Specialist

High School or College

Position Description

Audiovisual production specialists plan, supervise, and direct the production and editing of motion pictures; film strips; live, taped, and filmed television productions; live, taped, and recorded radio productions; and other productions, such as prerecorded slide lectures and sound accompaniments to exhibits and scenic or historic views.

Job responsibilities include directing the work of many other individuals, including writers, actors, narrators, or other speakers, musicians, set designers, recording and sound technicians, and motion picture and television camera operators. They also edit tapes and films to create the finished product, and rehearse and direct live performances.

Because radio, television, and film media all require different techniques, many audiovisual production specialists specialize in one medium. Both television and motion picture specialists deal with two basic types of productions. One largely concerns instructional material, such as how to operate pieces of equipment or how to perform various job duties. It is the simplest type of production. The second type involves more complex projects—educational, instructional, or public-information productions for domestic or foreign audiences. Subjects may be highly technical, theoretical, or abstract, and require great skill and imagination in conceiving and presenting visual information.

Radio production specialists also handle two basic types of productions. One type presents information in a straightforward manner, using one voice or simple dialogue, with a minimum of sound or special effects. The second type is more creative, involving dramatic plays, documentaries, variety programs, interviews, round-table discussions, special events reports, or news analysis programs. Skills include extemporaneous speaking ability and interviewing techniques.

Some audiovisual-specialist positions may be only part-time. Others may be combined with writing and editing jobs.

Salaries

Most audiovisual specialists have incomes ranging from about $16,305 to $55,381.

Employment Prospects

Openings are limited and arise largely due to turnover or retirement.

Advancement Prospects

Job advancement can be achieved by moving to a higher grade classification, becoming a supervisor, or moving to another communications- related position.

Education

A high school education is the minimum requirement, but this must be augmented by several years' work experience. Applicants who have earned undergraduate degrees in communications, broadcasting, or film have an advantage. College education may be substituted for work experience in meeting minimum job requirements.

Experience/Skills

College graduates should have at least one year of job experience, and high school graduates should have at least three years for many audiovisual positions. Qualifying experience includes production work in radio, movies, television, or a combination of those fields.

Many audiovisual-specialist positions, particularly those with responsibility for directing productions, require the ability to lead, supervise, and direct teams of specialists and technicians in various fields, and to make full use of their talents and skills. Foreign language skills may be necessary for some positions. Talent, creativity, and a knowledge of scriptwriting are paramount.

Unions/Associations

Major unions and associations representing federal white collar workers include the American Federation of Government Employees; American Federation of State, County and Municipal Employees; National Association of Government Employees; National Association of Government Communicators; National Federation of Federal Employees; and Federally Employed Women, Inc. Audiovisual specialists may also belong to other professional associations.

VISUAL INFORMATION OFFICER AND SPECIALIST

CAREER PROFILE

Duties: Develop and coordinate visual material for exhibits, speeches, briefings, television and film

Alternate Title(s): None

Salary Range: $16,305 to $55,381

Employment Prospects: Fair

Advancement Prospects: Fair

Prerequisites:

Education—High school diploma minimum; bachelor's degree in art, art history, design, or related fields preferred

Experience—Three to six years' visual information experience for most jobs

Special Skills—Ability to think in visual terms; artistic ability; production knowledge

CAREER LADDER

Supervisory Visual Information Officer or Specialist

Visual Information Officer or Specialist

College; Other Job

Position Description

Visual information officers and specialists plan and develop visual information for printed materials, exhibits and presentations. Printed materials include books, pamphlets, magazines and posters; exhibits may be either two-dimensional or three-dimensional and may involve models, dioramas, panels, film strips, slides, sound, music and spoken narration; presentations include formal speeches and briefings at training conferences, news conferences, or for television or film programs.

These employees generally are not involved in determining the subject matter content of the information or the audience. However, they take into consideration the nature of the project in planning their materials, such as whether or not the visual information will be the primary means of communication or merely will supplement information that will be given orally. Visual information officers and specialists also should be familiar with the audience in order to communicate effectively. Work may involve layout and production responsibilities.

Visual-information-officer positions tend to be more managerial in nature than visual information specialists, often involving planning in conjunction with public information programs. Officers' work covers all aspects of a visual information program, including long-range planning, participation in policy and program determinations, selection of the means of communicating information through visual means, and management of the visual program.

Specialists are more concerned with development of materials and in working with others on production.

Salaries

Pay for visual information officers and specialists ranges from about $16,305 to $55,381, depending on grade and level.

Employment Prospects

Job prospects are fair. Competition is always strong for federal jobs, but budget cutbacks have limited new job growth.

Advancement Prospects

Prospects for advancement are at least fair, ranging to good. Employees may move up grade levels, which increases responsibilities and pay, or to supervisory jobs or related communications positions.

Education

A high school education is the minimum requirement, but applicants with a bachelor's degree or degree from an art institute in art, art history, design, or related fields have an advantage. Education should also include courses in communications and English.

Experience/Skills

No previous job experience is required for entry level positions if the applicant has a college degree. High school graduates should have three to six years' experience in visual information work. College-level courses may be substituted for some work experience requirements.

Skills include the ability to communicate information visually, a knowledge of the principles of artistic design and display, and the ability to apply these principles to the field of visual communications.

Unions/Associations

Major unions and associations include the National Association of Government Employees; National Association of Government Communicators; National Federation of Federal Employees; American Federation of State, County and Municipal Employees; American Association of Government Employees; and Federally Employed Women, Inc. Visual information officers and specialists may also belong to related professional groups outside the federal government.

THEATER SPECIALIST

CAREER PROFILE

Duties: Write, plan, supervise, and administer productions for the stage and festivals; coach; promote productions

Alternate Title(s): None

Salary Range: $16,305 to $55,381

Employment Prospects: Poor

Advancement Prospects: Fair

Prerequisites:

Education—Undergraduate degree in drama or theater preferred

Experience—Experience in any aspect of theater work helpful

Special Skills—Playwriting and scriptwriting; acting, directing, and production ability; creativity; interpersonal skills

CAREER LADDER

Supervisory Theater Specialist

Theater Specialist

College

Position Description

Theater-specialist positions require a thorough knowledge of one or more of the theater arts, such as producing, staging, technical direction, techniques of rehearsal and performance, and theatrical literature and history. Some theater specialists plan, supervise, administer, or carry out educational, recreational, cultural, or other programs in theater, such as children's theater, acting workshops, or creative dramatics. Some produce, stage, or direct theatrical productions such as plays, documentary or thematic productions, variety shows, musicals, pageants, contests, or festivals.

Others serve as specialists or instruct in one or more areas of theater arts, such as direction; technical production (including lighting design and execution, scenic and costume design and construction, and makeup); dance production (including choreography, dance drama, and ritual theater); performance techniques (including acting, dancing, and dramatic pantomime); playwriting; play or music production; and theater management, administration, and promotion.

Still other theater specialists review, evaluate, and act upon requests for federal financial support in theater; others carry out research in the technology, history, or literature of theater.

Salaries

Most salaries fall between $16,305 and $55,381.

Employment Prospects

The government employs few theater specialists. The number of openings has decreased in the last few years, and estimates are that this field will remain small, at least through the next decade.

Advancement Prospects

Theater specialists may advance in grade classification or to supervisory positions. They may also qualify for other related communications positions.

Education

An undergraduate degree in drama or theater is preferred for this type of job. In lieu of a college education, applicants should have at least three years' experience in theater work, in such activities as acting, producing, directing, technical production, coaching, teaching, or theater administration.

Experience/Skills

A background in theater work is desirable for theater specialist. Applicants should be familiar with all aspects of dramatical production, including scriptwriting. One to three years' experience in theater work is required for jobs at grades 7 through 11. Skill in interpersonal relationships is vital to success in most theater-specialist positions.

Unions/Associations

Major unions and associations representing federal white collar employees include the National Association of Government Employees; American Federation of State, County and Municipal Employees; American Federation of Government Employees; National Association of Government Communicators; National Federation of Federal Employees; and Federally Employed Women, Inc. Theater specialists may also belong to other professional organizations.

SCHOLASTIC, ACADEMIC, AND NONPROFIT INSTITUTIONS

JOURNALISM TEACHER

CAREER PROFILE

Duties: Teach secondary-school classes in journalism, creative writing, and English; advise student publications

Alternate Title(s): None

Salary Range: $13,000 to $35,000+

Employment Prospects: Fair

Advancement Prospects: Fair

Prerequisites:

Education—Undergraduate degree in communications, journalism, education, liberal arts; graduate degree preferred

Experience—None to several years

Special Skills—Ability to help and motivate others; organization; speaking skills; ability to handle problems smoothly

CAREER LADDER

Administrator

Teacher

College

Position Description

A journalism teacher in a junior or senior high school usually has a wide range of responsibilities. Only one or two classes may be devoted to teaching news gathering, writing, and editing, or work on student publications. The teacher may also conduct classes in English and creative writing, plus supervise study hall, homeroom, or lunch periods.

Journalism teachers are responsible for all or most student publications, such as newspapers, creative writing magazines, and yearbooks. They advise the student staffs on content and layout, and give final approval to the finished product before it is published.

Disciplinary problems must be handled with sensitivity and tact. Classroom presentations must be designed to meet the individual needs and abilities of students. Instructional materials can include films, slides, and computer terminals, as well as books. Teachers may bring in journalism and editorial professionals as guest speakers, as well as arrange field trips to visit local newspapers, magazines, or printing companies.

In addition to developing and teaching regular classes, teachers supervise extracurricular activities, meet after hours with students and parents, and are expected to participate regularly in classes and workshops, to stay current in their field. Most teachers work more than 40 hours a week, but have at least two months off during summer break.

Salaries

The average public school teacher earns about $25,000 a year. Beginners with only undergraduate degrees earn less in many areas; graduate degrees bring higher pay.

Employment Prospects

Overall job prospects in teaching will improve through the 1990s as the children of the baby boom generation enter school.

Advancement Prospects

Experienced teachers may qualify for promotion to administrative, curriculum-development, or guidance-counseling positions. Qualifications include several years of teaching, at least one year of graduate study, and in some cases, a special certificate. Advancement is becoming increasingly difficult because of declining enrollments and budget cutbacks.

Education

An undergraduate degree, preferably in English, liberal arts, communications, or journalism, is the minimum educational requirement. Approximately half the states in the nation require graduate degrees. In addition, teachers must be certified by state boards of education.

Experience/Skills

Beginning teachers start right after graduation from college. Previous work as a journalist or editor is helpful for specializing as a journalism teacher. Teachers should be comfortable speaking to groups, able to organize class content, materials, and tests, and interested in helping and instructing others.

Unions/Associations

The National Education Association and American Federation of Teachers are the major professional and wage-bargaining unions for secondary- school teachers. The AFT is affiliated with the AFL-CIO. Teachers may also subscribe to the AFL-CIO's Academic Corrective Bargaining Information Service.

ASSISTANT PROFESSOR

CAREER PROFILE

Duties: Teach college-level classes in all or various aspects of communications

Alternate Title(s): None

Salary Range: $21,000 to $33,000+

Employment Prospects: Good

Advancement Prospects: Fair

Prerequisites:

Education—Ph.D. usually required

Experience—Four to five years working in the field

Special Skills—Skill in instructing and helping others; speaking ability; organization

CAREER LADDER

Associate Professor

Assistant Professor

Instructor

Position Description

Assistant professor is an entry-level untenured teaching position in colleges and universities. Candidates have worked several years as journalists or advertising or public-relations professionals, and have earned graduate degrees, usually Ph.D.'s.

Assistant professors teach undergraduate courses, many of them large lecture classes of several hundred students. They may specialize in certain areas of communications, such as print or broadcast journalism, advertising, or public relations. Their courses may include introductions to mass communications and mass-communications law and theory, as well as practical instruction in news or copy writing, editing, composition, and layout. They may coordinate course materials and lectures with other faculty members. Teaching loads average nine to 12 hours a week. Besides lecturing, assistant professors make reading and writing assignments, and develop and grade exams.

Assistant professors, as well as their colleagues, are expected to stay abreast of developments in the field and to write and publish articles or books. They may also supervise or help supervise intern programs and have advisory roles on student publications.

Assistant professors should enjoy instructing and helping others in their career preparation. Their schedules are flexible and change from one quarter or semester to another. Their days can be long, from morning classes to night ones. In addition, they maintain office hours for consultations with students.

Salaries

Assistant professors earn an average salary of $21,000 to $33,000 or more at state and major private universities.

Employment Prospects

Demographics indicate an increasing need for college-level teachers.

Advancement Prospects

Assistant professor is an untenured position. Tenure—continued employment and freedom from dismissal without cause—is becoming increasingly difficult to obtain, due to declining enrollments and budget cutbacks. Tenure is required for promotion to associate professor and full professor.

Education

Assistant professors must have earned graduate degrees, preferably in communications, English, or liberal arts. Doctorates are usually preferred for most positions.

Experience/Skills

In addition to advanced degrees, assistant professors must have had four to five years working in the field as journalists, editors, or advertising or public-relations professionals. Knowledge of video display technology is essential.

Skills include the abilities to organize course direction and materials, to instruct and help others, and to speak to large audiences.

Unions/Associations

Associations and unions include the American Association of University Professors and National Education Association.

HISTORIAN

CAREER PROFILE

Duties: Describe, analyze, and evaluate the past through research, writing, speaking, and teaching

Alternate Title(s): Biographer

Salary Range: $14,800 to $38,000+

Employment Prospects: Poor

Advancement Prospects: Poor

Prerequisites:

Education—Graduate degree in history, political science, economics

Experience—Background in research or teaching helpful

Special Skills—Analytical ability; public speaking; clear writing; teaching; foreign language

CAREER LADDER

Associate Professor

Instructor; Assistant Professor

Teaching Assistant

Position Description

The job of the historian is to describe and evaluate the past for today's society. Historians do painstaking research of documents, artifacts, and historical evidence, and sometimes develop theories to explain the significance of their findings.

Nearly all historians specialize by devoting themselves to the study of a particular time period, country, or culture. Some specialize in fields such as military history, science, or religion. Historians try to publish their work in papers, articles, and books.

Most historians work at colleges or universities where they lecture and teach in addition to research. Some do only research. Other historians work in a wide variety of jobs, for such institutions and groups as museums, libraries, historical societies, environmental and public-interest groups, businesses and industries, media, and the federal government. Depending on the job, duties can include cataloging historical documents and artifacts, writing biographies, working to preserve historical buildings and sites, and assisting in the preparation of environmental impact statements and other community development plans.

Historians spend long hours in independent study, researching and writing. At academic institutions, they have flexible work schedules built around classes and administrative duties. Beginners in the field are likely to start out as teaching assistants and work their way up to full professorships.

In nonacademic institutions, historians are likely to work regular business hours. Travel may be occasionally required for research.

In addition, historians may:

- edit historical publications;
- consult on development of historical exhibits, films, and scripts;
- develop academic curricula.

Salaries

Starting salaries range from $14,800 to $18,400 for those with undergraduate degrees. Master's degrees bring an average $22,500, while doctorates command an average $27,200 to $32,600. Average federal government pay is $38,800.

Employment Prospects

Little growth is expected in job opportunities for professional historians through the 1990s. An oversupply of history graduates will compete for few jobs. Those with Ph.D.'s from prestigious institutions will have the best advantage.

Most historians in the U.S. work for colleges and universities. New job opportunities may increase in nonacademic institutions. Persons with computer backgrounds and training in quantitative methods of analysis will have the best advantage in business, industry, government, and research firms. Other favorable areas are historic preservation, public historical studies, and public administration.

Advancement Prospects

At academic institutions, advancement from instructor or assistant professor to full professor is made by earning a Ph.D. and gaining tenure. But some institutions require a Ph.D. for entry-level positions. Tenure is increasingly difficult to obtain, due to the staff and budget cutting at many colleges and universities.

At nonacademic institutions, historians can advance to managerial posts, such as curators or directors of museums or libraries, or directors of historical, preservation, or environmental societies. Some historians gain recognition on their own as writers or self-employed consultants.

Education

A master's degree in history is the minimum requirement for college instructor; many institutions require a Ph.D. Advanced degrees are not required by the federal government and many nonprofit institutions, but because of keen competition, most historians employed in these areas do have Ph.D.'s or their equivalent in training and experience.

Experience/Skills

No work experience is required for many entry-level positions. Students who gain experience in the field with part-time jobs while attending school probably have a competitive advantage for jobs.

Basic skills necessary for all historians include good research methods, plus writing and public speaking abilities. Quantitative methods of analysis or statistics and computer techniques are also important. Historians who earn Ph.D.'s must be competent in at least one foreign language.

Unions/Associations

Professional historians may belong to the American Historical Society; Society of American Archivists; Organization of American Historians; Society of Architectural Historians; American Association of Museums; American Association of University Professors; National Education Association; or American Federation of Teachers.

LIBRARIAN

CAREER PROFILE

Duties: Acquire, catalog, and maintain collections of books, records, and other sources of information

Alternate Title(s): Information specialist; information scientist; information manager

Salary Range: $10,000 to $60,000+

Employment Prospects: Fair to good

Advancement Prospects: Fair

Prerequisites:

Education—Graduate degree in library science

Experience—None to several years for entry-level jobs

Special Skills—Knowledge of book publishing and computer data bases; attention to detail; good organization

CAREER LADDER

Senior Librarian

Librarian

Library Assistant/Clerk

Position Description

Librarians perform a vital role of information management. They acquire, catalog, maintain, and provide access to collections of information, either to the general public or to business, scientific, and technical professionals. In addition, they may develop media and educational programs.

Most librarians work either in schools, colleges, and universities, or in public or special libraries. A growing number work in business and industry, managing computerized data bases of highly specialized information.

Tasks are varied. Some librarians specialize in certain areas, such as acquisitions or media development, but most handle a wide range of responsibilities.

After materials are acquired, they must be cataloged, indexed, and shelved or filed. Much information is transferred to microfilm. Librarians must be able to handle many requests to locate specific information. They may assist teachers in developing educational programs, or compile bibliographies for researchers. They may prepare computer abstracts for scientists and engineers. Librarians also may develop community programs and speakers' forums on issues and topics of interest. They often develop their own publicity materials.

Most librarians work a five-day week of thirty-five to forty hours, including evenings and weekends for public and college libraries.

Salaries

The more specialized the job, the better the pay. Most librarians work for a federal, state or municipal system, and can expect to average $16,000 to $30,000. University librarians typically earn around $29,000, but those at large institutions can earn $50,000 to $70,000 or more. Specialist librarians earn an average $30,000 to $39,000. Part-time librarians can earn as little as $4 to $8 an hour.

Employment Prospects

Job prospects may be limited in academia and government due to budget restrictions, but new opportunities are opening in business, law, industry, science, engineering, and medicine, where the "information explosion" in computer data bases is creating a need for information management.

Advancement Prospects

Advancement to senior librarian, manager, and director depends heavily on the area of work. Business and technical fields offer the best opportunities for promotion.

Education

Education should include an undergraduate degree in liberal arts, English, social sciences, or business, plus at least a master's degree in library science (M.L.S.) The M.L.S. includes advanced courses in cataloging, indexing, computer automation, abstracting, and library administration. A Ph.D. is advantageous for teaching or academic administration. Specialized technical or research work requires additional education.

Experience/Skills

For entry-level positions, experience or internships as a library assistant are helpful. In some localities where jobs are few and applicants many, several years' experience is required for entry-level positions. Public librarians must be state-certified, and requirements vary widely in each state.

Skills include attention to detail; knowledge of publishing, current events, or specialized subjects; and ability to work with the public. Knowledge of computer data bases is becoming increasingly important in all types of librarian jobs.

Unions/Associations

The American Library Association; American Society for Information Science; and Special Libraries Association are major support groups serving the profession. Specialized associations and groups serve educational, technical, music, medical, and other library fields.

PUBLIC-INFORMATION SPECIALIST

CAREER PROFILE

Duties: Disseminate information about a university, college, or nonprofit organization to prospective students, faculty, parents, corporations, the government, and the press; write stories and articles

Alternate Title(s): Public-Affairs Specialist; Public- Relations Specialist; Public-Affairs Director; Public-Relations Officer

Salary Range: Mid-teens to $50,000+

Employment Prospects: Fair to good

Advancement Prospects: Fair

Prerequisites:

Education—Undergraduate degree in English, communications, or other liberal-arts field; advanced course work in writing

Experience—Previous work in public relations; background in journalism or newswriting

Special Skills—Good writing skills; ability to work with people; pleasant telephone manner; organizational ability

CAREER LADDER

Public-Affairs Director; Public-Affairs Manager

Public-Information Specialist

Assistant Public-Affairs Specialist; Journalist; College

Position Description

The public-information specialist acts as a spokesperson for a college or nonprofit organization, handling such duties as college-entrance requirements, departmental information, telephone inquiries, fundraising details, and any other items of interest to the press and public.

Frequent news releases might concern promotion of a professor or administrator, receipt of a large grant, or offer of a definitive study on some new topic to interested journalists. The work of a public-information specialist is no different than for most other public-relations or promotion staffers, except that the employer is a private or public organization or government agency, which is often nonprofit. Besides informing the public or press, a public-information specialist advises his employer about how a particular event or announcement could impress the public, thereby bringing favorable attention to the organization.

In addition, public-information specialists may:

- act as lobbyists in the state capital or Washington, D.C., on behalf of the organization;
- handle fundraisers and banquets for the university or agency;
- represent the university, agency, or organization in the community and at industry functions.

Salaries

Salaries typically start at less than $20,000 and rise to $40,000 to $50,000 or more with ten years or more of experience. PR officers at large public universities typically earn $35,000 to $50,000. Jobs in the nonprofit sector pay less than average.

Employment Prospects

Although the need for public-affairs and information specialists is growing, there are still fewer jobs than the demand for them. Work in public relations with a nonprofit organization is considered a good way to break into the field.

Advancement Prospects

Once employed as a public-information specialist, advancement is a little easier. Many public-affairs professionals for nonprofit groups go on to private industry or start their own firms. Government jobs have a definite career path, with ascending classifications and salaries. Many individuals comfortably ensconced in a public-information post, particularly for a college or university, may stay there until retirement. Advancement prospects are fair and are influenced by budgets.

Education

The best preparation for a public-information career is an undergraduate degree in English, communications, journalism, or other liberal- arts field. Advanced course work in writing and marketing communications is quite helpful.

Experience/Skills

Entry-level staff positions require a college degree; prior experience as a public-relations writer is necessary for higher-level jobs. Most work experience as a public-information specialist for one nonprofit group or government agency will stand you in good stead for another such position. The best skills a public-information specialist can possess are a good command of English and grammar; a clear writing style; an excellent rapport with all sorts of people; tact; good telephone manners; and organizational and clerical abilities.

Unions/Associations

Public-information specialists have no union. As with other public-relations professionals, many choose to join the Public Relations Society of America, Inc., or other professional communications organizations. Public- relations staffers representing colleges, universities, or hospitals may want to join local civic and business groups, to meet the members of the supporting community.

FREELANCE SERVICES AND SELF-PUBLISHING

FREELANCE WRITER

CAREER PROFILE

Duties: Write nonfiction articles for magazines and businesses, or publicity, promotion, and ad copy

Alternate Title(s): Writer

Income Potential: $10 to $100 per hour+; $200 to $800 per day; also per piece

Work Prospects: Excellent

Prerequisites:

Education—No minimum education required; undergraduate degree in journalism, communications, or liberal arts preferred

Experience—Background as a journalist helpful

Special Skills—Good writing ability; persistence; self-motivation; salesmanship

Position Description

Freelance writing is a difficult way to make a living, but the rewards are great for those who succeed: the satisfaction of bylines and credits, ongoing relationships with editors, perhaps even retainers, and increasing income as one's reputation is established.

Most freelance writers begin their freelancing part-time while holding full- or part-time jobs. They send queries and manuscripts to magazines, or write brochures or slide show scripts for businesses. Eventually, business builds to a point where the writer is able to begin freelancing full-time.

General-interest magazines are a very tough market to crack, and many rejection slips may be collected before a sale is made. Freelancers who approach magazines with ideas for articles must first study a publication for its content, style, and slant. With the exception of a very few publications, most magazines do not pay well for the time a writer invests in researching, writing, and revising an article.

Trade and special-interest magazines that cover such topics as home computing, advertising, and business often are easier to break into than general-interest magazines, but they require that the writer have a background in the subject area.

Many freelancers rely heavily on business writing for regular income, which pays much better than most magazines. Business writing for corporations includes press and publicity material, trade stories, speeches, film scripts and slide shows, and internal newsletters and magazines. Some freelancers are able to work on retainers for businesses—a flat monthly fee in exchange for a specified amount of work, such as production of a newsletter. Many advertising and public-relations agencies also rely on freelancers.

Freelance writers must be highly self-disciplined to work on their own. Most put in long hours, and work tends to come unevenly, bringing frequent deadline pressures at the same time. Writers usually have many projects going concurrently in various stages of development—queries or proposals sent out for consideration, researching and interviewing for assignments, writing, and revising. It is essential to maintain a constant pursuit of assignments, because writers never know how long it will take to sell a particular idea. It could sell to the first magazine queried, or it could sell to the tenth after many months.

Many freelance writers find steady work contributing to textbooks, encyclopedias, and other reference books. This work usually is "work for hire," that is, the writer receives a flat fee from the publisher in exchange for all rights. No royalties are paid.

Writers must keep their own business records. They bill clients and keep track of tax deductible expenses.

Additionally, freelance writers may:

- write fiction stories or novels;

- write plays or screenplays;
- work as public-relations consultants;
- edit manuscripts.

Income Potential

A freelance writer's income depends on his or her geographic location and type of projects. Major cities, where more business, magazine, and publishing headquarters are located, offer more fruitful hunting grounds. Yet many freelance writers earn a fair amount of money by sending manuscripts through the mail to distant publications.

Many successful freelance writers earn $20,000 or more, and some who work mostly for businesses and industries earn $40,000 and up.

Pay for trade and general-interest magazine articles can range from $50 to $3,000; top-rated freelancers who work for prestigious publications can command more.

Many freelancers, especially those serving corporate clients, charge by the hour or by day; rates vary according to the job. Typical day rates range from $200 to $800, and hourly rates range from $10 to $100.

Work Prospects

Thousands of trade and general-interest periodicals and businesses rely on freelance writers, yet competition remains stiff, especially for the premium markets. The best bet for beginners is to look to small publications or businesses with which to build the experience and credentials sought by larger markets. It usually takes a freelance writer several years to become established and build a fairly steady income.

Education

Most freelance writers have undergraduate degrees in liberal arts, journalism, or communications. Specialized fields may require certain educational or work credentials. In general, however, a magazine editor looks for good ideas and good writing, not for degrees.

Experience/Skills

Many freelance writers start with no experience other than school writing courses. Others begin freelancing after spending several years as journalists, public-relations writers, or editors. To succeed against the competition, freelancers must be good writers and deliver on time. They must be persistent in selling themselves and should not be easily discouraged by rejections. Freelancers must have a strong entrepreneurial drive.

Unions/Associations

Major national associations include the Authors Guild; American Society of Journalists and Authors, Inc.; Associated Business Writers of America; National Writers Club, Inc.; Public Relations Society of America, Inc.; and Women In Communications, Inc. The Writers Guild of America is a union that represents scriptwriters for radio, television, and film; the National Writers Union represents writers and authors.

TECHNICAL WRITER

CAREER PROFILE

Duties: Interpret technical and scientific information for technical and nontechnical audiences; research and write a wide variety of material

Alternate Title(s): Publications Engineer; Staff Writer; Communications Specialist; Communicator; Industrial Writer; Instructional Materials Developer

Income Potential: $15 to $70/hour+

Work Prospects: Excellent

Prerequisites:

Education—Undergraduate degree in technical communications, science, engineering, computer science, journalism, liberal arts

Experience—Previous work as a technician, scientist, engineer, or writer is helpful

Special Skills—Understanding of complex technical subjects; logic; good writing and layout skills; curiosity

Position Description

Technical writing is a highly specialized field that combines technical, scientific, or engineering backgrounds with the ability to write. Technical writers use their specialized knowledge to translate complex information into readily understandable terms. Their audience may or may not have technical backgrounds.

Technical writing covers a wide variety of tasks. Technical writers prepare instruction manuals for equipment or computer software programs; catalogs and other materials used by industrial sales representatives; equipment specifications and instruction manuals for persons who assemble, operate, or repair machinery; or training aids. They write printed materials or scripts for films, film strips, or cassettes, and also write books.

Technical writers also prepare reports on scientific research; write papers and speeches for scientists and engineers; draft articles for technical publications; and write news releases, advertising copy, promotional brochures, and corporate annual reports. They also prepare exhibits for museums and trade shows.

Technical writers usually work closely with scientists and engineers. They research their subject by studying blueprints; diagrams; technical documents, studies, and journals; and the actual products. They become thoroughly familiar with their subject before writing about it.

Once they collect sufficient information, they prepare a draft for review by technical professionals—computer programmers, engineers, or scientists. A technical editor oversees changes and coordinates artwork and production.

Most technical writers do not begin work in the profession directly out of college. First they gain experience in their area of expertise, or as writers or research assistants. Those with writing ability gradually move into technical writing jobs, first by doing library research and drafts for established technical writers.

Technical writers are concentrated in the electronics, computer manufacturing and software development, aircraft, chemical and pharmaceutical manufacturing industries. Many freelance for research laboratories and hospitals. Others work for the federal government, technical publications, pharmacological and health-related industries, academic institutions, advertising and public-relations agencies, and technical publishing firms.

Income Potential

Freelance technical writers typically are paid by the hour. Some have day rates or else set flat fees by project. Hourly rates range from about $15 up to $70 or more, depending on the writer's expertise, the employer and the project. Businesses usually pay more than publishers.

Work Prospects

Freelance opportunities for technical writers are expected to be strong throughout the 1990s, particularly in the electronics, computer, pharmaceutical, and health-related industries, and in research and development. The Society of Technical Communicators reports that the number of freelancers and consultants has been increasing significantly since 1985. Most work opportunities are in major metropolitan areas.

Education

Most technical writers have undergraduate degrees in science, engineering, technical communications, journalism, or liberal arts. Some have advanced degrees. Most employers prefer thorough technical backgrounds.

Experience/Skills

Many employers look for freelance technical writers who have gained experience working in jobs related to their profession.

Technical writers should be curious, well-organized, and able to explain complicated information. They must be consistently accurate. Technical writers should have the patience and persistence to work long hours sifting through great quantities of details. They should be able to work well as part of a team and on their own.

Unions/Associations

The Society for Technical Communications represents technical writers, editors, scientists, engineers, educators, and others. Other major professional groups include the National Association of Science Writers, Inc., and American Medical Writers Association.

TECHNICAL EDITOR

CAREER PROFILE

Duties: Supervise preparation of technical information material; coordinate artwork; supervise production

Alternate Title(s): Technical Information Editor; Technical Communications Editor; Publications Editor; Instructional Materials Editor

Income Potential: $15 to $70/hour or more

Work Prospects: Excellent

Prerequisites:

Education—Undergraduate degree in science, computer science, technical communications, engineering, journalism, communications, or liberal arts

Experience—Several years' experience as technical writer

Special Skills—Ability to translate technical material into understandable terms; sense of layout and graphics; copy-editing skills; supervisory ability

Position Description

Technical editors are responsible for the content, accuracy, and production of a wide range of technical information materials. Many such editors freelance for technical and scientific journals and book publishers. Other technical editors work for businesses, industries, health professions, or the federal government, producing instruction manuals, sales and promotion literature, advertising copy, books, news releases, speeches, films, film scripts, and cassettes.

Freelance technical editors edit the work of technical writers. They may proofread galleys. Their work requires adherence to production schedules and deadlines.

Technical editors work closely with scientific and technical professionals, who review their material.

Technical editors must have thorough backgrounds in their specific areas. Many begin their careers as engineers, scientists, or other technical professionals before becoming technical writers and editors.

Income Potential

Freelance/technical editors generally are paid between $15 and $70 or more an hour, depending on their expertise and the assignment.

Work Prospects

The demand for technical editors is expected to be strong throughout the 1990s, especially in major metropolitan areas. Major growth areas include computer manufacturing and software development, health professions, electronics, and pharmaceutical manufacturing. Research and development organizations also should provide good opportunities.

Education

While there are no rigid requirements for technical writing and editing, most technical editors have at least an undergraduate degree in science, engineering, or computer science, or in English, liberal arts, or journalism. Many have undergraduate degrees in science or engineering, and graduate degrees in journalism or English. A degree in almost any field is often acceptable with a good technical background and writing skills.

Experience/Skills

A professional background as a technician, scientist, engineer, or programmer is helpful for technical writing and editing. Most editors have had several years' additional experience as technical writers.

Creativity and interest in problem-solving are important traits of technical editors. They must be able to supervise others and work as part of a team. They must always be conscious of deadlines, production schedules, and budgets. They should be good editors as well as writers, and be knowledgeable in graphics and layout.

Unions/Associations

The Society for Technical Communication is the professional association. The National Association of Science Writers, Inc., and American Medical Writers Association are two other organizations to which many technical editors belong.

COPY EDITOR

CAREER PROFILE

Duties: Edit manuscripts and copy for book and periodical publishers, trade and industry publications and corporate communications and publications

Alternate Title(s): None

Income Potential: $10 to $100/hour or more

Employment Prospects: Good

Prerequisites:

Education—Undergraduate degree; graduate degree may be preferred for technical subjects

Experience—Background and previous employment in communications helpful

Special Skills—Grammar, spelling and style skills; knowledge of subject areas helpful or may be required

Position Description

Freelance copy editors edit a wide range of copy for grammar, style, spelling, punctuation, consistency and clarity. They work within the house style guidelines provided by the employer. They improve awkwardly written sentences, correct spelling, and flag suspected errors or inconsistencies in numbers, dates, context and content for double-checking by the author. Their work requires them to be familiar with numerous standard reference works, which they consult frequently when verifying facts.

Copy editors are hired to review book manuscripts (including appendices, indices and bibliographies), periodical articles, newsletters and copy for manuals, advertisements, press kits, in-house communications and more. They work primarily from manuscripts or typeset galleys or proofs and mark corrections directly on the pages. With the increase in electronic text preparation, some copy editors edit online or with a disk.

Income Potential

Freelance copy-editing fees usually are based on an hourly rate. Freelancers set their own rates for various types of jobs, but generally are limited to going rates established by industry or employer. The average rate range in book publishing, magazines, journals and packaging ranges from about $10 to $40 per hour. Copy editors who work in advertising, public relations and corporate communications command up to $100 an hour or more.

Employment Prospects

Work prospects for freelance copy editors are consistently good, for employers can cut staff costs by contracting work out. Good copy editors can build ongoing relationships for steady work.

Education

Copy editors should have an undergraduate degree, preferably in English or communications. Advanced degrees may be preferred or required for technical and scientific work.

Experience/Skills

Previous employment as an editor, copy editor, proofreader or writer is desirable, or may be required, for freelance copy-editing work. Technical or scientific backgrounds may be required for specialized work (see Technical Communicator).

Copy editors are meticulous, good at detail work and have a good command of grammatical rules and spelling. They are versed in production symbols and language and use them in editing. They are quick to grasp content and to spot weaknesses, errors and inconsistencies. They use good judgment and do not impose their own prejudices on the writing. They are diplomatic in pointing out errors and inconsistencies. Copy editors frequently must work under great deadline pressure.

Unions/Associations

Editorial Freelancers Association is open to freelance copy editors. Those who also are writers may belong to a variety of writers' organizations, such as the American Society for Journalists and Authors and National Writers Union.

PROOFREADER

CAREER PROFILE

Duties: Check typeset galleys, page proofs, mechanicals and blue lines for errors prior to printing

Alternate Title(s): None

Income Potential: $8 to $50 per hour

Work Prospects: Fair to good

Prerequisites:

Education—Undergraduate degree in communications or other field; technical or scientific study for work in these areas

Experience—Prior work as writer, editorial assistant, editor, production assistant helpful

Special Skills—Good command of grammar and style; eye for detail

Position Description

The proofreader provides the final check for errors before copy and text of all kinds—from books to periodicals to annual reports to brochures to advertisements—are sent to the printer. Thus, the proofreader carries a great deal of responsibility.

Proofreaders may be called in at different or multiple production stages: when copy is typeset in galleys, when typeset galleys have been arranged into pages; when copy and art are pasted onto boards (mechanicals); or when a dummy is printed (typically in blue ink, hence the name "blue line" or "blues"). They check the typeset copy against the corrected manuscript or corrected galleys to make sure that all changes have been executed as marked. They also look for typographical errors, unevenness in printed lines and other typesetting or printing imperfections. In addition to text, proofreaders make sure that captions, tables, etc. are correct, and that all pieces of art are in the right places. They mark all corrections on their proofs using printer's symbols. Proofreaders also may find inconsistencies or factual errors, which they bring to the attention of the editor.

Freelance proofreaders usually are writers and editors who perform other services, of which proofreading may be a part. Proofreading may be done on an employer's premises or out of a freelancer's home or office.

Income Potential

Proofreaders usually charge an hourly rate that varies according to industry and the type of material being proofed. Book and magazine publishers typically pay the lowest rates, from about $8 to $30 an hour. Corporations and advertising and public relations agencies pay up to $50 or more an hour. If proofreading is part of an overall job done by a freelancer, especially for a corporation, the work may be billed at much higher rates.

Work Prospects

Freelancers have fair to good chances of frequent or steady proofreading work, especially in business and industry, where much communications production work is contracted out. Publishing work opportunities are greatest in the East, but exist wherever there are book and periodical publishers.

Education

Proofreaders usually are communications professionals who hold undergraduate degrees in communications or other fields. Scientific and technical employers may require graduate degrees.

Experience/Skills

Proofreaders must be careful readers and be meticulous in attention to detail. They should have a thorough knowledge of the rules of grammar, punctuation and style. Since they may work directly with typesetters and printers, they should be versed in production procedures.

Proofreading is largely clerical in nature and can be tedious work. Proofreaders should be careful not to move through type too quickly or cut corners, as they may miss errors.

Unions/Associations

Depending on other communications services provided, proofreaders may belong to a variety of organizations, such as Editorial Freelancers Association, American Society of Journalists and Authors; Women In Communications, Inc.; National Writers Union, etc.

FACT CHECKER

CAREER PROFILE

Duties: Check the accuracy of manuscripts prior to publication

Alternate Title(s): Researcher

Income Potential: $10 to $25 per hour

Employment Prospects: Fair

Prerequisites:

Education—Undergraduate degree in journalism, mass communications or other field

Experience—None required, but prior work as writer or researcher helpful

Special Skills—Attention to details, knowledge of how to use library and reference works

Position Description

The publishers of articles, reports and books rely heavily upon the author's accuracy, but many pass manuscripts on to fact checkers to doublecheck for errors. The depth of fact checking varies from verification of dates and spellings of names, titles and places to verification of nearly every detail.

Fact checkers work from a copy of the manuscript and may be given all the author's original notes and tapes. They make heavy use of libraries and reference works. For example, if a writer states that a battle took place on a certain date and at a certain place, a fact checker would look it up, perhaps in an encyclopedia, to verify the information. Fact checkers also call persons interviewed to verify the accuracy of their quotes and statements, and research topics to ascertain whether or not the statements and claims in a manuscript can be validated. They may query the author to find out the sources of certain facts. They report their findings back to the editor.

Fact checking carries a great deal of responsibility but can be tedious work.

Income Potential

Freelance fact checkers typically earn $10–$25 per hour. Some may work on a flat fee basis, or on retainer.

Employment Prospects

Work opportunities are fair at book publishing houses and magazines. However, fact checking is seen as expendable by many publishers, who are constantly looking for ways to cut costs. Increasingly, publishers rely on authors' statements that information in their manuscripts is accurate. Fact checking is still rigorously pursued at some publications, such as *Reader's Digest*, which has fact checkers on staff who immerse themselves in every article the *Digest* seeks to publish. Articles that do not stand up to fact checking are killed. Other publishers check only selected manuscripts.

Education

There are no specific educational requirements for fact checking. An undergraduate degree in journalism, mass communications, English or other field is desirable.

Experience/Skills

Prior experience as a writer, editor, researcher or librarian's assistant is advantageous to obtaining freelance fact checking work.

Fact checkers must be diligent in their search for verifications and unwilling to let minor discrepancies go by. Their attention to detail is required to catch inconsistencies. They must be polite and sensitive in dealing with sources. In some cases, knowledge of the subject at hand is advantageous.

Unions/Associations

There is no professional association of fact checkers, but freelancers who offer this service usually provide other communications services, and may qualify for membership in the Editorial Freelancers Association; American Society of Journalists and Authors; Society for Technical Communications; or Women In Communications, Inc., among others.

INDEXER

CAREER PROFILE

Duties: Compile indices to books, newspapers, periodicals, journals, databases, maps and software

Alternate Title(s): None

Income Potential: $1.50 to $4.00/manuscript page; $10 to $20/hour; 30 cents to 75 cents/index line; several hundred to several thousand dollars flat fee

Employment Prospects: Fair to good

Prerequisites:

Education—Undergraduate degree in humanities, social science or liberal arts; graduate degree in library science or in scientific or technical areas may be required

Experience—Background in scholarly research or as librarian helpful

Special Skills—Organization, grammar, detail, logic, accuracy, reading skills, perception, ability to make connections, predictive ability

Position Description

Indices are the road maps of information—they guide a reader in a direct manner to a logical sequence of information and help the reader discover new information. Without indices, it would be difficult, if not impossible, to conduct research efficiently, and vast quantities of information would go unexplored and unused.

There is a misconception that indexing is clerical work and can be done with little or no experience. On the contrary, indices are complex constructions that require skill and training to produce. A poor index that confuses the reader is worse than no index at all.

Indices are compiled by professional indexers, many of them freelance, who work for libraries, publishers, databases and corporations. They are familiar with the different formats of indices and with international style standards. Rules and practices are in constant change, and professional indexers must stay abreast of them.

Prior to beginning work on an index, an indexer finds out the job requirements. The length and depth of the index is determined by the number of pages allotted, the number of columns per page, the type size, and the format and style rules to be followed. Ideally, the length of the index should be between 1/50 and 1/20 the length of the text. Large reference works such as encyclopedias require the most complex indices, with up to 100,000 or so entries. A short and simple index, on the other hand, may have fewer than 1,000 entries. The more complex the index, the greater the skill required on the part of the indexer, who must cross-reference and spot associations that will lead readers to specific information.

Once the job requirements are known, the indexer carefully reads the entire text and begins compiling entries. The indexer keeps track by marking the text, by keeping alphabetical lists manually, or by using a computer software program. Numerous changes are made as work progresses and the indexer gets new ideas for referencing the information. In the final edit, the indexer checks the index to make sure that all entries lead the reader to the right information, and that the length fits the publisher's requirements. Sometimes indexers can obtain more space for an index by convincing the publisher to increase the number of pages or, more likely, to decrease the type size and leading (space between lines).

Indexers also provide a valuable service by spotting inconsistencies and errors in the writing and typographical errors overlooked by editors.

The average book index is compiled in two to four weeks. Large reference works may take months of work. Indexers often work under a great deal of pressure, as they are called in at the last minute to provide an index as quickly as possible.

With the proliferation of personal computers and software programs, many indexers now compile indices electronically. Some, however, still prefer to work manually, constructing indices with a stack of 35-inch cards and a shoebox, and typing the final copy. In fact, there are some opinions among indexers that any index with fewer than 9,000 entries need not be done on computer. Increasingly, however, publishers are requiring indices to be submitted on disk or transferred electronically via modem.

In addition to indexing, some indexers provide other services, such as researching, abstract writing, updating databases, writing, editing and proofreading.

Income Potential

Earnings depend on the type of indexing and one's expertise. Technical and scientific work pay more than consumer work. Freelance fees are negotiated according to the project, the employer's pay scales and the indexer's scale of fees. Indexers may be paid by each line in an index, by the manuscript page indexed, by the hour, or by a flat fee. The average consumer book brings a fee of $200–$500. Some indexers work on retainer and give that employer first priority. Court rulings on work-for-hire have enabled many indexers to retain rights to their work, and thus to earn additional monies for new editions, reprints and foreign translations.

Employment Prospects

There is an increasing need for indexers due to the proliferation of information and the need to organize and manage it. More and more, people want speedy access to information and do not want to wade through texts in search of facts. In book publishing, some publishers still forego an index as an optional expense, but book reviewers are paying more attention not only to the inclusion of indices, but their quality as well. Databases, libraries, corporations, newspapers and periodicals require indexes to keep track of their collections.

Education

In addition to an undergraduate degree, many indexers have graduate degrees in library science. Some also have advanced degrees in technical or scientific areas. Graduate degrees, especially in library science, may be required for highly complex indexing work.

Experience/Skills

A background in library science and information management is helpful to a freelance career as an indexer. Indexing is precise work and should not be undertaken without some training. Graduate schools of library science may offer non-credit or credit seminars, workshops and courses for the novice indexer.

Indexers bring a wide range of skills to the job. They must be careful readers who get a quick grasp of material. They must be able to anticipate how a reader might look for a specific piece of information. Though indices are logical, the reader does not always approach them logically. Indexers also must be knowledgeable on the latest rules and practices concerning index formats and grammatical style. In addition, indexers are good at seeing patterns, organizing information, paying attention to detail and accuracy, and working under pressure.

Unions/Associations

The American Society of Indexers, Inc. is the only professional association in the U.S. devoted to the advancement of indexing; it is affiliated with professional indexing societies in Canada, the United Kingdom, and Australia. Membership is open to anyone interested in the field. Indexers who provide other freelance communications services may belong to societies for authors, writers, editors, technical writers and editors, public relations professionals, etc.

STRINGER

CAREER PROFILE

Duties: Provide frequent copy to newspapers and/or magazines

Alternate Title(s): Correspondent; Contributing Writer; Contributing Editor

Income Potential: $25 + per article

Work Prospects: Fair

Prerequisites:

Education—Undergraduate degree in communications, journalism, English, or liberal arts, or at least a high school diploma

Experience—Background as a journalist helpful

Special Skills—Ability to work independently and meet deadlines; good writing; sense for news

Position Description

Many newspapers and magazines cover broad geographic areas but are not able to maintain writing staff to monitor far-flung events. Instead, they rely on stringers or correspondents, writers who are expected to monitor local news of interest to the publication and provide timely, frequent stories. Some magazines pay writers to provide copy on specialized topics for columns and departments, such as computer technology or personal health. These writers are usually called contributing writers or contributing editors.

Stringers are expected to keep abreast of news developments and inform their editors of important or special events, or ideas for in-depth or feature stories. Their duties may include reporting on local government and school-board meetings, providing local material for roundup stories and reader surveys, and filing reports on conventions, exhibits, and conferences.

Deadlines depend on publication frequency. A newspaper stringer may be expected to cover an evening meeting and then dictate a story over the telephone. Some transmit copy by telecopier or other facsimile device, and others may only be required to mail articles. A stringer may be required to submit a certain number of stories a week or month, or just report on an as-needed basis. Assignments are given by home-base editors.

If a disaster strikes, such as a flood or tornado, stringers may be called on short notice to provide news coverage. Occasionally they may be asked to travel.

Stringers may hold writing or reporting jobs on other, noncompetitive publications, or they may be part- or full-time freelancers. Their editors depend on them the same way they depend on their immediate reporting or writing staff.

Income Potential

Most stringers do not earn a great deal of money, but the pay can be steady. Major national news magazines pay hourly rates to stringers, from about $10 to $15, or day rates up to $80 or more, plus expenses; stringers submit time records. Other publications pay per story, $25 and up, and some pay by the published inch, usually $1 to $5. Some stringers can earn flat monthly retainer fees of $50 to $500 and up, depending on the publication and work involved.

Work Prospects

Publications covering broad areas, particularly newspapers, and weekly trade and news magazines, are the best bets for stringing.

Education

Most stringers, like other journalists and writers, have undergraduate degrees in communications, journalism, or liberal arts. Those who specialize may have advanced degrees.

Experience/Skills

Stringers generally are established writers, either freelance or employed by another, noncompetitive publication, with several years' experience as journalists. They must be dependable, accurate, and self-motivated.

Unions/Associations

Major national associations include the Society of Professional Journalists, Sigma Delta Chi; American Society of Journalists and Authors, Inc.; National Writers Union; National Association of Black Journalists; National Association of Media Women; National Federation of Press Women, Inc.; and Women In Communications, Inc.

BOOK REVIEWER

CAREER PROFILE

Duties: Write book reviews for newspapers, periodicals and newsletters

Alternate Title(s): Columnist

Income Potential: $0 to several hundred dollars

Work Prospects: Poor

Prerequisites:

Education—Undergraduate degree in communications, English, liberal arts or in area of specific expertise; graduate degree may be preferred in some cases

Experience—Recognition as expert in subject areas or in literature; knowledge of other and current books

Special Skills—Good writing ability, criticism skills

Position Description

Book reviewers help readers choose books by providing summaries of their contents, plot synopses (without giving away surprises and endings) and opinions on their merits and flaws.

Reviewing books can provide a small but often steady source of income for freelance writers and authors. Most newspapers, consumer and trade periodicals and industry newsletters carry book review columns in each issue; many rely on freelancers to provide the reviews. The column itself may be produced on a regular basis by a freelancer, or an editor may assign reviews to a variety of writers. Since the majority of publications are specialized and thus limit reviews to books of specific interest to their audiences, expertise in a subject area is often required of book reviewers. Some writers work regularly or often as reviewers, while others write occasional reviews upon invitation by publications.

Unless a writer is given responsibility for developing a book review column and generating his or her own material, a publication will ask a writer to review a certain book. The writer is given the book as well as instructions on length and format, and a deadline.

There are several types of review, which depend upon the publication and the importance of the book. Straight descriptive reviews are short and give the reader the title, author, publisher, price and a brief description of the contents with no evaluation. Short reviews of several paragraphs provide the pertinent information with a brief evaluation. Essay reviews can be up to one or two thousand words in length and include comparisons of the book to previous works by the same author and similar works by other authors, and an evaluation on the part of the reviewer. Critique reviews are even broader in scope, discussing an entire genre or literary movement.

Income Potential

Most writers are paid small fees for individual book reviews—$10 to $25 are typical fees. In some cases, a free book and a byline are the sole compensation. Large and prestigious consumer publications pay up to several hundred dollars for essay and critique reviews, but rely primarily upon well-known writers and experts.

Work Prospects

Many book reviews are assigned on the basis of the reviewer's credentials, expertise and sometimes name recognition. The best prospects for regular work as a reviewer are in local markets, and through establishing a relationship with a publication by writing articles first. Aspiring reviewers also can query publications with a letter outlining credentials and expertise and, if available, sample review clips.

Education

No education is required to become a book reviewer. Most writers have an undergraduate degree in communications, liberal arts, English or other subjects. Graduate degrees may be preferred for certain specialized areas or publications.

Experience/Skills

Book reviewers should be knowledgeable about the subjects covered in a book, if nonfiction, or the genre, if fiction. One need not be an expert to write straight descriptive and short reviews, but expertise enhances the prospects for higher-paying reviews. Reviewers should be objective, fair and sensitive and have good criticism skills.

Unions/Associations

There are no associations specifically for book reviewers. Those who are writers may belong to one or more writers' organizations, such as the Authors Guild; American Society for Journalists and Authors; Mystery Writers of America; Poets, Essayists and Novelists (P.E.N.); National Writers Union; etc.

CONTRIBUTING EDITOR

CAREER PROFILE

Duties: Suggest and write articles for periodicals

Alternate Title(s): Contributing Writer; Correspondent

Income Potential: Up to $40,000+

Work Prospects: Poor

Prerequisites:

Education—Undergraduate degree preferred; graduate degree may be preferred or required for specialized areas

Experience—Extensive published credits or name recognition with audience; thorough knowledge of subject areas

Special Skills—Excellent writing; dependability; self-discipline

Position Description

Contributing editors are hired by periodicals to write an article for every issue, or a certain number of articles per year. They generally are not part of the periodical's staff, but work on a freelance, contract basis. Pay is set per article or annually, depending on the contributing editor's responsibilities.

Contributing editors usually have extensive experience as writers. They have an established expertise and a reputation for dependability. They are invited to become contributing editors by writing regularly for periodicals. Some well-known or celebrity writers may be invited by a periodical to become contributing editors in order to draw readers. Many small periodicals use contributing editors as a way of stretching their staffs, particularly if they require coverage of far-away areas.

Contributing editors may be responsible for providing coverage of certain topics or geographic areas, or may be roving. They suggest their own ideas and are given assignments by their superior editors. Duties can range from writing articles, reviews and columns to attending staff meetings to supervising other writers. Distant contributing editors usually are not expected to attend staff meetings.

A contributing editorship usually is but one of many sources of income for a writer.

Income Potential

Earnings depend on the size and nature of publication, the responsibilities of the position, and the contributing editor's credentials and reputation. Contributing editors can earn as little as a few thousand dollars a year to $40,000 a year or more at prestigious publications. Celebrity writers may earn more.

Work Prospects

A solid track record of published credits and a good reputation as a writer usually are required to become a contributing editor at major periodicals. A writer may work into this position over time by writing regularly on a topic or for a periodical, and developing a good working relationship with the staff. However, small periodicals in need of dependable, freelance contributors may provide the best prospects for writers in the early stages of their careers.

Education

Most writers have an undergraduate degree in communications, liberal arts, English or social sciences. Graduate degrees may be advantageous or required in technical and specialized areas.

Experience/Skills

Contributing editors usually have demonstrated their expertise over a period of years before becoming contributing editors. They must be creative, self-disciplined, reliable, knowledgeable about their areas and good writers.

Unions/Associations

Contributing editors can belong to organizations for writers, such as the American Society of Journalists and Authors; the Society for Technical Communication; the National Writers Union and Women in Communications, Inc. They may also belong to trade or professional associations related to the areas and topics they cover.

SYNDICATED COLUMNIST

CAREER PROFILE

Duties: Write, self-edit, and deliver columns to client newspapers; prepare sales material; sell column

Alternate Title(s): None

Income Potential: $5 to $75 + per piece

Work Prospects: Poor

Prerequisites:

Education—Depends on need for expertise; most have undergraduate degrees

Experience—Background as journalist or writer helpful; knowledge of subject area important

Special Skills—Concise writing; self-editing; sales and entrepreneurial ability; self-discipline; perseverance

Position Description

All newspapers publish columns on a wide variety of subjects, including self-help pieces, feature articles, news analyses, and puzzles. Some of the columns are written by the newspaper's own staff, but most are purchased through syndication.

Writers who have ideas for columns can try to market them to syndicates—organizations that in turn sell to the newspapers—or market them directly to newspapers in self-syndication.

The proliferation of columns makes it appear deceptively easy to become syndicated. Almost anyone with a novel idea, it seems, can become wealthy and famous. In reality, syndication, by either route, is difficult and highly competitive work; few columnists become famous or wealthy.

A prospective columnist must be able to offer something new, or be able to write about a subject better than established columnists. The idea should be strong enough to generate interesting material at least once or twice a week over a long period of time. Syndicates and newspapers are not interested in fads. What's more, the columnist should have experience in writing and a background in the subject area.

Most columns are short, 500 to 1,000 words or so. They must be tightly written and deliver good information.

There are more than 60 major syndicates that handle all kinds of columns. A prospective columnist should submit to such syndicates at least six sample columns, along with a pitch letter that describes the writer's qualifications, the potential audience, and the column's appeal. Syndicates keep anywhere from 40 to 60 percent of the gross revenues of a column.

In addition to columns, syndicates also purchase single articles, called "one-shots," which have wide appeal and can be sold to newspapers for one-time use. A typical one-shot might be a feature story on a prominent person, or a topic or issue of great current interest. The author is usually paid a flat fee of about 20 to 50 cents a word.

Self-syndication is much costlier and more time consuming, but the writer keeps all of the profits. Sample columns and pitch letters are sent directly to newspaper editors and usually followed up by phone calls. Several hundred newspapers may have to be approached in order to net a few dozen clients. Some columnists start out by establishing themselves with one or two newspapers, and then expanding.

The self-syndicated columnist is responsible for writing, editing, and delivering the copy to all clients by their deadlines, and for billing them. Self-syndication can easily be a full-time job or more, requiring 40 to 80 hours of work per week.

Income Potential

Most columns are sold for $5 to $75 per piece to each client. Rates depend on the popularity of the column and writer. A few columnists earn over $100,000 a year, including Jack Anderson (well over $200,000), William Safire, Russell Baker, Art Buchwald, Abigail Van Buren (Dear Abby), Ann Landers, and others. A self-syndicated columnist who is published in about 60 or 70 newspapers and charges $10 per piece can clear about $30,000 a year. Most columnists earn far less than that.

Work Prospects

Syndicates and newspapers receive far more queries for columns than they can possibly use. Writers who can identify new and developing trends in popular interests have the best chances for successful sales. Self-syndication is an alternative for those willing to put in long hours to get established, a process that usually involves giving columns away on free trials. Most aspiring columnists will find their best bets in their own local markets, and among the nation's many small daily and weekly newspapers.

Education

Little attention is paid to education unless it is necessary to establish the columnist as an authority. However, an undergraduate degree in journalism or any subject is desirable.

Experience/Skills

Most columnists are already established writers or journalists with several to many years of experience. Regardless of previous writing experience, columnists must demonstrate good writing ability. They must be able to research and develop fresh, concisely written material on a regular schedule. Persistence and a flair for sales and promotion is helpful to self-syndicators.

Unions/Associations

There are no associations specifically for syndicated columnists. Related groups include the Society of Professional Journalists, Sigma Delta Chi; Women In Communications, Inc.; American Society of Journalists and Authors, Inc.; National Association of Media Women; and National Federation of Press Women.

COMMUNICATIONS CONSULTANT

CAREER PROFILE

Duties: Advise clients on ways to improve writing and communications skills, or editorial operations

Alternate Title(s): Editorial Consultant

Income Potential: $200 to $1,000+ per day

Employment Prospects: Fair

Prerequisites:

Education—Undergraduate degree in communications, liberal arts, or related field; graduate degree advantageous

Experience—Sufficient background to provide expertise

Special Skills—Excellent written and oral communications skills; teaching ability; salesmanship; self-motivation

Position Description

Consulting is viewed as a highly glamorous, prestigious occupation. Consultants enjoy a reputation for high compensation relative to work performed, as well as complete independence. While it is true that consultants can earn high pay, most work very hard for it, putting in long hours searching for and pitching clients. Their work and reputation must be good enough to earn repeat clients, for it is virtually impossible to stay in business on one-shot efforts.

Consultants exist in just about every profession, discipline, and occupation. In communications, consultants perform a variety of services. They assist businesses, publications, and newspapers in special projects, in streamlining and improving editorial operations, and in launching new publications. They conduct research and studies of potential advertisers, markets, and subscribers. They help pinpoint weaknesses. They conduct seminars for staff on how to improve writing and editing skills, or training sessions on new technology. Consultants may also assume responsibility for such publications as corporate newsletters, handling the editing and production involved.

To be successful, consultants must have expertise and credentials to attract and satisfy clients. Such a reputation usually comes after years of work in the field as a writer, editor, or publishing executive. Some people enter consulting on a part-time basis, handling projects that are not conflicts of interest with their jobs. Part-time consulting allows for a base of clients and references to be built with a minimum of financial risk; however, it does limit the types of assignments that can be accepted. Part-time consulting can be built into a full-time occupation.

Most consultants have a strong desire to be self-employed and are highly motivated to succeed. Building a client base requires persistence and good sales skills. They must identify their target audience and develop direct-mail, telephone, and advertising campaigns to promote their particular skills and abilities.

Hours can be very long, especially in the beginning. Consultants spend a great deal of time prospecting for clients, by attending professional meetings and conferences, accepting speaking engagements, and soliciting on the telephone. Work loads are seldom spread evenly, which creates many deadline pressures. Some consultants travel extensively.

Income Potential

Consultants usually work on a per diem or project basis. Per diem rates range from $200 to $1,000 and up—some top consultants charge as much as $2,000 a day. Rates depend on experience and expertise; the average is about $550 per day. Flat fees for projects depend on the nature of the work and time spent.

Other common types of fees include: retainer fees (a flat monthly rate in exchange for a specified amount of time); percentage fees (a percent of the value of a product that is to be offered for sale); and equity fees (an interest in a business in lieu of cash).

Employment Prospects

Overall, there are some 50,000 full-time consultants in all fields, with an additional 2,000 persons setting up shop every year. The industry totals more than $32 billion a year. About half of all consultants are sole proprietorships.

In communications, the best employment prospects are among corporations, many of which use consultants regularly for ongoing staff education and training. Many newspapers also use consultants. In addition to editorial experience, many newspaper consultants also have some background in production, advertising, or circulation.

Education

High academic credentials carry weight in consulting. An undergraduate degree in communications, liberal arts, or a specialized area is the minimum requirement. A master's degree won't guarantee success, but it can help attract clients. A background in finance or accounting is advantageous in all areas of consulting.

Experience/Skills

Besides expertise, consultants should possess good problem-solving ability. They should be quick at grasping situations and in seeing solutions.

Excellent writing and speaking skills are a must for consultants. Pitch letters, proposals, reports, and studies must be well researched, organized, and written. Consultants do a great deal of public speaking, either in instruction to small groups or to larger audiences at conventions and professional meetings.

Sales skills also are essential to success. Consultants must sell themselves to potential clients, and sell their ideas and proposals to existing clients. Consultants must be well organized, ambitious individuals with a strong desire to succeed on their own.

Unions/Associations

Membership in professional associations and organizations is wise because of the contacts and referrals that can be made. Which organizations to join depends on the individual's area of expertise.

DESKTOP PUBLISHER

CAREER PROFILE

Duties: Produce or publish newsletters, magazines, brochures, reports and other small publications

Alternate Title(s): Communications consultant; freelance publisher

Income Potential: $1,000 and up per job

Work Prospects: Fair to good

Prerequisites:
Education—Undergraduate degree in mass communications, journalism, English or other field
Experience—Prior work in writing, editing and publications production essential
Special Skills—Good writing and editing skills; knowledge of desktop publishing software; management skills; organization; ability to meet deadlines; salesmanship

Position Description

Sophisticated computer technology has enabled the freelance writer and editor to expand in new directions and produce a finished product end to end. With an investment in the right computer hardware and desktop publishing (DTP) software, the freelancer becomes producer or publisher.

The desktop publisher works with businesses, associations, agencies and organizations to produce publications that have a professionally published look. These usually are newsletters, magazines and reports for either an inhouse or external audience.

Desktop publishers work with a staff editor or communications manager who provides specifications for the publication's content, design, size and length. The desktop publisher may be given the copy, produced in-house or by freelancers, or may have to generate it in accordance with an assignment list. If the copy is hard (printed on paper), it is keyed or scanned into the computer. Some copy may be provided on disk or transferred by modem. The copy is edited, and the pages are formatted on-screen to accommodate graphics and design. The pages can be printed out exactly as they appear on the screen. Art must be screened and added.

Simple documents such as a single-sheet newsletter can be printed in quantity directly on a high-quality printer (laserjet is preferred). The printer also can be used to produce proofs, which are mounted on mechanicals and sent to a printer. The desktop publisher either delivers the finished product or the mechanicals, or sends the mechanicals to a printer.

Desktop publishers wear all hats—writer, editor, copy editor, designer, typesetter—or supervise others who perform those tasks. All facets of producing a publication must be coordinated in order to meet deadlines. The task involves periodic meetings with the in-house person in charge of the publication, to review progress and get the necessary in-house approvals on content and design.

Some desktop publishers found their own newsletters and periodicals. The success of these ventures relies in the astute meeting of a market need and the marketing of the product to paying subscribers. Fulfillment—the management of mail lists and the mailing of the publication—is time-consuming, as is collecting money and keeping track of accounts. New publications may operate in the red for a considerable period of time. If successful, self-published newsletters can be rewarding in terms of income and creative satisfaction.

Income Potential

Desktop publishers set individual fees, usually by establishing a day rate and estimating the time required to complete a job. Certain expenses may be billed in addition to the fee. The production of even a simple quarterly newsletter can bring in several thousand dollars annually.

An initial investment in equipment and software is necessary, however. One needs a personal computer with sufficient built-in memory to handle DTP programs, a word processing program, a DTP program and a high quality printer that can handle different fonts.

Work Prospects

Opportunities for desktop publishers are fair to good and are increasing due to downsizing in the business world. Businesses are trimming their staffs or keeping them small, yet their need to communicate remains the same or increases. It's more economical for many businesses to hire freelance desktop publishers than to assign staff to produce certain publications. The DTPer is to business communications what the packager is to book publishing.

The best DTP opportunities are at corporations of all sizes, professional or trade organizations and associations, and the nonprofit sector, though pay is lower at the latter.

Education

An undergraduate degree in mass communications, journalism, English, or other field is desirable.

Experience/Skills

Previous experience as a writer or editor, and knowledge of production, are essential. Though DTP programs do not require graphics design skill, some knowledge of layout and design is helpful, and may be essential for larger and more complex publications.

DTPers must be well organized and able to coordinate people and tasks to bring the pieces together into a whole. Personal interaction skills are important, as DTPers typically work with a variety of people who must provide material, art or approvals. DTPers also must have good sales skills to sell their services.

Unions/Associations

DTPers may belong to a number of communications organizations, such as the International Association of Business Communicators; Public Relations Society of America; Women In Communications, Inc.; the American Society of Journalists and Authors; Editorial Freelancers Association; and more.

PACKAGER

CAREER PROFILE

Duties: Create books for publishers

Alternative Title(s): Book producer

Income Potential: $0 to no limit

Work Prospects: Poor to fair

Prerequisites:

Education—Undergraduate degree in English, communications, liberal arts, humanities; publishing and marketing courses desirable

Experience—Prior work as author or editor essential

Special Skills—Creativity; innovation; ability to sense marketing opportunities; salesmanship; marketing and finance savvy; familiarity with production

Position Description

Packagers provide complete book preparation services to publishers, from the outline to the finished product. Some also provide marketing and distribution services. By offering package deals to publishers, packagers save publishers money and reduce staff time. Most publishers pay packagers according to a percentage of the book's retail price and the number of copies ordered. The usual percentage is 20 percent. Thus, a packager is paid $5 for a book that will sell to the public for $20. To make a profit, the packager must hold production costs to less than $5 per book. Mistakes can make the difference between profit or loss.

Packagers conceive ideas for books and then write proposals, which they use as sales tools to interest editors. The proposal includes a summary of the book's contents, sample material, market potential, and, if the packager provides the finished product, the production specifications (number of pages, trim size, type of paper, etc.). The editor and packager then negotiate a price. The packager must take into account anticipated production expenses and build in a profit margin.

Some packagers write, edit and produce their own books. Others work with authors, whom they pay on a flat fee or royalty basis. Unless a packager has production equipment, work is subcontracted to typesetters and print shops. The services of a graphic artist or illustrator usually are necessary. The packager consults with the editor at numerous points along the way. Depending on the contract, the editor may have a significant voice in how the book is produced.

Packagers devise production schedules and must coordinate a variety of personnel and activities. They are familiar with production. Many packagers retain rights to their books, which they sell piecemeal to publishers, periodicals and other outlets. Selling these rights is time-consuming and requires knowledge of the publishing marketplace. Some packagers have agents to help them sell proposals and rights.

Most packagers have had extensive prior experience as authors or editors. They know the business and have numerous contacts in the publishing world. They may opt to specialize in certain kinds of books, such as art books or lavishly illustrated coffee-table and gift books, or in serial fiction.

Packaging can provide the satisfaction of self-publishing without the distribution worries, unless the packager opts to provide marketing and distribution services. However, it can be difficult to get started, and vagaries in cash flow from typically slow-paying publishers can strain a tight budget.

Income Potential

Earnings depend on the type of books packaged, the end product provided (finished books fetch more money but consume more money to produce) and the success of books sold. Profit margins vary depending on individual negotiations. The profit from a book may be only a few thousand dollars. Big sellers can go on to earn hundreds of thousands of dollars over a period of time.*

Packaging requires startup investment on the part of the packager. In a typical contract, a packager is paid in thirds by the publisher (one-third on signing, one-third on delivery, and one-third on publication) or in halves (half on signing, half on delivery). Payment from a publisher can come months after signing or delivery; meanwhile, work must be done on the book and suppliers and authors expect to be paid. Packagers who work out of an office must factor in rent and other office expenses.

Work Prospects

It is difficult to get started in packaging without personal contacts in the publishing world, but it can be done. Packagers can work anywhere, but the overwhelming majority are concentrated near New York City, where they can have easy access for face-to-face meetings with major publishers. A good-quality, professional product is paramount to success.

Education

Most packagers have an undergraduate degree in liberal arts, English, communications, humanities, or other area. They may have taken additional courses in publishing, business administration, marketing, advertising, and promotion.

Experience/Skills

Prior work as an author or editor is virtually essential to packaging. The packager functions almost as a publisher, and must be familiar with the market. The ability to make convincing proposals, both in writing and in person, is important. Packagers must manage cash flow, staff and suppliers, and juggle tight deadlines.

Unions/Associations

The American Book Producers Association is the primary organization for packagers. Some may also belong to the Association of American Publishers, Inc., or various writers' organizations.

SELF-PUBLISHER

CAREER PROFILE

Duties: Write and publish one's own books, monographs, periodicals, etc.

Alternate Title(s): Independent publisher, private publisher

Income Potential: $0 to no limit

Work Prospects: Fair

Prerequisites:

Education—Undergraduate degree in English or communications; courses in business and finance helpful

Experience—Work as writer and editor helpful; familiarity with production essential; sales experience, financial acumen desirable

Special Skills—Innovation; willingness to take risks; ability to predict trends and market opportunities; salesmanship and marketing skills; self-promotion; organization; financial planning; good records keeping.

Position Description

In times past, self-publishing once carried a stigma—it was the mark of an author who failed to sell his or her work to a publisher. That stigma no longer exists. In fact, many a self-published author is considered a savvy businessperson, someone who retains total control over the product and stands poised to keep all the profits, not a small percentage of them.

Self-publishing became viable with the explosion in personal computing and desktop publishing software. For a moderate investment, an individual can purchase the equipment and programs needed to produce manuscript copy, galleys and page mechanicals ready for the printer. At the same time, the consolidation of large publishing houses has left openings in the market to be filled by small presses (many of which began as self-publishing operations and expanded) and self-publishers. Self-publishing is not to be confused with vanity publishing, in which an author pays a publisher to publish a work.

Self-publishing requires a great deal of business planning and organization, for the self-publisher bears all the expenses of producing and marketing a book. The author wears many hats, and must plan and budget for every step along the way. Prior to writing the book, the self-publisher must try to estimate production costs and market potential. A marketing plan is drawn up. The book is then written, and then must be typeset, proofread and corrected, paginated, and made ready for mechanicals for the printer. The self-publisher must be familiar with production shop operations and able to work with those personnel. A cover must be designed, which may require hiring a graphic artist. If the text is illustrated, the art must be collected or commissioned and positioned in the text. Any legal questions must be resolved with the help of an attorney.

Once the book is produced, the self-publisher takes delivery and must be able to sell the copies through channels of distribution, which include book and specialty stores, catalogs, direct mail, and wholesale distributors. Orders are placed; prices and terms must be negotiated; books must be delivered and monies collected. In addition, publicity and reviews must be solicited and advertisements, if desired, placed. Many of these activities are time-consuming, and authors find themselves working more as business managers than as writers. Furthermore, not all markets are eager to do business with self-publishers, and it is at the point of distribution that many self-publishers fail and lose money.

Success, however, is a heady experience. Sufficient profits enable self-publishers to produce other books. Once track records of sales are established, distribution becomes easier. Many authors who have been published by large publishing houses have found great satisfaction in self-publishing, even if profits are small or modest. They enjoy having complete control and in seeing immediate financial results, instead of waiting months to years to earn royalties.

Income Potential

A successful self-published book is one that earns at least enough income to cover production costs. Profits may range from several hundred dollars to several thousand dollars, depending on the profit margin per copy and the number of copies sold. Some very successful self-published books have made hundreds of thousands of dollars in profits. A trade paperback of about 155 pages with no illustrations and a simple cover might cost about $3 per copy to produce, and could sell for up to $9.95 or $10.95.

Minimum press runs typically are 1,000 or more copies. Depending on costs, the self-publisher must invest up front an average of $8,000–$12,000 or more for a typical book. Depending on how quickly a book sells, recovering costs and making a profit may take several months to years. Those who succeed have researched in advance the potential market for their books and potential distribution channels.

Additional income may come from the sale of subsidiary rights, such as foreign sales, audio tapes, condensations, serializations, film and television production, etc. Occasionally a successful self-published book is purchased for larger distribution rights by a major publisher.

Nonfiction self-published books, especially those that are self-help, guides or subjects for specialty markets, are much more likely to succeed than fiction and poetry.

Work Prospects

The ranks of self-publishers have swelled since affordable desktop computing arrived in the early 1980s. Market opportunities depend upon trends and perceived needs as seen by the aspiring self-publisher. It is possible to get started in self-publishing on a part-time basis while one continues to work at a full-time job, though the time demands can be grueling. Successful self-publishing can lead to the establishment of a small press, which publishes several titles a year, including the works of others. Thousands of small presses operate in the U.S. alone.

Education

Most self-publishers are authors-turned-publishers and have undergraduate degrees in communications, English, liberal arts, and the humanities. Additional courses in business, marketing, and finance are recommended prior to launching a self-publishing venture.

Experience/Skills

Self-publishers are good writers and are creative and innovative. They are not afraid to take risks. Editing skills are advantageous, though self-publishers can always hire editors on a project basis. Self-publishers also have a working knowledge of production and printing requirements and procedures. Financial, sales, and promotion skills also are necessary. A great deal of advance business planning must be done in order to be successful.

Unions/Associations

The Committee of Small Magazine Editors and Publishers (COSMEP) is the leading association of independent book and periodical publishers. Many self-publishers also belong to the Publishers Marketing Association, a national nonprofit cooperative, and to various regional small-press associations. Self-publishers also may belong to local business organizations and writers' organizations, such as the American Society for Journalists and Authors; Authors Guild; National Writers Union; etc.

APPENDICES

APPENDIX I
EDUCATIONAL INSTITUTIONS

The minimum educational requirement for most salaried jobs featured in this guide is an undergraduate degree in communications, with emphasis in a particular sequence, such as print journalism, broadcasting, advertising/public relations, etc. The following is a list of some of the four-year colleges and universities that offer such undergraduate degrees; in addition, some offer courses in book publishing. The listings include addresses, telephone numbers and the majors or sequences offered, in random order. In addition, the institutions whose programs have met the standards set by the Accrediting Council on Education in Journalism and Mass Communications (ACEJMC) have been marked with an asterisk (*). For more information about course descriptions, admissions requirements, and the availability of scholarships, call or write to the institutions of interest.

Many major professional associations have information on scholarships and internships; consult Appendix IV. The Dow Jones Newspaper Fund publishes a comprehensive annual *Journalism Career and Scholarship Guide*. For information, contact:

The Dow Jones Newspaper Fund
P.O. Box 300
Princeton, NJ 08543-0300
609-452-2820

ALABAMA

Alabama State University
Montgomery, AL 36101-0271
205-293-4493
Print journalism, radio-TV, public relations

Auburn University
Auburn, AL 36830
205-826-4607
News-editorial, public relations

Samford University
Birmingham, AL 35229
Broadcasting, print, public relations, advertising

Troy State University
Troy, AL 36802
205-566-3000 ext. 289
Broadcasting, news-editorial

University of Alabama
Tuscaloosa, AL 35487
Journalism, broadcast and film communications, advertising/public relations, speech communication
Courses in publishing

ALASKA

University of Alaska-Anchorage
Anchorage, AK 99508
907-786-1329
News-editorial, photojournalism, public relations and advertising, telecommunications, general communications

University of Alaska-Fairbanks*
Fairbanks, AK 99775
907-474-7761
Broadcasting, news-editorial

ARIZONA

Arizona State University*
Tempe, AZ 85287-1305
602-965-5011
Journalism (news-editorial, photojournalism, public relations), broadcasting (broadcast journalism, telecommunication management, production analysis)

Northern Arizona University
Flagstaff, AZ 86011
602-523-3671
News-editorial, public relations, advertising, journalism education, photojournalism, mass communications, broadcast news, broadcast production
Courses in publishing

University of Arizona*
Tucson, AZ 85721
602-621-7556
News-editorial (newspaper, magazine, public information, community journalism, photojournalism)
Courses in publishing

ARKANSAS

Arkansas State University*
State University, AR 72467
501-972-2468
Broadcasting, news-editorial, advertising, public relations, community journalism, photojournalism
Courses in publishing

Arkansas Tech University
Russellville, AR 72801
501-968-0640
Broadcast news, news-editorial

Henderson State University
Arkadelphia, AR 71923
501-246-5511

News-editorial, secondary school, broadcasting

John Brown University
Siloam Springs, AR 72761
501-524-3131

Broadcasting, news-editorial, public relations

Ouachita Baptist University
Arkadelphia, AR 71923
501-246-4531 ext. 207

News-editorial, broadcast news, broadcast production, public relations, photography

University of Arkansas*
Fayetteville, AR 72701
501-575-3601

News-editorial, advertising, public relations, magazine journalism, broadcast journalism

University of Arkansas*
Little Rock, AR 72204
501-569-3250

News-editorial, broadcast journalism, professional and technical writing, public information

University of Central Arkansas
Conway, AR 72032
501-450-3162

Mass communications, news-editorial, magazine

CALIFORNIA

California Polytechnic State University
San Luis Obispo, CA 93407
805-756-2508

News-editorial, broadcast news, agricultural journalism, public relations
Courses in publishing

California State Polytechnic University
Pomona, CA 91768

Public relations, telecommunications, journalism, organizational communications, specialized communications
Courses in publishing

California State University
Chico, CA 95929
916-895-5751

News-editorial, public relations

California State University
Dominguez Hills
Carson, CA 90747
213-516-3313

Journalism, television studies, public relations

California State University*
Fresno, CA 93740-0010
209-294-2087

News-editorial, radio-TV news communications, photocommunications, advertising, public relations

California State University*
Fullerton, CA 92634-4080
714-773-3517

Journalism, public relations, advertising, photocommunications, radio-TV-film

California State University
Hayward, CA 94542
415-881-3292

Mass communications

California State University*
Long Beach, CA 90840
213-985-4981

News-editorial, magazine journalism, broadcast journalism, public relations, journalism, photojournalism, secondary school teaching

California State University
Los Angeles, CA 90032
813-224-3626

Broadcast journalism, news-editorial, public relations, advertising

California State University*
Northridge, CA 91330
818-885-3135

News-editorial

California State University
Sacramento, CA 95819-2694
916-278-6353

Journalism, government-journalism

Humboldt State University*
Arcata, CA 95521
707-826-4775

News-editorial, public relations

Pacific Union College
Angwin, CA 94508
707-965-6437

News-editorial, communications, international communications, public relations

Pepperdine University Seaver College
Malibu, CA 90265
213-456-4211

Journalism (news-editorial), advertising, public relations, communications theory, international studies, organizational communications, communications theory, telecommunications (production, news and management)

San Diego State University*
San Diego, CA 92182
619-594-6635

News-editorial, advertising, radio-TV news, public relations

San Francisco State University*
San Francisco, CA 94132
415-338-1689

News-editorial, photojournalism, magazine journalism

Santa Clara University
Santa Clara, CA 95053-2999
408-554-2798

News-editorial, broadcast production

Stanford University
Stanford, CA 94305
415-723-1941

Communications (undergraduate), mass communications (masters), journalism, documentary film production (doctorate), communications research
Courses in publishing

University of California*
Berkeley, CA 94720
415-642-3383

Graduate programs in news-editorial and television news

University of La Verne
La Verne, CA 91750
714-593-3511

Broadcast news, photography, news-editorial

University of San Francisco
San Francisco, CA 94117-1080
415-666-6680

Broadcasting, news-editorial

University of Southern California*
Los Angeles, CA 90089-1695
213-743-5662

Broadcasting, print journalism, public relations

COLORADO

Adams State College
Alamosa, CO 81102

News-editorial

Colorado State University*
Fort Collins, CO 80523
303-491-6310

News-editorial, public relations, electronic reporting, agricultural/natural resources journalism, technical-specialized

University of Colorado*
Boulder, CO 80309
303-492-5007

News-editorial, advertising journalism, broadcast news, broadcast production management

University of Denver
Denver, CO 80208
303-871-2166

News-editorial, broadcasting, critical studies, public relations
Courses in publishing

University of Northern Colorado
Greeley, CO 80639
303-351-2726

Telecommunications, news-editorial, advertising, public relations

University of Southern Colorado
Pueblo, CO 81001
303-549-2811

News-editorial, public relations, advertising, telecommunications

CONNECTICUT

Southern Connecticut State University
New Haven, CT 06515
203-397-4311

News-editorial, magazine journalism, broadcast journalism, public relations

University of Bridgeport
Bridgeport, CT 06601
203-576-4128

News-editorial, advertising

University of Connecticut
Storrs, CT 06268
203-486-4221

Journalism (news-editorial)
Courses in publishing

University of Hartford
West Hartford, CT 06117
203-243-4333

Communications (includes studies in American journalism, mass communications, magazine journalism, advertising, broadcasting, organizational communications, interpersonal communications)

University of New Haven
West Haven, CT 06516
203-932-7208

Journalism, public relations, managerial and organizational communications, international business, marketing, mass communications (TV, radio, film)

DISTRICT OF COLUMBIA

American University
Washington, DC 20016
202-885-2060

Print journalism, broadcast journalism, public communications, visual media
Graduate programs in journalism and public affairs (broadcast or print), film and video, economic communications, public communications

George Washington University
Washington, DC 20052
202-994-6225

News-editorial
Courses in publishing

Howard University*
Washington, DC 20059
202-636-7690

Broadcast journalism, news-editorial, public relations

FLORIDA

Florida A&M University*
Tallahassee, FL 32307
904-599-3379

Newspaper journalism, broadcast journalism, magazine journalism, public relations, photography and graphic design

Florida International University
North Miami, FL 33181
305-940-5625

Public relations, advertising, telecommunications (production and management), journalism (print and broadcast)

Florida Southern College
Lakeland, FL 33801-5698
813-680-4168

Journalism, public relations, advertising

University of Central Florida
Orlando, FL 32816
305-275-2681

News-editorial, radio-TV, film, advertising/public relations

University of Florida*
Gainesville, FL 32611
904-392-5970

News-editorial, public relations, magazines, technical communications, photojournalism, advertising

University of Miami
Coral Gables, FL 33124
305-284-2265

News-editorial, photocommunications

University of South Florida*
Tampa, FL 33620
813-974-2591

Broadcast programming and production, film, visual communications, broadcast news, public relations, news-editorial, advertising, magazine journalism
Courses in publishing and printing

University of West Florida*
Pensacola, FL 32514
904-474-2880

News-editorial, public relations/advertising, broadcast journalism, radio-television-film

GEORGIA

Brenau College
Gainesville, GA 30501
404-534-6290
Broadcasting, news-editorial, public relations

Clark/Atlanta University
Atlanta, GA 30314
404-880-8309
Radio-film-TV, journalism, public relations

Georgia Southern College
Statesboro, GA 30460
912-681-5138
Public relations, news-editorial, broadcast production

Georgia State University
Atlanta, GA 30303
404-651-3200
Broadcast news, broadcast production, print, public relations, film and video, theater, magazine journalism, speech

Savannah State College State College Branch
Savannah, GA 31404
912-356-2169
Media management and performing arts, radio and TV, print journalism

University of Georgia*
Athens, GA 30602
404-542-3000
Newspapers, magazines, public management

HAWAII

University of Hawaii*
Honolulu, HI 96822
808-948-8881
Public relations, news-editorial, broadcast journalism

IDAHO

Boise State University
Boise, ID 83725
208-385-3320
Mass communications (general), journalism (general)

Idaho State University
Pocatello, ID 83209
208-236-3295
Media studies, print media, television, photography

University of Idaho
Moscow, ID 83843
208-885-6458
News-editorial, organizational communications, advertising, public relations, communications, telecommunications, photography/film

ILLINOIS

Bradley University
Peoria, IL 61625
309-677-2354
Radio-video-photo, speech, public relations/advertising, news

College of St. Francis
Joliet, IL 60435
815-740-3696
News-editorial, advertising/public relations, broadcasting/graphic design

Columbia College Chicago
Chicago, IL 60605
312-633-1000 ext. 366
Advertising, public relations, news-editorial, magazine editing, photojournalism, broadcast journalism, science writing and reporting

Eastern Illinois University
Charleston, IL 61920
217-581-6003
News-editorial

Illinois State University
Normal, IL 61761
309-438-3671
Public relations, journalism, broadcasting

Lewis University
Romeoville, IL 60441
312-242-0015 ext. 362
News-editorial, radio-TV broadcasting

Loyola University of Chicago
Chicago, IL 60611
312-670-3116
News-editorial-journalism, radio/television/film
Courses in publishing

Northern Illinois University*
De Kalb, IL 60115
815-753-1925
Journalism (news-editorial, public relations, photojournalism, broadcast news)

Northwestern University*
Evanston, IL 60208
312-491-5091
News-editorial (undergraduate), magazine journalism, advertising, TV news, corporate public relations, direct marketing (graduate)

Roosevelt University
Chicago, IL 60605
312-341-3813
Broadcast journalism, news-editorial, public relations

Southern Illinois University*
Carbondale, IL 62901
618-536-3361
News-editorial, advertising

Southern Illinois University
Edwardsville, IL 62026
618-692-2230
Journalism, television and radio (general)

University of Illinois*
Urbana, IL 61801
217-333-2350
News-editorial, broadcast news, media studies, advertising

Western Illinois University
Macomb, IL 61455
309-298-1424
News-editorial, advertising, public relations

INDIANA

Anderson University
Anderson, IN 46012
317-641-4340
News-editorial, public relations, broadcasting

Ball State University*
Muncie, IN 47306
317-285-8200
Public relations, news-editorial, newspaper advertising, photojournalism, magazine journalism, secondary school journalism

Butler University
Indianapolis, IN 46208
317-283-9357

Broadcast production, news-editorial, photography, public relations

Calumet College of Saint Joseph
Whiting, IN 46394
291-473-7770

News-editorial, radio-TV, photography

De Pauw University
Greencastle, IN 46135
317-658-4675

Print journalism

Franklin College
Franklin, IN 46131
317-736-8441 ext. 133

News-editorial, broadcasting, advertising–public relations

Indiana State University
Terre Haute, IN 47809
812-237-3027

News-editorial, photojournalism, magazine journalism, secondary teaching

Indiana University
Bloomington, IN 47405
812-855-9247

News-editorial, broadcast news, photojournalism, public relations, advertising, magazine journalism, education, professional graduate

Indiana University
Indianapolis, IN 46202
317-274-2773

News-editorial, magazine journalism, public relations, advertising

Purdue University
West Lafayette, IN 47907
317-494-3429

Mass communications, journalism, public relations, telecommunication, advertising, graduate program

St. Mary-of-the-Woods College
St. Mary-of-the-Woods, IN 47876
812-535-5210

News-editorial, public relations/advertising, secondary education

University of Evansille
Evansville, IN 47722
812-479-2377

News-editorial, advertising, interpersonal communications, public relations, telecommunications, broadcast journalism

Valparaiso University
Valparaiso, IN 46383
219-464-5271

Print journalism, advertising/public relations, broadcast journalism, communicative disorders, theatre and television arts

IOWA

Drake University*
Des Moines, IA 50311
515-271-3194

News-editorial, broadcast sales and management, broadcast news, high school journalism teaching, radio-television, magazine journalism, media graphics, public relations, advertising
Courses in publishing management

Grand View College
Des Moines, IA 50316
515-263-2800 ext. 2914

Print journalism, radio-TV, mass communications

Iowa State University*
Ames, IA 50011
515-294-4340

News-editorial, broadcast news, advertising, agricultural journalism, secondary journalism education, magazine journalism, public relations, engineering journalism, science writing journalism, general journalism, family and consumer journalism

Loras College
Dubuque, IA 52001
319-588-7400

News-editorial, public relations, public address, secondary education, media, photography

Marycrest College
Davenport, IA 52804
319-326-9343

Newspaper/magazine journalism, photojournalism, public relations, advertising, communications (general), broadcast journalism, broadcast production, media management, organizational communications

University of Iowa*
Iowa City, IA 52242
319-335-5821

News-editorial, mass communications laboratory, mass communications inquiry
Courses in publishing

KANSAS

Benedictine College
Atchison, KS 66002
913-367-6110 ext. 243

Print journalism, broadcast journalism

Fort Hays State University
Hays, KS 67601
913-628-4359

Public relations/advertising, news-editorial

Kansas State University
Manhattan, KS 66506
913-532-6890

News-editorial, human ecology, mass communications, advertising, public relations, general, agricultural journalism, radio-TV

Pittsburg State University
PIttsburg, KS 66762
316-231-7000

News-editorial, public relations, broadcasting, advertising, photojournalism

St. Mary-of-the-Plains College
Dodge City, KS 67801
316-225-4171

News-editorial, broadcasting

University of Kansas*
Lawrence, KS 66045
913-864-4755

News-editorial (community journalism, newspaper journalism, photojournalism, business communications, advertising, magazine journalism, radio-TV)
Courses in publishing

Washburn University
Topeka, KS 66621
913-295-3600 ext. 426

Electronic/print journalism, public relations, broadcasting/mass media, speech

communications
Courses in publishing

Wichita State University
Wichita, KS 67208
316-689-3185

Journalism, advertising–public relations, electronic media/visual communications

KENTUCKY

Eastern Kentucky University
Richmond, KY 40475
606-622-1871

Broadcasting, news-editorial, public relations

Morehead State University
Morehead, KY 40351
606-783-2694

News-editorial, advertising–public relations, photojournalism, community newspapering, journalism education

Murray State University*
Murray, KY 42071
502-762-2387

News-editorial, public relations, radio-TV, advertising

Northern Kentucky University
Highland Heights, KY 41706
606-572-5435

News-editorial, organizational communications, radio/TV, advertising, public relations

Union College
Barbourville, KY 40906
606-546-4151 ext. 251

News-editorial

University of Kentucky
Lexington, KY 40506
606-257-2786

General editorial, communications, advertising–public relations

Western Kentucky University*
Bowling Green, KY 42101
502-745-4143

News-editorial, advertising, public relations, photojournalism

LOUISIANA

Grambling State University
Grambling, LA 71245
318-247-2189 or 247-2403

News-editorial, technical writing, visual communications, advertising–public relations, broadcast news, broadcast production

Louisiana College
Pineville, LA 71359
318-487-7211

News-editorial, public relations

Louisiana State University*
Baton Rouge, LA 70803-7202
504-388-2336

News-editorial, broadcast journalism, advertising

Louisiana Tech University
Ruston, LA 71212
318-257-4427

News-editorial

Loyola University
New Orleans, LA 70118
504-865-3430

News-editorial, film studies, photojournalism, public relations, advertising, broadcasting (news, production), communications studies

Nicholls State University
Thibodaux, LA 70301
504-448-4136

Print journalism, broadcasting, advertising-public relations

Northeast Louisiana University
Monroe, LA 71209-0320
318-342-4095

News-editorial, public relations, photojournalism, public relations/advertising

Northwestern State University of Louisiana
Nachitoches, LA 71497
318-357-5213 or 357-6272

Broadcast journalism, news-editorial, public relations

Southeastern Louisiana University
Hammond, LA 70402
504-549-2100

Journalism (news-editorial, journalism education, broadcasting)

Southern University
Baton Rouge, LA 70813
504-771-5790 or 771-5791

News-editorial, broadcast production, mass communications

University of Southwestern Louisiana
Lafayette, LA 70504
318-231-6358 or 231-6103

Print journalism, radio-TV, public relations, media advertising, interpersonal and public communications

MAINE

University of Maine
Orono, ME 04409
207-581-1283

News-editorial, advertising, broadcast news, broadcasting

MARYLAND

Bowie State University
Bowie, MD 20715
301-464-7250

News-editorial, advertising, public relations, cinematography, photography

University of Maryland*
College Park, MD 20742
301-454-2228

News-editorial (news, magazine, literary journalism, photojournalism, and science communications specializations) public relations, advertising, broadcast news

MASSACHUSETTS

Boston University
Boston, MA 02215
617-353-3484

News-editorial, photojournalism, broadcast journalism, magazine journalism, science communications
Courses in publishing

Emerson College
Boston, MA 02116
617-578-8805

Broadcast journalism, news-editorial

Simmons College
Boston, MA 02115
617-738-2215
Communications, graphic design, advertising, public relations
Courses in publishing

Suffolk University
Boston, MA 02108
617-573-8500
Journalism and English, broadcast communications, public relations/marketing communications, bilingual communications, science and technical communications

University of Massachusetts
Amherst, MA 01003
413-545-1376
News-editorial

MICHIGAN

Central Michigan University
Mt. Pleasant, MI 48859
517-774-3196
Advertising, managing, news-editorial, photojournalism, public relations, magazine journalism

Eastern Michigan University
Ypsilanti, MI 48197
313-487-4220
Journalism (print), public relations, technical writing

Madonna College
Livonia, MI 48150
313-591-5064
News-editorial, public relations, communications arts, video communications

Michigan State University*
East Lansing, MI 48824
517-353-6430
News-editorial, public relations, radio-TV news, photojournalism, magazine

Oakland University
Rochester, MI 48309
313-3700-4120
News-editorial

University of Michigan
Ann Arbor, MI 48109-1285
313-764-0420
Communications (news-editorial, broadcast news, broadcast production)

Wayne State University
Detroit, MI 48202
313-577-2943
News-editorial, radio-TV, public relations–advertising

MINNESOTA

Bemidji State University
Bemidji, MN 56601-2699
Broadcast, public relations, journalism

College of St. Thomas
St. Paul, MN 55105
612-647-5632
News-editorial, public relations, advertising, broadcasting

Mankato State University
Mankato, MN 56001
507-389-6417
News-editorial, public relations

Moorhead State University
Moorhead, MN 56560
218-236-2983
Advertising, broadcast journalism, print journalism, public relations, English/mass communications, photojournalism

St. Cloud State University*
St. Cloud, MN 56301
612-255-3293
Advertising, news-editorial, broadcasting, public relations

St. Mary's College
Winona, MN 55987
507-457-1502
Journalism, public relations, broadcasting

University of Minnesota*
Minneapolis, MN 55455-0418
612-625-9824
News-editorial, advertising, broadcast journalism, visual communications

Winona State University
Winona, MN 55987
507-457-5230
Advertising, broadcasting, journalism, photojournalism, public relations

MISSISSIPPI

Jackson State University*
Jackson, MS 39127
601-968-2151
News-editorial, news-editorial and public relations, creative advertising, advertising sales, broadcast production, broadcast journalism

Mississippi State University
Mississippi State, MS 39762
601-325-3320
News-editorial

Mississippi University for Women
Columbus, MS 39701
601-329-7249
Journalism (general), broadcasting, broadcast journalism

Rust College
Holly Springs, MS 38635-2328
601-252-4661 ext. 259
Journalism (general), mass communications (general), radio/TV

Tougaloo College
Tougaloo, MS 39174
601-956-4941 ext. 304
Journalism (general)

University of Mississippi
University, MS 38677
601-232-7146
News-editorial, broadcast journalism, journalism/advertising

University of Southern Mississippi
Hattiesburg, MS 39406
601-266-5650
News-editorial, public relations, photojournalism, advertising

MISSOURI

Central Missouri State University
Warrensburg, MO 64093
816-429-4840
Broadcasting and film, journalism (news-editorial), mass communications, public relations

Culver-Stockton College
Canton, MO 63435
314-288-5221 ext. 382
Journalism (print)

Evangel College
Springfield, MO 65802
417-865-2811 ext. 383

News-editorial, broadcasting, journalism, education

Lincoln University
Jefferson City, MO 65101
314-681-5437

News-editorial, advertising/public relations

Lindenwood College
St. Charles, MO 63301
314-949-2000

Mass communications, (print journalism, public relations, radio-TV), corporate communications

Northeast Missouri State University
Kirksville, MO 63501
816-785-4483

Communications media (general)

Northwest Missouri State University
Maryville, MO 64468
816-562-1361

Journalism, broadcasting

Park College
Parkville, MO 64152
816-741-2000 ext. 320

Radio-TV film, journalism, communications theory and human resources

Southeast Missouri State University
Cape Girardeau, MO 63701
314-651-2241

News-editorial, corporate video, radio, advertising, public relations, media studies, journalism education, community journalism

Stephens College
Columbia, MO 65215
314-876-7014

Broadcasting, public relations, journalism, communications studies

University of Missouri*
Columbia, MO 65205
314-882-4821

News-editorial, advertising, magazine, broadcast news, newspaper publishing, photojournalism, graduate professional program

Webster University
Webster Grove, MO 63119
314-986-6924

News-editorial, media communications, broadcast journalism, photography, public communications, video/film, media communications (graduate)

MONTANA

University of Montana*
Missoula, MT 59812
406-243-4001

News-editorial, radio-TV (general)

NEBRASKA

Creighton State University
Omaha, NB 68178-0119
402-280-2825

News-editorial, broadcasting, advertising, public relations

Hastings College
Hastings, NB 68902
402-463-2402 ext. 367

Writing, news-editorial, advertising, public relations, theatre and film, speech, broadcasting, communications management

Kearney State College
Kearney, NB 68849
308-234-8537

News-editorial, advertising, secondary school, public relations

Midland Lutheran College
Fremont, NB 68025
402-721-5480 ext. 5078

News-editorial, photography, public relations/advertising, broadcasting

University of Nebraska*
Lincoln, NB 68588
402-472-3041

Advertising, news-editorial, radio-TV (general), graduate professional program Courses in publishing

University of Nebraska
Omaha, NB 68182
402-554-2601

News-editorial, broadcasting, public relations

NEVADA

University of Nevada
Las Vegas, NV 89154
702-739-3325

Broadcasting, communications theory, journalism, public relations, rhetoric, advertising

University of Nevada*
Reno, NV 89557-0040
702-784-6531

News-editorial, public relations, advertising, broadcast journalism

NEW HAMPSHIRE

Keene State College of the University System of New Hampshire
Keene, NH 03431
603-352-1909 ext. 224

Print journalism, broadcast media

NEW JERSEY

Glassboro State College
Glassboro, NJ 08028
609-445-7186 or 7187

News-editorial, advertising, public relations, radio/TV/film, speech communications, mass communications (general)

Rider College
Lawrenceville, NJ 08648
609-896-5089

Journalism, public relations, communications, radio-TV, business and professional communications

Rutgers, The State University of New Jersey
New Brunswick, NJ 08903
201-932-7500

News-editorial, broadcast journalism, environmental and technical writing, mass media and government, advertising, magazine journalism

Rutgers, The State University of New Jersey
Newark, NJ 07102
201-648-5431 or 648-1107

Print journalism, photojournalism, public relations, broadcast journalism

Seton Hall University
South Orange, NJ 07079
201-761-9474
News-editorial, public relations/advertising, communications/computer graphics, broadcast/film, theatre/speech

NEW MEXICO

Eastern New Mexico University
Portales, NM 88130
505-562-2113 or 562-2130
News-editorial, radio-TV, public relations, speech communications

New Mexico Highlands University
Las Vegas, NM 87701
505-425-7511
Print media, broadcast production

New Mexico State University
Las Cruces, NM 88003
505-426-1034
Journalism/public relations, advertising, broadcasting

University of New Mexico*
Albuquerque, NM 87131
505-277-2326
News-editorial, broadcast journalism

NEW YORK

College of New Rochelle
New Rochelle, NY 10805
914-654-5576
News-editorial, advertising, broadcast production, film

College of White Plains Pace University
White Plains, NY 10603
914-422-4134
Print journalism, broadcast journalism, publishing (graduate)

Columbia University (graduate only)
New York, NY 10027
212-280-4150
News-editorial

Cornell University
Ithaca, NY 14853
607-255-2111
Public communications, publications, interpersonal communications, electronic communications, science communications

Fordham University
Bronx, NY 10458
212-579-2533
Print journalism, radio-TV (news), media and society
Courses in publishing

Hofstra University
Hempstead, NY 11550
516-560-5424
Print journalism, electronic journalism, Tv production, radio production

Hunter College of CUNY
New York, NY 10021
212-772-4949
Journalism (general), broadcasting, public relations
Courses in publishing

Long Island University—Brooklyn Campus
Long Island, NY 11201-5372
718-403-1053
News-editorial (magazine journalism, advertising, public relations, mass media emphasis)

Medaille College
Buffalo, NY 14214
716-884-3281
Broadcasting, advertising, public relations, print journalism, photography/graphics

Mercy College
Dobbs Ferry, NY 10522
914-693-4500
News-editorial, broadcast production

New York University*
New York, NY 10003
212-998-7980
News-editorial, broadcast news, magazine journalism, public relations, mass communications
Courses in publishing

C.W. Post Center of Long Island University
Brookville, NY 11548
516-299-2382
News-editorial, public relations, radio-TV, photojournalism

St. Bonaventure University
St. Bonaventure, NY 14778
716-375-2520
News-editorial

St. John Fisher College
Rochester, NY 14618
716-385-8191
Print journalism, advertising/public relations, electronic media

St. John's University
New York, NY 11439
718-990-6161 ext. 6442
Journalism, communications arts

State University College at Buffalo
Buffalo, NY 14222
716-878-6008
News-editorial, public relations, broadcasting (general)
Courses in publishing

Syracuse University*
Syracuse, NY 13244-2100
315-443-2301
Newspaper, advertising, broadcast journalism, magazine journalism, public relations, photojournalism, TV-radio-film management, TV-radio-film writing, TV-radio-film production, illustration, photography
Courses in publishing

Utica College of Syracuse University
Utica, NY 13502
Journalism public relations, journalism/public relations

NORTH CAROLINA

Johnson C. Smith University
Charlotte, NC 28216
704-378-1173
Publishing and graphic arts (print), public relations and organizational communications, telecommunications

University of North Carolina
Asheville, NC 28804
704-251-6411
Mass communications (general), broadcasting, print journalism
Courses in publishing

University of North Carolina*
Chapel Hill, NC 27599-3365
919-962-1204
News-editorial, advertising, broadcast journalism, public relations, visual communications, graduate news-editorial

NORTH DAKOTA

North Dakota State University
Fargo, ND 58105
701-237-7295
Print, broadcast, public relations

University of North Dakota*
Grand Forks, ND 58202
701-777-2159
Journalism, advertising, public relations, broadcasting, speech

OHIO

Bowling Green State University*
Bowling Green, OH 43403
419-372-2076
News-editorial, public relations, magazine journalism, photojournalism, broadcast journalism

Kent State University*
Kent, OH 44242
216-672-2573 or 2572
News-editorial, broadcast news
Courses in publishing

University of Dayton
Dayton, OH 45469
513-229-2028
Journalism, broadcasting, communications management, public relations, communications arts (general)

University of Toledo
Toledo, OH 43606
419-537-2005
Broadcasting, print media, public relations

OKLAHOMA

Central State University
Edmond, OK 73034
405-341-2980 ext. 5122
Newspaper, phoographic arts, public relations, education, professional writing, magazines, advertising, journalism (general), business journalism

East Central University
Ada, OK 74820-6899
405-332-8000 ext. 482
News-editorial, radio-TV, advertising

Northeastern Oklahoma State University
Tahlequah, OK 74464
918-456-5511 ext. 2801
News-editorial, broadcasting, advertising-public relations, photojournalism, education (teaching)

Oklahoma Baptist University
Shawnee, OK 74801
405-275-2850 ext. 2236
News-editorial, public relations

Oklahoma City University
Oklahoma City, OK 73106
405-521-5252
News-editorial, advertising-public relations, radio-TV, magazine journalism, media management

Oklahoma State University*
Stillwater, OK 74078
405-744-6354
News-editorial, photojournalism, radio-TV advertising, public relations

OREGON

Oregon State University*
Corvallis, OR 97331
503-754-3109
Technical journalism

Southern Oregon State College
Ashland, OR 97520
503-482-6424
Print journalism, broadcasting

University of Oregon*
Eugene, OR 97403
503-686-3738
News-editorial, advertising, radio-TV news, public relations, magazine journalism
Courses in publishing

PENNSYLVANIA

Bloomsburg University of Pennsylvania
Bloosburg, PA 17815
717-389-4184
News-editorial, broadcast production, magazine journalism, public relations

Duquesne University
Pittsburgh, PA 15282
412-434-6460
News-editorial, broadcast news, advertising, public relations, magazine journalism, photojournalism

Indiana University of Pennsylvania
Indiana, PA 15705
412-357-4411
News-editorial, public relations

Lehigh University
Bethlehem, PA 18015
215-758-4180
News-editorial, science writing
Courses in publishing

Mercyhurst College
Erie, PA 16546
814-825-0464
Journalism, radio/TV

Pennsylvania State University*
University Park, PA 16802
814-865-6597
Journalism, advertising, broadcast/cable, film and video, mass communications

Point Park College
Pittsburgh, PA 15222
412-392-3422
News-editorial, broadcast media, advertising, public relations, photojournalism, journalism and communications/secondary education (undergraduate), journalism and communciations news—editorial, public relations, advertising (graduate)

Shippensburg University
Shippensburg, PA 17257
717-532-1521
News-editorial, radio/TV, public relations

Temple University*
Philadelphia, PA 19122
215-787-8346
News-editorial, advertising, public relations, magazine journalism, broadcast journalism, photography
Courses in publishing

University of Pittsburgh
Johnstown, PA 15904
814-266-9661 ext. 367
News-editorial
Courses in publishing

RHODE ISLAND

University of Rhode Island
Kingston, R.I. 02881
401-792-2195

News-editorial, radio-TV, journalism, public relations

SOUTH CAROLINA

Benedict College
Columbia, SC 29204
803-256-4220 ext. 5164

News-editorial, broadcasting, public communications/marketing

University of South Carolina*
Columbia, SC 29208
803-777-4105

News-editorial (newspaper, photojournalism), advertising/public relations (management, creative advertising), broadcasting (radio-TV)

SOUTH DAKOTA

Black Hills State University
Spearfish, SD 57783
605-642-6861

Journalism (general), broadcasting

South Dakota State University*
Brookings, SD 57007
605-688-4171

News-editorial, broadcast journalism, advertising, science and technical writing, printing management, agricultural journalism, home economics, journalism, printing journalism, printing education

TENNESSEE

East Tennessee State University*
Johnson City, TN 37614
615-929-4308

Journalism, public relations/advertising, broadcasting

Memphis State University*
Memphis, TN 38152
901-678-2401

News-editorial (magazine, newspaper and photojournalism), advertising, public relations, broadcast news

Middle Tennessee State University*
Murfreesboro, TN 37132
615-898-2814

Advertising/public relations, journalism, graphic communications

Tennessee Technological University
Cookeville, TN 38505
615-528-3060

News-editorial, technical communications

University of Tennessee
Chattanooga, TN 37403
615-755-4400

News-editorial, broadcast journalism, broadcasting and electronic media, advertising, public relations

University of Tennessee*
Knoxville, TN 37996
615-974-3031

News-editorial, broadcast journalism, advertising, public relations, graduate professional program

University of Tennessee
Martin, TN 38238
901-587-7550

News-editorial, broadcasting (radio, broadcast news, TV production), public relations

TEXAS

Abilene Christian University
Abilene, TX 79699
915-674-2298

News-editorial, telecommunications, advertising, public relations, photojournalism, corporate video

Angelo State University
San Angelo, TX 76909
915-942-2322

News-editorial

Baylor University
Waco, TX 76798
817-755-3261

News-editorial, public relations

East Texas State University
Commerce, TX 75428
214-886-5239

News-editorial, photojournalism, advertising-public relations, secondary school, photography, printing

Hardin-Simmons University
Abilene, TX 79698
915-670-1436

Journalism, public relations

Howard Payne University
Brownwood, TX 76801
915-646-2502 ext. 412

Journalism, radio/TV, speech, drama

Midwestern State University
Wichita Falls, TX 76308-2099
817-692-6611

Journalism (print, advertising, public relations, radio-TV news, radio-TV production, photojournalism)

Prairie View A&M University
Prairie View, TX 77446-0156
409-857-2229

Journalism, radio-TV, speech communications, general communications

Sam Houston State University
Huntsville, TX 77341
409-294-1495 or 294-1340

News-editorial, advertising, community journalism, public relations, broadcasting, photojournalism

Southern Methodist University
Dallas, TX 75275
214-692-2629

News-editorial, advertising management, public relations, broadcast news, TV-radio

Southwest Texas State University
San Marcos, TX 78666
512-245-2656

News-editorial, advertising, public relations, secondary school, broadcasting, magazine journalism, agriculture-journalism

Stephen F. Austin State University
Nacogdoches, TX 75962
409-568-4001

Photojournalism, public relations, speech, broadcasting, reporting and writing

Texas A&I University
Kingsville, TX 78363
512-595-3499

News-editorial, journalism teaching

Texas A&M University
College Station, TX 77843
409-845-4611
Journalism, agricultural journalism

Texas Christian University*
Ft. Worth, TX 76129
817-921-7425
News-editorial, broadcast journalism, advertising/public relations, photojournalism

Texas Southern University
Houston, TX 77004
713-527-7360
News-editorial, advertising-public relations, broadcast journalism

Texas Tech University*
Lubbock, TX 79409
806-742-3385
News-editorial, advertising, telecommunications, public relations, photocommunications, broadcast journalism, corporate telecommunications, graduate professional program

Texas Wesleyan University
Ft. Worth, TX 76105-1536
817-531-4928
News-editorial, broadcasting, advertising-public relations

Texas Woman's University
Denton, TX 76204
817-898-2181
News-editorial, advertising, radio-TV

Trinity University
San Antonio, TX 78282
512-736-8112
Communications (news-editorial, broadcasting)

University of Houston
Houston, TX 77004
713-749-1745
News-editorial, radio-TV (general)

University of North Texas
Denton, TX 76203
917-565-2205
News-editorial, advertising, public relations, business journalism, photojournalism, teaching journalism, broadcast news

University of Texas-Arlington
Arlington, TX 76019
817-273-2163
News-editorial, advertising, public relations, photojournalism, radio-TV news

University of Texas-Austin*
Austin, TX 78712
512-471-1845
News-editorial, magazine journalism, public relations, photojournalism, radio-TV news

University of Texas-El Paso
El Paso, TX 79968-0639
925-747-5129
News-editorial, photojournalism, advertising, broadcast journalism

University of Texas-Pan American
Edinburg, TX 78539
512-381-3583
Journalism (print, advertising, public relations, broadcasting)

West Texas State University
Canyon, TX 79017
806-656-2410
News-editorial, radio-TV news, journalism education

UTAH

Brigham Young University*
Provo, UT 84602
801-378-2077
Journalism (print, advertising, public relations, radio-TV news, broadcast production)

University of Utah*
Salt Lake City, UT 84112
801-581-5324
News-editorial, public relations, broadcast journalism, telecommunications and film
Courses in publishing

Utah State University
Logan, UT 84322
801-750-3292
New-editorial, public relations, secondary school, broadcast journalism, photography

Weber State College
Ogden, UT 84408-1903
801-626-6426
News-editorial, broadcast, public relations

VERMONT

St. Michael's College
Colchester, VT 05446
802-655-2000
News-editorial

VIRGINIA

Emory & Henry College
Emory, VA 24327
703-944-3121
News-editorial, mass communications (general), journalism

Hampton University
Hampton, VA 23668
804-727-5405
News-editorial, broadcast, advertising–public relations, mass media comprehensive

James Madison University
Harrisonburg, VA 22807
703-568-6228
Journalism (news-editorial, magazine journalism, public information), public relations, telecommunications (production, management, electronic journalism, media studies)

Liberty University
Lynchburg, VA 24506
804-582-2508
News-editorial, advertising, public relations, magazine journalism, journalism graphics

Norfolk State University
Norfolk, VA 23504
804-683-8330
News-editorial, photojournalism, public relations, advertising

Radford University
Radford, VA 24142
703-831-5282
Journalism (news-editorial, public relations), speech communications (radio/TV, speech)

University of Richmond
Richmond, VA 23173
804-289-8323
News-editorial

Virginia Commonwealth University*
Richmond, VA 23284-2034
804-367-1260

News-editorial, broadcast news, advertising/public relations

Virginia Polytechnic Institute and State University
Blacksburg, VA 24061
703-231-7136

Journalism, broadcasting, public relations, speech communications, popular culture and film

Virginia Union University
Richmond, VA 23220
804-257-5655

Journalism

Washington & Lee University*
Lexington, VA 24450
703-463-8432

News-editorial, radio-TV news

WASHINGTON

Central Washington University
Ellensburg, WA 98926
509-963-1066

News-editorial, radio-TV, public relations

Eastern Washington University
Spokane, WA 99204
509-458-6395

Journalism/mass communications, broadcast news

Gonzaga University
Spokane, WA 99258
509-328-4220 ext. 3262

News-editorial, broadcast studies, public relations

Pacific Lutheran University
Tacoma, WA 98447
206-535-7632

Journalism, broadcast journalism, public relations, communications theory

Seattle University
Seattle, WA 98122
206-626-5797

News-editorial, public relations, communications studies

University of Washington*
Seattle, WA 98195
206-543-2660

News-editorial, advertising, broadcast journalism, communications

Walla Walla College
College Place, WA 99324
509-527-2832

Journalism, mass communications, broadcast/film

Washington State University
Pullman, WA 99164-2520
509-335-1556

Broadcasting, journalism, advertising, general communications, public relations, speech communications

WEST VIRGINIA

Bethany College
Bethany, WV 26032
304-829-7877

General mass communications (news-editorial, advertising, public relations, radio-TV)

Marshall University*
Huntington, WV 25701
304-696-2360

News-editorial, advertising, public relations, broadcast journalism, magazine journalism

West Virginia University*
Morgantown, WV 26505-6010

News-editorial, advertising, public relations, broadcast news

WISCONSIN

Marquette University*
Milwaukee, WI 53233
414-288-5608

News-editorial, magazine journalism, photojournalism

University of Wisconsin
Eau Claire, WI 54701
715-836-2528

News-editorial, advertising, radio-TV, secondary school

University of Wisconsin
La Crosse, WI 54601
608-785-8368

Mass communications

University of Wisconsin*
Madison, WI 53706
608-262-3690

Advertising, broadcast news, news editorial, public relations, mass communications
608-262-1464
Agricultural journalism, family and consumer communications

University of Wisconsin
Milwaukee, WI 53201
414-229-4436

Print journalism, broadcast journalism, broadcast programming and management

University of Wisconsin*
Oshkosh, WI 54901
414-424-1042

News-editorial, advertising–public relations

University of Wisconsin*
River Falls, WI 54022
715-425-3169

News-editorial, broadcast journalism, agricultural journalism, secondary journalism education

University of Wisconsin
Whitewater, WI 53190
414-472-1634

News-editorial, broadcast journalism

WYOMING

University of Wyoming
Laramie, WY 82071
307-766-3122

Journalism, telecommunications, general speech

APPENDIX II
PROFESSIONAL, INDUSTRY, AND TRADE ASSOCIATIONS AND UNIONS

Note: Since many of these organizations operate on limited funds, please enclose a self-addressed, stamped envelope when querying for information.

Academic Collective Bargaining Information Service
1321 H Street NW Suite 210
Washington, DC 20005
202-727-2326

The Academy of American Poets
177 East 87th Street
New York, NY 10028
212-427-5665

Academy of Television Arts and Sciences
3500 West Olive Avenue Suite 700
Burbank, CA 91505
818-953-7575

Advertising Club of New York
155 East 55th Street Suite 202
New York, NY 10022
212-935-8080

Advertising Women of New York
153 East 57th Street
New York, NY 10022
212-593-1950

American Advertising Federation (AAF)
1400 K Street NW Suite 1000
Washington, DC 20005
202-898-0089

American Association of Sunday and Feature Editors
Box 17407
Dulles International Airport
Washington, DC 20041
703-648-1109

American Association of University Professors
1012 14th Street Suite 500
Washington, DC 20005
202-737-5900

American Black Book Writers Association
P.O. Box 10458
Venice, CA 90295
213-822-5195

American Book Producers Association
211 East 51st Street #11D
New York, NY 10022
212-308-0181

American Business Women's Association
Box 8728
9100 Ward Parkway
Kansas City, MO 64114
816-361-6621

American Federation of Government Employees (AFGE)
80 F Street NW
Washington, DC 20001
202-737-8700

American Federation of State, County and Municipal Employees (AFL-CIO)
1625 L Street NW
Washington, DC 20036
202-452-4800

American Federation of Teachers (AFL-CIO)
555 New Jersey Avenue NW
Washington, DC 20001
202-879-4400

American Federation of Television and Radio Artists (AFTRA)
260 Madison Avenue
New York, NY 10016
212-532-0800

American Guild of Authors and Composers
See Songwriters Guild of America

American Historical Association
400 A Street SE
Washington, DC 20003
202-544-2422

American Library Association (ALA)
50 East Huron Street
Chicago, IL 60611
312-944-6780

American Management Association
135 West 50th Street
New York, NY 10020
212-586-8100

American Medical Writers' Association
5272 River Road
Suite 370
Bethesda, MD 20816
301-493-0003

American Newspaper Publishers Association (ANPA)
Box 17407
Dulles International Airport
Washington, DC 20041
703-648-1000

American News Women's Club
1607 22nd Street NW
Washington, DC 20008
202-332-6770

American Society for Information Science
1424 16th Street NW
Suite 404
Washington, DC 20036
202-462-1000

American Society of Business Press Editors
4445 Gilmer Lane
Cleveland, OH 44143
216-531-8306

American Society of Composers, Authors and Publishers
1 Lincoln Plaza
New York, NY 10023
212-595-3050

American Society of Indexers
1700 18th Street NW
Washington DC 20009
718-990-6200

American Society of Journalists and Authors, Inc.
1501 Broadway
Suite 1907
New York, NY 10036
212-997-0947

American Society of Magazine Editors
575 Lexington Avenue
New York, NY 10022
212-752-0055

American Society of Newspaper Editors (ASNE)
P.O. Box 17004
Washington, DC 20041
703-648-1144

American Theatre Critics Association
c/o Clara Hieronymus
The Tennessean
1100 Broadway
Nashville, TN 37202
1-800-351-1752

American Women in Radio and Television, Inc. (AWRT)
1101 Connecticut Avenue NW
Suite 700
Washington, DC 20036
202-492-5102

American Writers Theatre Foundation
Box 810
Times Square Station
New York, NY 10108
212-581-5295

Associated Business Writers of America, Inc.
1450 South Havana Street
Suite 620
Aurora, CO 88012
303-751-7844

Associated Writing Programs
Old Dominion University
Norfolk, VA 23508
804-440-3839

Association for Business Communication
University of Illinois
Urbana IL 61801
217-333-1007

Association of American Advertising Agencies (AAAA)
666 Third Avenue
New York, NY 10017
212-682-2500

Association of American Publishers
220 East 23rd Street
New York, NY 10010
212-689-8920

Association of Petroleum Writers
c/o Katherine Reese
Oil & Gas Journal
Box 1260
Tulsa, OK 74101
918-835-3161

Association of Radio-Television News Analysts (ARTNA)
190 Riverside Drive
Suite 6-B
New York, NY 10024
212-799-2528

The Authors Guild (See **The Authors League of America, Inc.**)

The Authors League of America, Inc. (Includes The Authors Guild, Inc., and **The Dramatists Guild, Inc.)**
234 West 44th Street
New York, NY 10036
212-391-9198

Aviation/Space Writers' Association
17 S. High Street
Suite 124
Columbus, OH 43215
614-221-1900

Broadcast Music, Inc. (BMI)
320 West 57th Street
New York, NY 10019
212-586-2000

Broadcast Promotion and Marketing Executives
6255 Sunset Boulevard #624
Los Angeles, CA 90028
213-465-3777

Business/Professional Advertising Association (BPAA)
100 Metroplex Drive
Edison, NJ 08817
201-985-4441

Construction Writers Association
P.O. Box 259
Poolesville, MD 20837
301-972-8100

Committee of Small Magazine Editors & Publishers
See **COSMEP**

Computer Press Association
1260 25th Avenue
San Francisco, CA 94122
415-681-5364

COSMEP, the International Association of Independent Publishers
Box 703
San Francisco, CA 94101
415-922-9490

Council of Biology Editors
9650 Rockville Pike
Bethesda, MD 20814
301-530-7036

Dance Critics Association
Box 47 Planetarium Station
127 West 83rd Street
New York, NY 10024
212-477-5457

The Dramatists Guild (See **The Authors League of America, Inc.**)

Editorial Freelancers Association
P.O. Box 2050
Madison Square Station
New York, NY 10159
212-677-3357

Education Writers Association
1001 Connecticut Avenue NW Suite 310
Washington DC 20036
202-429-9680

Feminist Writers Guild
1742 West Melrose
Chicago IL 60657
312-929-1326

Garden Writers Association of America
c/o W. J. Jung
1218 Overlook Road
Eustis, Fl 32726
904-589-8888

Greeting Card Association
1350 New York Avenue NW
Suite 615
Washington, DC 20005
202-393-1778

International Association of Business Communicators (IABC)
870 Market Street
Suite 940
San Francisco, CA 94102
415-433-3400

International Black Writers
P.O. Box 1030
Chicago, IL 60690
312-995-5195

International Newspaper Advertising and Marketing Executives
Box 17210
Dulles International Airport
Washington, DC 20041
703-648-1168

International Newspaper Promotion Association
Box 17422
Dulles International Airport
Washington, DC 20041
703-648-1094

International Radio and Television Society (IRTS)
420 Lexington Avenue
New York, NY 10170
212-867-6650

International Society of Weekly Newspaper Editors
Department of Journalism
Northern Illinois University
DeKalb, IL 60115
817-753-1925

International Women's Writing Guild
Box 810
Gracie Square Station
New York, NY 10028
212-737-7536

Investigative Reporters and Editors
Box 838
Columbia, MO 65211
314-882-2042

Journalism Education Association
Kedzie Hall 104
Kansas State University
Manhattan, KS 66506
913-532-5532

Kappa Tau Alpha
c/o William Taft
107 Sondra Avenue
Columbia, MO 65202
314-443-3521

Magazine Publishers Association
575 Lexington Avenue
New York, NY 10022
212-752-0055

Manhattan Publishing Group
c/o Cheryl Joan Jenkins
842 Blake Avenue
Brooklyn, NY 11207
718-385-4945

Music Critics Association
6201 Tuckerman Lane
Rockville, MD 20852
No telephone number available

Mystery Writers of America, Inc.
236 West 27th Street
New York, NY 10001
212-255-7005

National Academy of Television Arts and Sciences
110 West 57th Street Suite 1020
New York, NY 10019
212-586-8424

National Association for Young Writers
P.O. Box 228
2151 Hale Road
Sandusky, MI 48471
313-648-4070

National Association of Black Journalists
Box 2089
Washington, DC 20013
703-648-1270

National Association of Black Professors
c/o Sarah Miles Woods
Dept. of Chemistry
430 S. Michigan Avenue
Roosevelt University
Chicago IL 60605
312-341-3817

National Association of Broadcast Employees and Technicians (NABET)
7101 Wisconsin Avenue Suite 800
Bethesda, MD 20814
301-657-8420

National Association of Broadcasters (NAB)
1771 N Street NW
Washington, DC 20036
202-429-5300

National Association of Composers, USA
Box 49652, Barnington Station
Los Angeles CA 90049
213-541-8213

National Association of Farm Broadcasters (NAFB)
Box 119
Topeka, KS 66601
913-272-3456

National Association of Government Communicators (NAGC)
Box 7127
Alexandria, VA 22307
703-823-4821

National Association of Government Employees (NAGE)
1313 L Street NW
Washington, DC 20005
371-6644

National Association of Media Women
1185 Niskey Lake Road SW
Atlanta, GA 30331
404-344-5862

National Association of Science Writers, Inc.
Box 294
Greenlawn, NY 11740
516-757-5664

National Black Public Relations Society
30 West Washington Rm. 503
Chicago, IL 60602
312-782-7703

National Book Critics Circle
c/o Alida Becker
756 S. 10th Street
Philadelphia, PA 19147
215-925-8406

The National Broadcasting Society/Alpha Epsilon Rho
c/o Dr. John Lopiccolo
College of Journalism
University of South Carolina
Columbia, SC 29208
803-777-3324

National Conference of Editorial Writers
6223 Executive Boulevard
Rockville, MD 20852
301-984-3015

National Education Association
1201 16th Street NW
Washington, DC 20036
202-833-4000

National Federation of Federal Employees
1016 16th Street NW
Washington, DC 20036
202-862-4400

National Federation of Press Women, Inc.
1105 Main Street
Box 99
Blue Springs, MO 64015
816-229-1666

National Newspaper Association
1627 K Street
Suite 400
Washington, DC 20006
202-466-7200

National Newspaper Publishers Association
National Press Building Rm. 948
Washington, DC 20045
202-662-7324

National Press Club
National Press Building
529 14th Street NW
Washington, DC 20045
202-662-7500

National School of Public Relations Association
1501 Lee Highway
Arlington, VA 222009
703-528-5840

National Sportscasters and Sportswriters Association
Box 559
Salisbury, NC 28144
704-633-4275

National Turf Writers Association
2362 Winston
Louisville, KY 40205
502-452-6965

National Writers Club, Inc.
1450 South Havana
Suite 620
Aurora, CO 80012
303-751-7844

National Writers Union
13 Astor Place
Seventh Floor
New York, NY 10003
212-254-0279

The Newspaper Guild (AFL-CIO)
8611 Second Avenue
Silver Spring, MD 20910
301-585-2990

Organization of American Historians
Indiana University
112 North Bryan Street
Bloomington, IN 47401
812-855-7311

Outdoor Writers Association of America
2017 Cato Avenue
South College, PA 16801
814-234-1011

P.E.N.American Center
568 Broadway
New York, NY 10012
212-334-1660

The Poetry Society of America
15 Gramercy Park South
New York, NY 10003
212-254-9628

Poets & Writers, Inc.
72 Spring Street
New York, NY 10012
212-266-3586

The Public Relations Society of America, Inc. (PRSA)
33 Irving Place
New York, NY 10003
212-995-2230

Public Relations Student Society of America (See **PRSA** above.)

Publishers' Ad Club
c/o Cathy Grunewald
Street Martin's Press
175 Fifth Avenue
New York, NY 10010
212-674-5151

Publishers' Publicity Association
c/o Arlynn Greenbaum
Little Brown & Co.
205 Lexington Avenue
New York, NY 10016
212-683-0660

Quill and Scroll Society
School of Journalism
University of Iowa
Iowa City, IA 52242
319-335-5795

Radio and Television Correspondents Association (RTCA)
Senate Radio-Television Gallery
U.S. Capitol
Room S-325
Washington, DC 20510
202-224-6421

Radio-Television News Directors Association (RTNDA)
1717 K Street NW
Suite 615
Washington, DC 20006
202-659-6510

Religion Newswriters Association
c/o Ed Briggs
Richmond Times-Dispatch
P.O. Box C-32333
Richmond, VA 23293
804-649-6754

Romance Writers of America
5206 FM 19060 West
Suite 208
Houston, TX 77069
713-440-6885

Science Fiction Writers of America
Box 4236
West Columbia, SC 29171
803-791-5942

Small Press Writers and Artists Organization
c/o Audrey Parente
328 Timberline Trail
Ormond Beach. FL 32074
904-672-3085

Society for Collegiate Journalists
Institute of Journalism
CBN University
Virginia Beach, VA 23462
804-523-7091

Society for Scholarly Publishing
2000 Florida Avenue NW
Suite 305
Washington, DC 20009
202-328-3555

Society for Technical Communication
815 15th Street NW
Suite 506
Washington, DC 20005
202-737-0035

Society of American Archivists
600 S. Federal Street
Suite 504
Chicago, IL 60605
312-922-0140

Society of American Business Editors and Writers
P.O. Box 838
University of Missouri
Columbia, MO 65205
314-882-7862

Society of Architectural Historians
1232 Pine Street
Philadelphia, PA 19107
215-735-0224

Society of American Travel Writers
1100 17th Street NW
Suite 1000
Washington, DC 20036
202-785-5567

Society of Children's Book Writers
Box 296
Mar Vista Station
Los Angeles, CA 90066
818-347-2849

Society of Professional Journalists
53 West Jackson Boulevard
Suite 731
Chicago, IL 60604
312-922-7424

Songwriters Guild of America
276 Fifth Avenue
New York, NY 10001
212-686-6820

National Academy of Songwriters
6381 Hollywood Boulevard Suite 810
Hollywood, CA 90028
213-463-7178

Special Libraries Association
1700 18th Street/NW
Washington, DC 20009
202-234-4700

Television Critics Association
c/o Art Chapman
Ft. Worth Star Telegram
400 West 7th Street
Ft. Worth, TX 76102
817-390-7400

Western Writers of America
1753 Victoria
Sheridan, WY 82801
307-672-2079

Women Executives in Public Relations
P.O. Box 781
Murray Hill Station
New York, NY 10156
212-683-5438

Women In Cable
c/o P.M. Haeger & Assocs.
500 N. Michigan Avenue
Suite 1400
Chicago, IL 60611
312-661-1700

Women In Communications, Inc. (WICI)
2101 Wilson Boulevard
Suite 417

Alexandria, VA 22201
703-528-4200

Women In Scholarly Publishing
c/o Julia Sawabiui
MIT Press
55 Hayward Drive
Cambridge, MA 02142
617-253-586

Women's National Book Association, Inc.
160 Fifth Avenue Room 604
New York, NY 10010
617-720-3992

Writers Guild of America, East, Inc.
555 West 57th Street
New York, NY 10019
212-245-6180

Writers Guild of America, West, Inc.
8955 Beverly Boulevard
Los Angeles, CA 90048
215-550-1000

APPENDIX III MAJOR TRADE PERIODICALS

The following are some of the principal trade publications serving writers in various fields. For information on additional publications, consult these reference books at your public library. *Directory of Publications and Broadcast Media Literary Market Place*; and *Writer's Market*. In addition, most trade and professional associations and unions publish periodicals for their membership.

ACADEMIC, INSTITUTIONAL

The American Historical Review
American Historical Association
Indiana University
914 Atwater
Bloomington, IN 47405
812-855-7609

American Libraries
50 East Huron Street
Chicago, IL 60611
312-944-6780

School Library Journal
249 West 17th Street
New York, NY 10017
212-463-6759

ADVERTISING, PUBLIC RELATIONS

Advertising Age
Crain Communications
220 East 42nd Street
New York, NY 10017
212-210-0100

Adweek
A/S/M Communications, Inc.
49 East 21st Street
New York, NY 10010
212-995-7323

Madison Avenue
140 Riverside Drive, No. 7-F1.
New York, NY 10024
212-972-0600

Marketing & Media Decisions
401 Park Avenue South
New York, NY 10036
212-695-4215

Public Relations Journal
33 Irving Place
New York, NY 10003
212-995-2266

ENTERTAINMENT

Billboard
1515 Broadway
New York, NY 10036
212-764-7300

Hollywood Reporter
6715 Sunset Boulevard
Hollywood, CA 90028
213-464-7411

Show Business
1501 Broadway
New York, NY 10036
212-354-7600

Songwriter
Box 3510
Hollywood, CA 90028
213-464-7664

Variety
475 Park Avenue South
New York, NY 10016-6902
212-779-1100

JOURNALISM

Columbia Journalism Review
700 Journalism Building
Columbia University
New York, NY 10027
212-854-3431

Editor & Publisher
11 West 19th Street
New York, NY 10011
212-675-4380

Quill & Scroll
School of Journalism
University of Iowa
Iowa City, IA 52242
319-335-5795

Washington Journalism Review
2233 Wisconsin Avenue NW
Suite 442
Washington, DC 20007
202-333-6800

World Press Review
200 Madison Avenue
New York, NY 10016
212-889-5155

MAGAZINE AND BOOK PUBLISHING

Folio: The Magazine for Magazine Management
Cowles Media Co.
P.O. Box 4949
Stamford, CT 06907-0949
203-358-9900

Magazine & Bookseller
545 Madison Avenue
New York, NY 10011
212-463-6812

Publishers Weekly
249 West 17th Street
New York, NY 10022
212-916-1600

Small Press
11 Ferry Lane West
Westport, CT 06880-5808
203-226-6967

Small Press Review
Box 100
Paradise, CA 95967
916-877-6110

WRITING, POETRY, DRAMA

The Drama Review
55 Hayward Street
Cambridge, MA 02142
617-253-2889

Poets & Writers Magazine
Poets & Writers Inc.
72 Spring Street
New York, NY 10012
212-226-3586

The Writer
120 Boylston Street
Boston, MA 02116
617-423-3157

Writer's Digest
1507 Dana Avenue
Cincinnati, OH 45207
513-531-2222

APPENDIX IV BIBLIOGRAPHY

Becker, Lee B. and Thomas E. Engelman. "Survey of Journalism and Mass Communications Graduates 1988: Summary Report July 1989." Columbus, Ohio: Ohio State University, and Princeton, NJ: Dow Jones Newspaper Fund. (For a copy, send $3.00 to the School of Journalism, The Ohio State University, 242 W. 18th Ave., Columbus, OH 43210.)

Bly, Robert W., and Blake, Gary. *Dream Jobs: A Guide To Tomorrow's Top Careers*. New York: Wiley & Sons, 1983.

Busnar, Gene. *Careers in Music*. New York: Julian Messmer, 1982.

Butler, Susan Lowell. "What's Ahead for Communicators in the '90s." *The Professional Communicator*, Spring 1990, pp. 16–17+.

Click, J.W., and Baird, Russell N. *Magazine Editing and Production*. Dubuque, IA: Wm. C. Brown, 1974.

The Dow Jones Newspaper Fund, Inc. *1990 Journalism Career and Scholarship Guide*. Princeton, NJ: 1989.

Field, Shelly. *Career Opportunities in the Music Industry*. New York: Facts On File, 1986.

Field, Syd. *The Screenwriter's Workbook*. New York: Dell, 1984.

Goeller, Carl. *Writing and Selling Greeting Cards*. Boston: The Writer, Inc., 1980.

Gould, Jay, and Losano, Wayne. *Opportunities in Technical Communications*. Skokie, IL: VGM Career Horizons, National Textbook Co., 1980.

Groome, Harry C. Jr., *Opportunities in Advertising Careers*. Louisville, KY: Vocational Guidance Manuals, 1976.

Haas, Ken. *How to Get a Job in Advertising*. New York: Art Direction Book Co., 1979.

Haubenstock, Susan H. and David Joselit. *Career Oportunities in Art*. New York: Facts On File, 1988.

Heim, Kathleen, and Sullivan, Peggy. *Opportunities in Library and Information Science*. Skokie, IL: VGM Career Horizons, National Textbook Co., 1982.

Jerome, Judson. *The Poet's Handbook*. Cincinnati, OH: Writer's Digest Books, 1980.

Krefetz, Gerald, and Gittelman, Philip. *The Book of Incomes*. New York: Holt, Rinehart & Winston, 1981.

Johnson, Betty and Mary Esther Bullard Johnson. "Getting Ahead: A Profile of Black Media Managers." Published by the National Association of Black Journalists, Jan. 13, 1989. Kamerman, *Book Reviewing*. Boston: The Writer, Inc., 1978.

Lafky, Sue A. "Economic Equity and the Journalistic Work Force." Talk given for the Association for Education in Journalism and Mass Communication at Portland, OR, July 2–5, 1988; published in Sept. 1988 *Presstime*.

Mainstream Access, Inc. *The Public Relations Job Finder*. Englewood Cliffs, NJ: Prentice-Hall, Inc., 1981.

Mainstream Access, Inc. *The Publishing Job Finder*. Englewood Cliffs, NJ.: Prentice-Hall, Inc. 1981.

"PRJ's Fourth Annual Salary Survey." *Public Relations Journal*, June 1989, pp. 17–21.

Psivack, Jane F., ed. *Careers in Information*. White Plains, NY: Knowledge Industry Publications, Inc., 1982.

Reed, Robert M. and Maxine K. *Career Opportunities in Television, Cable and Video*. 3nd ed. New York: Facts On File, 1986.

Ross, Tom and Marilyn. *The Complete Guide to Self-Publishing*. Cincinatti: Writer's Digest Books, 1985.

Russman, Linda deLaubensfels. "WICI Job & Salary Survey Results." *The Professional Communicator*, Spring 1990, pp. 18–22.

Scherman, William H. *How to Get the Right Job in Publishing*. Chicago: Contemporary Books, Inc., 1983.

Shaffer, Susan E. *Guide to Book Publishing Courses*. Princeton, NJ: Peterson's Guides, 1979.

Tebbel, John. *Opportunities in Journalism*. Skokie, IL: VGM Career Horizons, National Textbook Co., 1977.

U.S. Department of Labor. Bureau of Labor Statistics. *Occupational Outlook Handbook 1982–83*. Washington, DC: U.S. Government Printing Office, 1982.

"Where the Money Is: PW's Second Annual Publishing Salary Survey." Survey conducted by Mary Connors,commentary by John F. Baker. *Publisher's Weekly*, Sept. 29, 1989, pp. 17–21.

Williams, Gurney, III. *Writing Careers*. New York: Franklin Watts, Inc., 1976.

Wilson, Jean Gaddy. "Special Report." *Presstime*, Oct. 1986, pp. 31–37.

Wright, John W. *American Almanac of Jobs and Salaries*, 3rd ed. New York: Avon Books, 1987.

Zeller, Susan L. *Your Career in Radio and Television Broadcasting*. New York: Arco Publishing, Inc., 1982.

INDEX